Water Wheels

North Star Kids of the River Mill Era

**CALUMET
EDITIONS**

Minneapolis

FIRST EDITION September 2023

Water Wheels: North Star Kids of the River Mill Era
Copyright © 2023 by Michael Barnes.

10 9 8 7 6 5 4 3 2 1
ISBN: 978-1-960250-95-7

Cover and interior design: Gary Lindberg

Cover painting: *St. Louis: Laclede's Landing* (1885) by John Stobart.

for Bill and Marge
and all the children of immigrants

Table of Contents

Prologue (1876) **Centennial**
The state of Minnesota on the United States' one hundredth birthday   1

Chapter 1 (1868) **Strawberry Picnic**
Oliver Kelley's "Grange" in Minnesota   3

Chapter 2 (1871) **Arbor Day**
Norwegian immigrant farmers meet Ignatius Donnelly   17

Chapter 3 (1871) **Meier Hardware and Lumber**
German immigrants meet Father John Ireland   37

Chapter 4 (1873) **Blizzard**
Stranded in Minnesota's killer "Blizzard of 1873"   53

Chapter 5 (1873) **Panic**
Surviving the financial "Panic of 1873"   73

Chapter 6 (1874) **Lumberjack Pony**
Halvor goes to work for lumber baron Isaac Staples   87

Chapter 7 (1875) **Wolves in the Woods**
Dangerous life in a logging camp   109

Chapter 8 (1876) **Fourth of July**
Emelia goes to work for brewer Theodore Hamm   131

Chapter 9 (1876) **Bank Raid**

Confrontation with the outlaw Jesse James   147

Chapter 10 (1876) **North Oaks**

Visit to James J. Hill's farm estate   159

Chapter 11 (1877) **Grasshoppers**

Governor John Pillsbury meets young Laura Ingalls Wilder   173

Chapter 12 (1878) **Explosion**

Eighteen people are killed by Minneapolis flour mill explosion   187

Chapter 13 (1880) **Graduation**

Halvor and Emelia get jobs with the
Twin Cities' most famous entrepreneurs   203

Chapter 14 (1882) **Steamboat Race**

Rivalry between Hill and Washburn goes to Lake Minnetonka   227

Questions for Readers   245

Acknowledgments   247

About the Author   248

Endnotes   249

Water Wheels

North Star Kids of the River Mill Era

Michael Barnes

**CALUMET
EDITIONS**

Minneapolis

Prologue
Centennial
1876

The United States of America celebrated its one-hundredth birthday on the Fourth of July in 1876. Centennial festivities were held to celebrate the occasion in all thirty-seven US states and ten western territories. Fireworks burst with parades, concerts, banquets, speeches and demonstrations, especially at the International Exposition in Philadelphia, the first World's Fair held in America.

Minnesota was in the middle of a decade of amazing change that thrust the state to world leadership in lumber and flour production. How? Factors of geography, migration and technology came together simultaneously in the 1870s, like five fingers forming a powerful fist. First, the state's fertile soil supported millions of acres of pine trees in the north and fields of grain in the south. Second, Minnesota's network of rivers provided an extensive natural source of watermill power. Third, our population doubled when people from Europe and the eastern United States poured into the state. Fourth, railroad transportation crisscrossed Minnesota, and fifth, new technology placed more productive machines onto farms and into saw and flour mills.

A pair of Minnesota kids entered this turbulent decade as ten-year-olds and exited as college graduates. Halvor Dahl and Emelia Meier were children of immigrants, his parents from Norway and hers from Germany. They met briefly at the age of eight, but 1876 was to contain another coincidence for Halvor and Emelia. In addition to their shared age and immigration status, they would each find themselves staring at the wrong end of the same outlaw's pistol.

Chapter 1
Strawberry Picnic
1868

"You're a mess."

Eight-year-old Halvor Dahl looked up to see a girl about his age. He was indeed a mess. Seated at the edge of Oliver Kelley's strawberry field, Halvor had gathered the bottom hem of his white shirt to form a sack, into which he mounded the fresh fruit as he picked. The sticky berry juice leaked through his shirttail, and more was smeared around his lips where his tongue had failed to reach. Although the boy was busily licking tasty residue from his fingers, red smudges on the breast of his shirt provided telltale evidence of hand wipes.

The girl's words had sounded like an accusation, but her face showed no antagonism. Instead, she had simply stated a fact, and her expression was more curious than hostile.

"*Unnskyld meg,*" Halvor blurted.

Now the girl's head tilted, jostling her long dark braids so that one swung around in front of her shoulder. "What did you say?"

"Sorry," he stammered. "We are only two years here from Norway. I meant to say excuse me." Halvor was caught off guard, not used to speaking with strangers. This girl made him especially nervous with her direct gaze and voice.

"That's okay," came her reassuring reply.

3

She had an honest face, Halvor thought. Her square and sturdy frame was attired in a plain but neat gray dress. She was eating strawberries from a bowl and spoon, so the dress and her fingers were perfectly clean. "My name is Emelia Meier," she stated. "Who are you?"

"Halvor," he responded. "Halvor Dahl."

"Well, Halvor Dahl, the Mississippi River is that way," Emelia announced, pointing south with her spoon. "You could rinse your hands and face down there."

* * *

The occasion of this strawberry feast was a picnic hosted on the farm of Oliver Kelley. The motivation for Kelley's generosity was three-fold. First, he was an active leader in scientific farming methods, founder of the county agricultural society, and an employee of the recently created US Department of Agriculture. Visitors to this event could see and discuss modern methods that Minnesota farmers used.

Second, Kelley was an entrepreneur acting as a sales representative for two St. Paul businesses: a farm machinery company and a nursery and seed store. The strawberry picnic provided a venue to display all those products to prospective buyers.

Third, and most famously, Kelley was a founder of the Grange, formally known as the National Grange of the Order of Patrons of Husbandry. He and eight other men had founded the Grange the previous year. They envisioned a national organization to benefit farmers both economically and socially. This picnic was a promotional event to recruit farmers into the Grange.

Halvor's father, Goran Dahl, was one of those farmers. He had remained near Mr. Kelley's house, visiting with other adults, when Halvor scampered off to feast on the free strawberries. The boy decided that Emelia Meier had made a good suggestion about cleaning himself up. He would try to rinse off in the river.

Halvor passed the edge of a fruit tree orchard, walking in the direction the girl had pointed. Before long, he began to hear a faint mechanical squeaking sound and looked up to see a tall windmill. It was spinning lazily with the gentle breeze of this sunny summer day. When the boy walked up beside the contraption, he could see a slender metal shaft plunging up and downward from the whirling wooden paddles on top of the tower. The shaft entered a vertical pipe as it came nearer the ground. Halvor gripped that pipe with his hand and could feel the vibration as the shaft pumped up and down inside. From the base of the windmill, he could see connected pipes which extended along the ground. In one direction, the pipeline led back toward Oliver Kelley's strawberry gardens. But the boy followed pipes in the opposite direction, which led him to the riverbank. He kneeled beside the pipe and touched its cool, wet surface glistening with water droplets. His eyes followed to the end of the pipeline, which extended beneath the surface of the Mississippi River.

The river was wide and calm here. Halvor descended a gradual slope to where the tall grass ended above a muddy bank. He sat in the grass, removed his shoes and socks, rolled his pant legs above the knees and waded into the gentle waves. He rinsed his hands and splashed water into his sticky face. Then, peeling the shirt over his tousled blonde hair, the boy swished it in the river and twisted it tightly to wring out the water. Halvor shook the shirt and held it up, happy to see most of the red stain had washed away. He repeated the dunking and wringing one more time before wiggling the wet garment back over his head and shoulders. Still soggy, the shirt clung to his skin, so the boy had to tug it down to cover his youthful pudgy torso. Returning to the grass, he used his still-moist fingers to wipe the mud off his toes before pulling socks and shoes back onto his feet.

Heading back toward the house and farm buildings, Halvor circled along a pasture where some of Oliver Kelley's livestock was grazing. There were a few dairy cattle and a pair of draft horses. The boy was fascinated by animals and was already demonstrating skill at working with livestock on the Dahl family farm. Halvor immediately recognized the breed of cows, for they looked just like their Jerseys back home. The mouse-colored hair was short and shiny in the sunlight. He knew these cattle were known for producing large quantities of milk rich in fat, ideal for making cream and butter. One of the cows stared curiously at him and walked right up to the fence where he stood. Halvor reached between the wooden rails and affectionately scratched behind her ears and between the short, dark-tipped horns. She happily licked her nose, then dipped down to crop off a mouthful of green grass that she chewed with satisfaction.

The boy stepped up onto the bottom rail of the fence and gazed across the pasture to see the horses. They were big and strong, bred for heavy farm work, as were the Dahl family's draft animals. Harald and Ragnhild, the Belgian horses Halvor helped care for, were chestnut in color with shaggy blond manes, tails and hair about their feet. But these horses were black, so he wasn't sure what breed they might be.

Halvor jumped down from the fence and noticed that his shirt billowed away from his body as he descended. The gentle breeze and bleaching rays of the sun had dried it out surprisingly fast. Flattening the fabric against his stomach, the boy was relieved to find the strawberry stains almost completely gone. Cheerfully, he skipped forward and broke into a jog back toward the house. Along the way, he passed immediately beside a chicken yard where many of the birds were spread about the enclosure, pecking the ground for seeds or insects. Several of them were startled by the running boy and scattered, squawking in alarm, running and flapping their wings. That commotion frightened the other chickens, who likewise scurried to escape.

Halvor realized his mistake and skidded to a stop. Gradually, the flock of agitated birds stopped scrambling, and their noisy cackling quieted down to the usual clucking. The boy resumed his route toward the Kelley family residence, trying to walk as if no disturbance had occurred. However, upon nearing the house, he saw the girl in the gray dress staring at him. From a distance, he couldn't tell if she was frowning in disapproval or smiling in amusement. He looked away, pretending not to notice her, and wondered why he cared what she might think.

Water Wheels

* * *

Emelia Meier was attending this event with her father. Heinrich Meier emigrated from Germany in 1851 at the age of seventeen. Now thirty-three years old, he owned a successful hardware store in St. Paul. Oliver Kelley's picnic was an opportunity for him to communicate with customers who might be interested in buying farm implements or machinery.

After her bowl of strawberries, Emelia walked to the top of a small knoll, where she could see a great distance to the horizon in every direction. This was an abnormal sensation for a girl from the city. In St. Paul, her vision across the landscape was interrupted by houses and buildings rising on the bluffs above the Mississippi River. This knoll was in a meadow of gently waving grass with random traces of white or yellow where prairie flowers were blooming. Her nose detected a hint of the blossoms, but the overwhelming aroma of fertile soil filled her nostrils. Again, this was an unusual sense for Emelia. The more prevalent city odors of coal smoke and human waste that ran through sewers to the river were missing from here. At last, she gazed back toward the farm buildings and the Kelley family's house. She could see people moving from that distance but could not hear them. Quiet. Except for a gentle breeze across the meadow, it was silent. This was a novel environment, Emelia realized, for her eyes, nose and ears.

Hiking back to the house, she gravitated toward a group of girls and women on the lawn. They turned out to be Oliver Kelley's wife and four daughters, plus Kelley's thirty-year-old niece, Caroline Hall. The group stood in the shade of a towering cottonwood tree near the two-story, plainly built family home. One of the girls appeared to be about Emelia's age, but the other three were older, up into their teens. Mrs. Kelley was fussing with her daughters' hair ribbons and smoothing their pretty dresses while the niece arranged the girls in a row before a small group of men and women. Miss Hall then handed a pair of song sheets for the girls to share and turned to address the gathering.

"Thank you for coming to our picnic," she began. "We have prepared this small bit of entertainment for your enjoyment." Then she turned, lifted her hands to get all the girls on cue, and led them in song:

The farmer's the chief of the nation.
The oldest of nobles is he.
How blessed beyond others his station,
From want and from envy how free.
His patent was granted in Eden,
Long ages and ages ago.
Oh the farmer, the farmer forever,
Three cheers for the plow, spade, and hoe!

The song was rewarded by a smattering of applause, which the girls acknowledged with a mixture of relief and shy smiles. Emelia suspected they were eager to escape. But Miss Hall pivoted back to the small audience. "Social gatherings like this are an important aspect of the Grange," she declared. "Farm families work long days, usually distant from neighbors. It is essential for us to gather occasionally, enjoy one another's company and share ideas. Just as the men discuss their most efficient ways to raise crops and livestock, we should help one another to support and guide our families."

A few women in the group nodded their heads in agreement. Some of the men seemed uncomfortable. Emelia was impressed with this young woman who stood tall and spoke with confidence.

"Women are not only welcome in the Grange," she continued, "but we are vital members."

When the gathering dispersed, Emelia followed Miss Hall to where her father spoke with Oliver Kelley and two other men. Kelley was a short, stout man with a merry face. His dark eyes seemed deeply set beneath black, bushy eyebrows. He happily welcomed his niece when she approached. "Caroline," he burst, "you already know our distinguished US House representative, Ignatius Donnelly." The politician grinned while Kelley continued introductions. "Meet Heinrich Meier and Goran Dahl."

Water Wheels

Miss Hall reached awkwardly for a handshake, seeing Heinrich's right sleeve pinned up to his shoulder. "I lost this arm in the war," he disclosed, extending his left hand with a reassuring smile. "It's a pleasure to meet you." Emelia moved in close beside her father, seemingly unnoticed by the men.

"Mr. Meier sells farm implements and machinery from his hardware store in St. Paul," Kelley announced. "Fine equipment," he proclaimed. "I hope the folks around here see the wisdom in purchasing his merchandise." Kelley neglected to mention it, but Caroline knew he had arranged to share a commission from selling Meier Hardware products to Grange customers.

Swiveling to the other man, Kelley continued, "Mr. Dahl has a farm in southern Minnesota."

Caroline took another step forward to shake hands with Goran. He awkwardly put his hand together with hers and hesitantly added, "Cannon River Valley." Emelia noted the farmer's heavy accent was like that of the Norwegian boy she had met in the strawberry field. She could also see he was uncomfortable shaking hands with Caroline. Probably, she thought, he had little experience with young women as bold and confident as Miss Hall. Emelia admired her.

"I am not familiar with the Cannon River," Caroline admitted. "Where is it?"

The politician Donnelly jumped in to answer for the bashful farmer. "The Cannon is a substantial river which begins in Rice County and flows into the Mississippi near Red Wing. It's a beautiful fertile valley where many immigrant farmers have settled."

Kelley looked impatiently at the congressman and attempted to refocus the conversation toward Mr. Dahl. "Goran came here today to represent other farm families in the Cannon Valley. They may be interested in starting their own chapter in the Order of Patrons of Husbandry."

Dahl nodded.

Caroline seemed to recognize the farmer's discomfort and stepped back beside her uncle. "The Grange is a wonderful organization for families," she offered.

Just then, young Halvor Dahl appeared at his father's side. They looked very much alike with blonde hair, blue eyes and stocky builds. Notwithstanding, the youth's soft round arms and torso were replaced by hardened muscles in his father. The man seemed to relax with the lad's arrival and curled a strong hand around his son's shoulder. "This is my boy Halvor."

Emelia and Halvor looked at each other across the small circle of adults, remembering their earlier encounter. The girl's dark brown hair and chocolate-colored eyes were completely different from the physical characteristics of Norwegian girls he usually saw. She looked to be about his age, but her posture and facial expression made her appear confident and more mature. In the background, he heard one of the men comment, "Fine-looking lad." But Halvor was so distracted by Emelia that he could not divert his attention.

Emelia noticed the boy's white shirt was remarkably cleaner. Also, the sticky red juice was gone from his face that was steadily directed toward hers. Without the strawberry residue around his lips, he was a good-looking boy. She felt self-conscious about his stare but did not look away. Not until hearing her father's voice did she look up. "And this is my Emelia," interjected Heinrich Meier. "She's smart as a whip."

Kelley capitalized on the hardware store owner's opening to bring the conversation back to the Grange. "Mr. Dahl, have you had a chance to look at the excellent machines from Meier Hardware?" He pointed toward the nearby farm implements. "The reaper and thresher are especially popular items with wheat farmers in this area."

"Wheat is a good crop," asserted Ignatius Donnelly.

Again, Oliver Kelley directed a look of irritation at the politician before turning back to Goran Dahl.

"We do raise wheat in the Cannon Valley," the farmer affirmed.

"The Grange is organizing cooperative buying groups to make purchasing modern equipment more affordable for farmers," Kelley boasted. "Furthermore, we will provide printed educational materials as well as extension agents so farmers in all of our Grange chapters can learn the best economic and scientific methods."

Suddenly, surprisingly, young Halvor spoke up. "I saw your windmill, Mr. Kelley," he blurted, "and the pipes leading from the river to your crop fields."

Everyone was silent for a moment, and Goran Dahl gripped his son's shoulder to indicate the youngster should hold his tongue. "I'm sorry if the boy spoke out of turn."

"On the contrary," Kelley chuckled, stepping forward to tousle Halvor's hair, "my irrigation system is exactly the kind of machinery and technology the Grange is promoting. The ten-acre fruit and vegetable garden watered by those pipes is the most profitable part of my entire farm."

Caroline exchanged a quick, private glance with Heinrich Meier. They both knew the garden was the *only* profitable part of Kelley's farm. He carried unpaid debt for modern equipment bought on credit and was behind on mortgage payments for his land. Kelley's side jobs with the agriculture department and writing for farm journals kept his family from bankruptcy. Emelia noticed the interchange between her father and Kelley's niece, but it was so quick and quiet, she thought little of it.

"Fresh fruits and vegetables are transported from here by railroad," Kelley explained, "north to St. Cloud and south to St. Paul. My produce can be picked today and sold in grocery stores tomorrow."

"Railroad tracks have been laid into the Cannon River Valley," announced Donnelly.

"Yes," Goran confirmed. "Halvor and I traveled here by train."

"The Grange is working to keep down the cost of transporting farm goods," commented Kelley, "by battling against the railroad monopolies."

Everyone nodded.

"Please, Mr. Dahl," Caroline requested, "when you return to the Cannon Valley, include the women in your consideration of forming a Grange chapter. As you know, wives and daughters are quite involved in the success of farm families."

Goran acknowledged a look of agreement from Halvor. "Ours are."

"We believe that women should be equal partners in raising happy families and contributing to farm prosperity," said Caroline.

Oliver Kelley clapped his hands. "My niece is a formidable young woman," he exclaimed. "She is a schoolteacher in this township and handles all of my business correspondence. In fact, leaders of the Grange between here and Washington, DC, consider Caroline Hall to be one of our founders."

The young woman lowered her eyes, humbly aware that everyone's focus was on her. However, none of those present were more stimulated than Emelia Meier, who suddenly saw a role model in the flesh. The girl knew that she herself was smart, and like Caroline Hall, she had courage and confidence in herself. Her future may not be in agriculture like Miss Hall, but she was destined to play an important role in some endeavor. Emelia Meier was going to make a positive mark.

* * *

At the end of the day, Goran and Halvor Dahl joined wagonloads of people being ferried from Kelley's homestead to the nearby railroad station. Tired father and son stepped into the first passenger car and plopped side-by-side into a pair of empty seats. As others boarded the waiting train, Halvor recognized Mr. Donnelly, whom they had met at the picnic. The politician slid into a seat immediately ahead of them. However, instead of sitting down, he perched on his knees, facing backward toward Goran and steadied himself by gripping the seat back with both hands. His face was alight with enthusiasm.

"Mr. Dahl," he beamed, "I'm glad for another chance to speak with you." A glance at his father's face told Halvor that Goran was more interested in rest than additional conversation, but Donnelly forged ahead. "Do you have other questions about the Grange that I might be able to answer for you and your fellow Cannon Valley citizens?"

"I have heard a lot," the farmer responded patiently. "I will share these ideas with our neighbors, and we will decide what is best for us."

Water Wheels

"Well, what's best for you is the Grange!" Donnelly erupted. "Let me be blunt, Mr. Dahl. It's all about power." He was on an unstoppable roll. "The bankers, the wealthy flour mill owners, the railroad tycoons—the people with money have the power. Against them, we poor farmers are power*less!* They capitalize on the fact that each of us is a single-family enterprise, often isolated from each other by many miles. And, if you don't mind my saying so"—he did not slow down to allow any objection—"we immigrants, my Irish relatives and your fellow Scandinavian settlers, are especially victimized. The bankers gouge us with high loan rates, the millers pay us too little for our crops, and the railroads over-charge us for goods coming and going."

He paused to read Goran's reaction. The farmer was attentive but simply gave a silent, understanding nod.

"To become power*ful,* we need to unite!" Donnelly exclaimed. "A political organization like the Grange, with thousands of voting members, could force the government to regulate bank rates, mill prices and railroad fees."

Words stopped flowing, but the politician's face continued to display excitement and anticipation of a response. Goran conceded, "You make a very convincing argument, Mr. Donnelly."

"Well, let me convince you of something else," he continued. "I am campaigning to represent Minnesota in the United States Senate, a position which will be refilled this year by our state legislature."

Goran looked perplexed. "Is Alexander Ramsey not running again?" Ramsey, a member of Donnelly's own political party, was a powerhouse in Minnesota government. He had been territorial governor, state governor, or US Senator for nearly twenty years.

"Ramsey is beholden to the big money bankers, millers and tycoons who are cheating us," Donnelly declared. "It's time for a change. Farmers should pressure their state legislators to stand with average Minnesotans and support me."

Just then, Heinrich Meier and his daughter boarded the train. There were open seats near Donnelly, who was still on his knees, facing backward. However, Mr. Meier nudged the girl to pass farther down the aisle, and they found a spot near the back of the passenger car. Emelia thought she detected an expression of disdain on her father's face. So, after they were seated, she looked at him again, trying to read his thoughts.

Recognizing his daughter's curiosity, Heinrich leaned to her with a dour whisper, "I do not wish to associate with that loudmouth turncoat. He became lieutenant governor on Alexander Ramsey's coattails, and now he wants to stab that great man in the back."

Knowing her father was referring to Ignatius Donnelly, Emelia stretched up to look at him. However, just then, the train lurched slightly and began to roll forward. The politician had turned and dropped into his seat. Instead, the only face looking back at her was that of Halvor Dahl.

* * *

Oliver H. Kelley (1826–1913)

Water Wheels

Caroline A. Hall (1838–1917)

Kelley and Hall are officially recognized as founders of the National Grange and Order of the Patrons of Husbandry, a farm organization that rose to prominence during America's populist movement of the late nineteenth century.[1]

Born in Boston, Kelley arrived in Minnesota newly married (Lucy) at the age of twenty-three. Though inexperienced with farming, the couple bought land along the Mississippi River in Benton County. Kelley was determined to succeed in agriculture by seeking local advice and reading countless farm publications. Two years later, his young wife died delivering their first child, who also died six months later. Kelley re-married the next year to Temperance Lane, a local schoolteacher, also from Boston. The couple raised four daughters, all born in the 1850s.[2]

Kelley founded the Benton County Agricultural Society in 1852. He experimented with new seed varieties and livestock breeds, and tested farm equipment and modern farm methods. Eventually, he began to write farm journal articles and took a part-time job with the US Department of Agriculture, which took him to Washington, DC, during the winter months. With contacts in the nation's capital, Kelley and several others founded the Order of the Patrons of Husbandry. That organization, commonly known as the Grange, was intended to help farmers economically and socially through education, rural events and political action. Kelley encouraged farmers to unify within the Grange to claim their fair share of profits against monopolies in agricultural business.[3]

Kelley's niece, Caroline Hall, became his assistant and played such an instrumental role in the Grange that she was officially designated one of the founders. Her extensive correspondence and attention to detail were indispensable to the organization's growth and influence. She is credited with insisting upon prominent leadership positions for women throughout its membership.[4]

The Grange started with four local chapters in 1868 and increased its power and popularity within six years to establish more than ten thousand chapters across rural America. However, the organization was unable to deliver prosperity to the nation's farmers and was virtually out of existence within a decade.[5]

Chapter 2
Arbor Day
1871

"Steady, Haakon... steady." Halvor was talking to his three-year-old colt in the most calm, low-pitched tone his eleven-year-old voice could muster. That was how his father spoke to their mature Belgian draft horses, Harald and Ragnhild.

In his native Norway, Goran Dahl had farmed with Fjord horses. But when he and Ingrid moved their young family to America in 1865, they spent their savings on land in Minnesota and the two Belgians. They named the big workhorses after legendary Norwegian royalty, King Harald and Queen Ragnhild. The mare had given birth to a female foal the following year, but Goran and Ingrid sold it because they needed the money.

When Ragnhild bore another colt, they named him Haakon after another Norwegian king and kept him because Harald was about halfway through his laboring years. If draft horses remain healthy, they can work from five to twenty years of age. When Haakon reached his working age of five, his sire would be fourteen.

The colt's physical appearance was like Ragnhild's reddish chestnut coloring with a nearly white mane and tail. Both mother and son had four white stockings and a wide white blaze from forehead to muzzle. Harald was slightly bigger than Ragnhild, but both adult horses weighed more than two thousand pounds and were so tall that Halvor's eyes were beneath their broad backs. The stallion was lighter in color, a tawny coat giving way to blond hair on his underside from lower chest to rump.

Both mature horses were gentle giants, loyal and affectionate to their human masters. However, when hitched to a heavy load, they went to work with determination, muscles rippling under their skin. They seemed to love the exertion, delighting in their opportunity to demonstrate the immense strength with which they were born. Harald carried himself like a Norwegian king—head held high with a stately, high-step stride. Ragnhild's working posture was slightly lower, her shoulders leaning forward into the harness collar.

Haakon was not really Halvor's horse, but there was a bond between the two young males. The boy had cared for the colt from the night of its birth when Goran had shown him how to rub the foal to familiarize it with human handling. Once weaned from Ragnhild's milk, Halvor fed and watered the colt, which was his usual chore with all the livestock. As a yearling, Haakon gained trust and affection for the boy, who frequently groomed him with soothing hands and words. The colt learned to lower his head into the halter that Halvor fastened behind his ears.

Once Haakon reached two years of age, the boy introduced him to a harness. At first, he simply allowed the young horse to sniff the leather, hear the buckles squeak, and feel the straps across his back. Eventually, Halvor's father helped him put a light harness on the colt, and the boy walked alongside, giving directions with reins and words. Haakon learned that "Get up" meant go and "Whoa" meant stop. He learned to turn right when told "gee," left for "haw," and to back up on the command "back."

* * *

This final Friday in April had been declared Arbor Day in Minnesota. The state legislature had passed the "tree bounty law," which authorized small financial rewards for farmers who planted trees on their naked prairie homesteads. This morning, after the cows were milked and livestock fed, the Dahl family ate an early breakfast of bread and coffee. Then Goran led his two oldest boys, Erik and Halvor, to harvest saplings from the moist banks of Wolf Creek. This tree-lined stream meandered through their land before flowing onward to the Cannon River.

Erik was thirteen, two years older than Halvor. The Dahl boys dug up trees two to three feet tall, plunging their shovels deep into the ground, trying to unearth most of the young tree roots. They found mostly maples, plus occasional oaks or cottonwoods. The saplings were then carried to where the horses waited. Harald and Ragnhild were harnessed to a large wagon. Haakon, now ready to do light work at three years of age, was hitched to a two-wheeled cart. When the cart and wagon were loaded, trees were hauled in two different directions. Goran and Erik drove Harald and Ragnhild back to their house and barn. Halvor directed Haakon toward the Lutheran Church, three miles away, where all their Norwegian neighbors were members.

Upon reaching their homesite, Halvor's father and older brother drove the wagon to the rows of holes that they had dug the day before. The holes had already been saturated with buckets of water, and beside each lay a small pile of excavated dirt, ready to be pushed back around the roots of every sapling. In a few years, with luck and care, these trees would grow to provide a protective shelter belt for the Dahl family house and barn. The rows of trees were planted on those two sides in the shape of an L because prevailing winds blew from the west, and winter storms howled out of the north.

The remainder of Halvor's seven-member family was already at the Lutheran Church. His mother, Ingrid, was there with other women of the valley, preparing a midday feast for all the families who would attend. It would be a full day. Trees were to be planted around the church, after which a Grange meeting was planned, followed by music and dancing before everyone returned home. Halvor's two younger sisters, Mathilde and Astrid, ages eight and three, would be helping Ingrid at the church. They provided much care for the youngest Dahl, one-year-old baby brother Thorvald.

Halfway from Wolf Creek to the church, Halvor scrambled to keep up with Haakon. The frisky colt was anxious to go faster and pulled the two-wheel cart as if it were no hindrance at all. The boy applied firm pressure with the reins, trying to slow the young Belgian to his own walking pace. "Steady... steady," he repeated.

Halvor was a stocky lad and stout for his age, but in size and strength, the draft horse was more than ten times greater than he. His father had often cautioned him to be careful of the danger posed by these powerful beasts. "They obey our commands because of their loyalty and desire to please us," Goran explained. "However, you must always remember they are animals. If provoked by fear or anger, they could trample us in an instant."

Upon reaching the crest of a ridge, Halvor was physically tired from exertion and determined to restrain the colt with his voice rather than his muscles. "Whoa," he commanded with a simultaneous tug on the reins. Haakon stopped and turned his big head to look back. When the boy affirmed a long, drawn-out "W-h-o-o-o-a," the young horse shook its neck, tossing its blonde mane back and forth. The colt's lips flapped as he expelled a snort and impatiently pounded one front foot onto the ground. Halvor felt the ground shiver when that hoof impacted the earth, but Haakon remained in place. The boy began to relax when his horse shifted its weight and cropped a mouthful of grass to chew.

Halvor wiped perspiration from his brow with one sleeve and shaded his eyes with the opposite hand. From atop this ridge, he could see the Lutheran church steeple in one direction and the roofs of the Dahl family house and barn in another. The shallow valleys that lay across this terrain reminded the boy of the Hallingdal region where he was born. Granted, the Norwegian mountains were not beyond this horizon, and fewer spruce trees grew in this part of Minnesota. But according to Halvor's memory from six years prior, the rolling farmland looked familiar to their former home.

Numerous factors had pushed the Dahls from Norway and pulled them to Minnesota in 1865. Their former country had experienced a decades-long population boom, resulting in too few jobs and too many mouths to feed. Poverty and starvation multiplied in the 1860s when the fish population and crop production plummeted simultaneously. Norwegians depend on plentiful herring along their ocean coasts to provide fishing jobs and seafood. When the herring runs diminished at the same time the crops failed in three successive years, people went hungry. Thousands of farmers abandoned the traditionally productive agricultural lands of southeastern Norway.

Many earlier immigrants to the United States had sent mail back to Europe, describing wonderful opportunities in their new land. Several of these so-called "America letters" caught the attention of Goran and Ingrid Dahl. These letters explained the Homestead Act, passed by the US Congress in 1862. The law allowed people to claim 160 acres of property—for free—if they lived and worked on that land for five years. This was an astonishing invitation for Scandinavian farmers whose typical landholdings were a mere two acres. Many America letters raved about economic opportunities in the American West. These letters also disclosed that many Norwegians from the Hallingdal region had already settled in Minnesota where the climate and terrain were similar to their homeland.

When America's Civil War ended, the Dahls decided it was time to leave Norway with their little family. Goran was thirty years old, and Ingrid was twenty-eight. Erik, their oldest, had just turned seven. Halvor was five and Mathilde three. Their steamship crossed the Atlantic, from Oslo to New York, in ten days. After the immigration process and two more days on a train, the family arrived in St. Paul, where they learned about a Norwegian settlement in the Cannon River Valley. Goran and Ingrid staked their claim to 160 acres along Wolf Creek within the week.

Today, six years later, Halvor scanned the horizon from his ridge-top vantage point. While Haakon peacefully grazed, the boy's memory drifted back in time. He could recall only fleeting visions from his few years in Norway. The most vivid image of his grandpa was not the man's face but his hands. The skin was rough and calloused, a pair of the fingers oddly bent. Nonetheless, there

21

was a loving tenderness in those hands that had held the little boy. Now, occasional letters were exchanged across the ocean between his parents and grandparents. However, they never expected to see one another again.

His memory of their voyage across the Atlantic focused on the steamship. Approaching the vessel from shore, it looked larger than anything Halvor could imagine. Three masts extended upward, providing sail capacity to supplement the powerful and noisy steam engines. The boat reached four hundred feet long and forty feet wide. The boy remembered his amazement, looking at more than a thousand passengers on the pier, that the entire throng would fit onto the steamer. Later at sea, when the ship was rocked by massive storm-driven swells, their vessel, which had seemed enormous at dockside, appeared tiny on the vast ocean.

Halvor's recollection of their brief transfer through New York was of chaotic activity. Hordes of people swarmed out from streets between tall buildings, and other hordes dispersed through similar avenues. His senses became so overwhelmed with strange sights, unpleasant odors, constant bumps from a melee of elbows, and the startling sounds of squeaks, knocks and shouts, that the entire experience was a blur.

The twelve-hundred-mile train ride from New York to St. Paul was at first a novelty for the five-year-old boy. However, the *clackety-clack* of wheels turning over the rails and the *chug-a-lug* from the locomotive soon became monotonous. Views from the train window turned into a series of pastures, forests and river crossings that looked pretty much alike. Frequent stops at a series of matching small-town depots seemed like never-ending delays. When the family finally reached their destination, Halvor could clearly see excited anticipation in his father's face, but the boy only felt relief.

Suddenly, Halvor was thrust out of his daydream by a shove in his back from Haakon's substantial nose. The colt had intended only a gentle nudge, but the boy was caught off guard, distracted by his memories. Stumbling forward, his foot caught in a tangle of weeds, and Halvor landed on the ground with a thump. He rotated onto the seat of his pants to look at the guilty horse. "Don't know your own strength, huh?"

Haakon tossed his head and emitted a whinny as if to say, "*Let's go.*"

"Okay," the boy consented, using a newly acquired American expression, "Hold your horses."

* * *

Halvor soon came to a well-worn trail that led to the Lutheran Church. The building served triple duty for the people of the valley as their place of worship, school and meeting house. It was a simple rectangular structure, painted white, with three tall windows evenly spaced along each side. The pointed steeple tower, its most notice-able feature, rose above the roof from a small entryway that jutted out from one end of the church. The tower contained a bell that rang to announce the beginning of Sunday religious services or weekday morning school sessions.

The bell was silent this morning, but the church and surrounding lawn were a beehive of activity. Approaching the churchyard, Halvor did not see his mother or younger siblings, so he assumed they were inside where the midday feast was being prepared. He steered Haakon toward a group of men and boys working to the west of the building. Glancing in the opposite direction, the boy remembered that several graves were arranged in an orderly cemetery on that side.

Drawing near the tree planters, Halvor recognized Lars Lund, a farmer in the valley and a leader of their Lutheran Church. During Sunday services, he, more than anyone, was most likely to read a Bible verse from the altar and preach a sermon about that passage. Halvor's mother and father usually agreed with Mr. Lund's interpretation of the holy gospel, and they tried to affirm his message to their children during wagon rides home from church.

Mr. Lund saw Haakon approaching with the cartload of trees and motioned for Halvor to steer his horse alongside. Two other men were shoveling dirt into holes where a row of saplings was being planted. A crew of youngsters were assisting, some of whom carried little trees. Others were on their knees, smoothing soil around each narrow tree trunk. Two older boys and Lars Lund's daughter carried buckets of water to pour around the fresh transplants. Their bucket brigade led back and forth from a nearby wagon loaded with wooden barrels of water. A few younger children were simply scampering around the churchyard, racing and playing with one another. Their shouts and laughter raised a clamor; nevertheless, it seemed to bother no one on this occasion.

"Welcome, Halvor," greeted Mr. Lund. "These are wonderful-looking trees you have brought us."

"Mostly maples from Wolf Creek," Halvor replied. "Father and brother are replanting others at our house. They will be coming here when they're done."

"Well, thank you for these," the older man expressed. Then, turning to a group of youngsters, he shouted, "Boys! Please come and help unload these trees from Halvor Dahl's cart."

Halvor grasped a pair of the saplings, but Mr. Lund took them from his hands. "Care for your horse, young man. Then come back to me. I've got a job for you."

There were no mature trees near the church to provide shade for Haakon, so Halvor led him to a hitching rail on the north side of the building. He removed the colt's harness and placed a half-full bucket of water beneath the wooden post. Finally, he tied the lead rope from Haakon's halter to the hitching rail with plenty of slack for the horse to take a drink.

Halvor ducked into the church's back door and found his mother at the banquet table. Ingrid gave her second son a broad, welcoming smile, which turned to a frown when she saw his dirty hands and arms. "Get away from this food, young man, until you have washed yourself."

"But I'm going right back out to do a job for Mr. Lund," he protested.

With a stern look, she pointed to a wash basin near the front door. Halvor knew there would be no arguing with that look. "Come back to me with clean hands before you leave," Ingrid instructed.

Water Wheels

While walking toward the wash basin, he saw his sister Mathilde helping several women prepare food. The eight-year-old girl had always seemed more mature than her actual age, and he was not surprised to see her working with the older ladies. She, like Halvor, had inherited their father's stocky physique, while Erik and Astrid were tall and slender like their mother. Thorvald was still a plump toddler, not yet revealing his future physique.

Upon his return, Halvor displayed scrubbed fingers for his mother's inspection. She took his hands in her own with a smile of amusement.

"Father and Erik are planting trees at home," the boy reported. "It could be hours before they get here."

"Don't worry," Ingrid assured. "I will make sure to save part of the feast for our family." With that, she thrust a pair of carrots into her son's clean hands. "Here is a snack."

On his way out the church door, he nearly collided with his little brother who was being chased by three-year-old Astrid. Thorvald was squealing in fake terror, and his giggling sister was happy to pursue the toddling tyke without actually catching him.

Halvor quickly consumed one of his carrots with several hungry bites before diverting behind the building to share the other one with Haakon. He returned to Mr. Lund, whose daughter was waiting beside him. Kjerstin was a few years older than Halvor and several inches taller. She was the smartest girl in school.

Lars Lund welcomed him back. "Young Mr. Dahl, we are nearly out of water. I need you to drive this wagon down to the creek, where Kjerstin will help you refill the barrels."

The boy glanced quickly around, expecting that someone older might be entrusted with this task. Mr. Lund detected his uncertainty and boosted the youngster's confidence. "I have witnessed your skill in handling horses. You'll have no trouble with my trusty team of old Percherons. Besides, Kjerstin tells me you're the smartest boy in school." Halvor stole a glance at the girl, who calmly looked him square in the face with an expression of confirmation.

Climbing aboard the wagon seat, Halvor grasped the reins and quickly learned that the Lunds' draft horses were indeed an easy pair to handle, calm and willing to work. Kjerstin, sitting next to him, broke the awkward silence. "You *are* the smartest boy in school." He turned for a momentary look at her face, which once again was steady and sincere. Neither of them spoke again until they reached Wolf Creek. Kjerstin directed Halvor to a gentle slope where the Percherons could walk right into the stream. "I will stay up on the wagon deck," she pronounced. "You dip water out of the creek and lift each bucket onto the flatbed." Picking up two wooden pails, she explained, "While you're scooping the next bucket, I'll dump the first one into a barrel and hand it back to you."

Halvor responded, with a Norwegian-sounding assent, "Yah." Whereupon he dropped beside the stream to remove his shoes and socks and rolled his pant legs above his knees. He waded into the creek, scooped the first pail full of water and set it onto the wagon bed where Kjerstin could grab it. By the time he repeated that action with the second bucket, she returned the first one. They continued that rotation at a steady pace, only pausing to put a lid on each of the four barrels when filled.

Within half an hour, their chore was done, and both were weary. Additionally, Halvor was thoroughly soaked from pails of water that splashed when he dipped them and sloshed when he lifted them. Kjerstin's face was streaked with perspiration, and wayward strands of hair had escaped from the clasp that held them in place behind her neck. Her hair was light brown, rather than blonde, like most of the girls in the valley. She slipped off her shoes, gathered the hem of her dress in one hand, and dropped from the wagon ankle-deep into the creek. Halvor saw the girl close her eyes in relaxation as the cooling stream rippled over her feet. Gradually, the skin on her neck and cheeks returned from flushed pink to its usual pale color. She bent forward and cupped a handful of water to rinse her face, then waded to a wagon wheel, which she climbed like a ladder, back up to the seat.

The horses were refreshed from standing in the creek and quenching their thirst. When Halvor flicked the reins and asked them to "Get up," they did not hesitate. The wagon was easily a thousand pounds heavier with the four barrels full of water. However, the big, powerful Percherons easily rolled it up out of the stream.

"How soon will your brother arrive at the church?" Kjerstin asked.

Halvor knew she was asking about Erik, who was almost her age. "It could be another hour or more. He and father are planting trees into a shelter belt to protect our house and barn."

"He is a very handsome boy."

Halvor peeked at the girl from the corner of his eye. She had loosened her long hair and was rearranging the tresses neatly back into the clasp behind her neck. He wondered if Kjerstin's opinion about Erik's attractive appearance was a comment she hoped he would share with his brother. He would not.

"What are his favorite foods?"

"He likes most everything," Halvor answered. "He eats a lot."

"For instance," she inquired, "if you're eating chicken, what's his favorite piece?"

He shrugged. "I don't know. He likes the legs, I guess."

Kjerstin smoothed the pleats of her dress, then folded hands in her lap, and conversation ceased for the remainder of their route back to the church.

* * *

It was early afternoon when the water wagon returned to the church. Halvor noticed that a greater number of people had arrived, including his father and older brother. They were helping to plant the remainder of the trees being brought by other late arrivals. When Halvor reined the Percherons to a stop beside Goran and Erik, Kjerstin said, "Hello, Erik."

Erik swiftly removed his hat and respectfully nodded in her direction. "Kjerstin," he acknowledged. His shy voice was barely loud enough to be heard. He quickly clamped the droopy, broad-brimmed hat back on his head and returned to work.

Halvor thought he detected a sparkle in Kjerstin's light brown eyes as she climbed down from the wagon seat and began walking toward the church. His view followed her route to the entryway, where several women surrounded one man whom they provided with a sandwich and glass of milk. Halvor recognized him as the politician Ignatius Donnelly. He must be here to promote the Grange, thought the boy. Donnelly was the only man present who was not helping to plant trees.

Soon, all the saplings were in the ground, and Halvor helped to pour buckets of water throughout the fledgling grove. He joined the force of tree planters who gathered around tubs of water to scrub their dirty hands and sweaty faces. Then everyone entered the church to line up for food. Halvor stood in single file with his family.

One and all carried their plates out into the sunshine. It was a cold lunch, typical for Norwegian settlers who normally consumed a small noon-time snack, often packed to eat at the job site. The family would eat their biggest meal and single hot-cooked daily dinner around their own table in the early evening. Now, Halvor's plate was covered by two generous slabs of ham, each upon a thick slice of whole-grain bread. He took a glass of milk and a big dollop of butter for this special occasion. Normally, his luncheon drink would be water, and the open-faced ham sandwich would be on dry bread. The Dahls gathered around their wagon to eat. Goran and Ingrid stood with the three older children while Astrid and Thorvald perched on the edge of the wagon bed.

As the family neared the end of their meal, Kjerstin Lund approached with a pair of trays. "Would you like a second helping?" she asked, addressing them all but extending one tray in front of Erik.

Halvor noticed there were several pieces of chicken legs on the tray. His brother took one and quietly said, "Thank you," barely making eye contact with the girl.

"Mother and I made *sandbakkels* for dessert," Kjerstin beamed. Toward Erik, she offered the other tray covered with the buttery scalloped cookies, a traditional Norwegian treat.

Goran stepped up beside his thirteen-year-old son, "Thank you," he said, plucking a *sandbakkel* from the tray and snapping a quick bite. "Delicious!" he exclaimed. "You're a good cook."

Water Wheels

Halvor shot a hasty glance at his mother, looking for approval to take a cookie, but she was staring at her husband with a mixed expression of wonder and amusement. The boy turned immediately to his father just in time to see an understanding twinkle in the man's eyes. Goran popped the remainder of the *sandbakkel* into his mouth and moaned, *"Mmm."* Both parents beheld their teenage boy's awkward reaction to Kjerstin Lund's flirting.

"Attention, everyone!" Lars Lund's booming voice was heard throughout the churchyard, and scattered conversations ended while people turned to face him. He had walked to the relative center of the gathering beside Ignatius Donnelly. Mr. Lund raised both hands. "Let us give thanks to the Lord for this wonderful day," he proclaimed, "for this wonderful feast and the loving company of our friends and family."

After a brief prayer, he extended one arm toward the politician. "We are blessed today by the presence of Ignatius Donnelly, our former lieutenant governor and US congressman. Please gather 'round while he shares a few words with us." There was a smattering of applause, and most people took a few steps forward. Mr. Lund noticed that Kjerstin was standing near the Dahl family, so he moved beside her and stood next to Goran.

Donnelly pivoted naturally to engage the people surrounding him on every side. "Thank you for welcoming a wayward Irishman into this beautiful valley," he joked. "Your generous Scandinavian hospitality is graciously appreciated." He had a broad belly and displayed an equally broad smile across his wide face. Halvor noticed some beads of perspiration on the man's forehead, which glistened in the afternoon sun. He must be warm, the boy thought, noting that the politician was the only man in attendance wearing a necktie.

"I am proud that our Minnesota legislature designated this final Friday of April to be Arbor Day," Donnelly announced. "The Tree Bounty Law, recently initiated in Nebraska and now established in our state, is a great idea. Happily, frontier farmers such as yourselves are capitalizing on the incentive to plant trees that will beautify our

29

landscape." He continued, pointing to the new rows of saplings nearby, "Someday, this windbreak will protect your house of worship from howling winter blizzards, and these trees will provide cooling shade for a chubby man standing in this churchyard." He paused, drew a handkerchief from his pocket to dab his brow, and cheerfully chuckled at his own expense.

Donnelly's willingness to poke fun at himself endeared him to the crowd. The politician was well-known for his powerful voice and articulate speech. Now, he demonstrated those nonverbal skills that made him a great orator. He was relaxed and confident with all eyes upon him. He seemed able to return eye contact with each one and everyone at the same time. In this case, he recognized the mood of his audience and knew precisely when and how to inject a note of humor.

Next, he praised them. "I congratulate you for embracing Arbor Day with such ingenuity and effort. I also admire the successful Grange organization you have established here in the Cannon Valley. I'm proud to boast of leadership in the Grange chapter that serves my own farm along the Mississippi River near Hastings. I believe that Oliver Kelley and I have been instrumental in making the Patrons of Husbandry particularly popular here in Minnesota. We now have more than fifty active chapters in the state."

"Our aim is to ensure that farmers are rewarded for the noble work we do to provide food for our fellow man. Too often, we are cheated from that reward by monopolistic middlemen between us and the hungry population—like grain moguls who underpay for our harvest, like railroad tycoons who overcharge for the transport of our goods, like bankers who collect excessive interest on our land." Donnelly's voice had steadily risen until he nearly shouted those words.

After a pause, he proceeded with a tone of quiet determination. "Our government needs to regulate those greedy monopolists. I hope your votes will help me regain a seat in the Minnesota legislature. I'm running for state senate as a member of the Anti-Monopoly Party. I promise to stand up for your benefit on every issue. Please vote for me in this year's election. Thank you."

Water Wheels

Polite applause followed the conclusion of Donnelly's speech, and a few individuals approached him to ask questions or extend wishes of good luck. Lars Lund leaned close to Goran Dahl. "Donnelly has lost favor with both the Democrats and Republicans," Lars murmured. "This Anti-Monopoly Party is the fourth switch he's made from one political party to another since coming to Minnesota from Philadelphia seventeen years ago."

Goran responded with hope, "I know. But I believe he's on our side. That he sincerely wants to work for the benefit of common rural people like us."

"He's a politician," Lars muttered skeptically. "He's on his own side."

* * *

People bid goodbye to Ignatius Donnelly before he departed to deliver another Arbor Day speech in Farmington. The dirty dishes were washed, and the leftover food was collected. As the chores were ending, Oskar Skogstad pulled his flatbed wagon near the flat, dirt-packed oval of ground in front of the church. Grass had been worn away from this space by years of schoolchildren's trampling feet. Oskar's wife Birget approached with a violin case clamped under one arm, and he nimbly hoisted her up to sit on the wagon's edge, his raw-boned hands encircling her waist.

Birget laid the case beside her and opened the latches to lovingly withdraw her beautiful Hardanger fiddle. At first glance, the traditional Norwegian instrument looked like an ordinary violin with a few decorations added. This one had black etchings surrounding the body, and a pattern of pearl inlay decorated the neck. Its top scroll was hand-carved into the head of a lion, symbolic of Norway's coat of arms. The maple body of Birget's instrument was narrower but deeper than a standard violin. However, the most significant difference was the number and location of its strings. There were four primary strings, like a typical violin. But a Hardanger fiddle has additional "sympathetic" strings beneath and between each of the higher ones. This requires a longer pegbox to hold double the number of tuning pegs.

31

Michael Barnes

Sitting on the edge of the wagon, Birget tucked the instrument under her chin and began to draw her bow across the strings. She played a traditional Norwegian folk song with an emotional melody. By simultaneously contacting multiple strings with her gliding bow, Birget produced dissonant, echoing notes, the haunting sound for which Hardanger fiddles are famous. Her shoulders swayed slightly with the song's slow rhythm, and one dangling toe tapped in midair. An audience converged around the Skogstads' wagon, and when Birget stroked her last note, people clapped and cheered, producing a humble smile from the soloist.

Before the applause died away, nimble Oskar leaped upon the wagon bed and extended the ovation with his own clapping. Straight away, he pulled a flat drum from under one armpit and withdrew a Y-shaped drumstick out of his back pocket. Tapping a tempo on the edge of the drum, he loudly and joyfully proposed, "How about a dance?" Oskar and Birget were well-known dance leaders in the Cannon Valley. She was the skillful musician. He was the enthusiastic "caller" who encouraged people to join the dance and occasionally sang lyrics. He always contributed to the fun and helped inexperienced participants by prompting them with easy-to-follow commands throughout the dance.

Oskar's homemade instrument was an imitation Sami drum. Scandinavian shamans used the authentic drums during ceremonies designed to see into the future by connecting with the spirit world. Historically, the drumheads were made from reindeer hide, and the hammers were carved from reindeer antlers. However, Oskar was no shaman. His Sami drum was designed to provide dance rhythm and percussion accompaniment to Birget's beautiful melodies. This drumhead was buckskin, stretched tightly around a pine bough bent into an oval that fit into the crook of Oskar's arm. His drumstick was carved from a white-tail deer antler.

Oskar was a thin, sharp-featured man with long arms and legs that sometimes seemed out of sync with each other. But now one of his boot heels thumped the wagon bed in perfect rhythm with the antler he clacked against the rim of his drum. This was a three-

32

beat tempo, typical for "walking dances" designed for couples the Norwegians called *springleik*. "Goran and Ingrid," he shouted with a broad grin. "Will you get us started?" He curled his arm in a beckoning gesture toward Mr. and Mrs. Dahl, likewise motioning other couples to step into the dusty oval.

Halvor saw his mother and father share consenting smiles in response to the caller's invitation. As they joined hands and walked forward, Birget's fiddle produced the first few notes for a *bygdedans,* a traditional Norwegian dance. Physically, the couple appeared mismatched. Long, slender Ingrid was taller than her compact, powerfully muscled husband. However, they had dismissed any discomfort with that peculiarity long ago. The music carried them gracefully around the oval. Now and then, at Oskar's direction, all the couples twirled with each other. Whether awkward or artful, each of these maneuvers were enjoyed by the dancers and onlookers.

By late afternoon, the dancing was done. Everyone had evening chores to perform and livestock to tend. Families gathered their children, said their goodbyes and rolled away toward their farms in various directions. Halvor harnessed Haakon to the two-wheeled cart. Goran mounted their wagon's bench seat alongside Erik, to whom he handed the reins. Ingrid dangled her feet from the tail of the wagon, holding Thorvald in her lap and flanked by Mathilde and Astrid. As the church steeple grew distant behind the Dahls, they listened to the fading echoes of one last melody from Birget Skogstad's Hardanger fiddle.

* * *

Michael Barnes

Ignatius Donnelly (1831–1901) was one of the most famous politicians in Minnesota history and was nationally known as a powerful orator and leader of the Populist movement.

Born in Philadelphia to an Irish Catholic immigrant, Donnelly became a well-educated lawyer. He married fellow Irish descendant Kate McCaffrey and moved to Minnesota at age twenty-five. The couple joined a group that tried to establish the utopian communal city of Nininger just upstream from present-day Hastings on the Mississippi River. The venture faltered, partly because of the economic Panic of 1857, leaving them deep in debt.[6]

A political Democrat when he arrived in Minnesota, Donnelly switched to the anti-slavery Republican party and became Alexander Ramsey's lieutenant governor in 1860. With Ramsey's backing, he was elected to three successive terms in the US Congress (1863–

69). However, when he attempted to unseat Ramsey as US Senator, he was defeated and lost favor with Republicans. Donnelly spent the rest of his political career alternating between the Democrats and several other minor parties. He was elected numerous times to the Minnesota legislature but never again held statewide office.[7]

During his fifties, Donnelly focused on writing rather than politics and authored three controversial and best-selling books. He boosted his income as a lyceum speaker and lobbyist, particularly on behalf of the Patrons of Husbandry (the Grange). He was a passionate supporter of farmers and, along with Oliver Kelley, helped to make Minnesota a hotbed of Grange support.[8]

In later years, Donnelly re-focused on politics and became a driving force within the Populist movement. He supported the People's Party, which failed to boost William Jennings Bryan into the presidency but achieved remarkable success in states throughout the upper Midwest.[9]

Chapter 3
Meier Hardware and Lumber
1871

"Fire!" Someone was banging on the Meiers' front door in the middle of the night. A man's voice yelled, "Heinrich, your lumber yard is on fire!" Emelia and her sisters sat up in bed. They heard their father's footsteps pound quickly down the stairs and opened the front door. "I've got a gig to take you there," the voice announced.

"Let me get some clothes on," Heinrich called over his shoulder. Bounding back up the staircase, he bolted between his oldest and youngest daughters, standing with their mother on the second-story landing. In less than a minute, he passed them again, going in the other direction, fastening pants and shirt as he hurried. As he landed on the main floor and burst out the door, his middle daughter dashed after him. While her mother and sisters stood frozen by the emergency, Emelia pulled on an old dress and flat shoes to give chase. Caught off guard, Hildegard shouted, "Get back here!" But it was too late. Her headstrong daughter was already leaping off the front porch, heading for the departing gig.

Alfred Kohler, a lumberyard workman, had sounded the alarm. He was driving the one-horse, two-wheeled buggy. As soon as Heinrich landed on the seat beside him, Alfred flicked the reins and urged his gelding forward. Running diagonally across the front yard, Emelia lost sight of the two men underneath the carriage canopy, which extended from above their heads down behind the bench seat. But she gained on them before the horse could accelerate to full speed. Approaching from behind, she saw apparatus for extra riders to stand on the rear of the gig. A horizontal rail reached from side-to-side at wheel hub height, and a handlebar extended behind the canopy roof. Despite her stocky frame, the girl nimbly leaped onto the foot rail and grabbed the handlebar with both fists. The muscles flexed in her sturdy arms. Her long brown hair, usually confined into neat braids, had been loosed at bedtime. It flew wildly in the wind.

Alfred directed the speeding horse westward from his boss's home on Dayton's Bluff, across a bridge over Phalen Creek and through downtown. The Meier Lumberyard was located a few blocks above St. Paul's lower levee on the Mississippi River. Emelia could hear the sound of her father's voice with his employee, although, with the wind whistling past her ears and horse hooves clip-clopping on the road, she was unable to distinguish their conversation through the canopy. She was confident, however, that her presence on the gig was unknown. Otherwise, Heinrich would undoubtedly have ordered her back home.

When Alfred slowed the horse a half-block from the lumberyard, Emelia dropped from the gig and blended into a crowd of onlookers. Her father's attention was focused on his property ahead and smoke billowing up into the dark night sky.

* * *

Twenty years earlier, young Heinrich Meier had immigrated to America from his native Germany. Born in the industrial Rhine River Valley, his merchant family was not poor, but they were "Forty-Eighters." Rebellion had erupted throughout the many disjointed, autocratic German states in 1848. Heinrich joined growing protests against heavy taxes, censorship and a feudal society enforced by dictatorial monarchs. He hoped for a unified German nation governed by a democracy that would ensure political and economic freedom. Unfortunately, military crackdowns crushed the protests.

Water Wheels

So, rebels like Heinrich, fearing punishment by vindictive rulers, fled central Europe in search of safety and freedom.

At seventeen, Heinrich joined thousands of "Forty-Eighters" who settled in the "Over the Rhine" neighborhood in Cincinnati, Ohio. He gained employment on the docks of the Ohio River, loading and unloading cargo from steamboats. That job enabled him to pay rent at a riverfront boardinghouse occupied primarily by German immigrants. He steadily saved an amount of his earnings but could not see opportunities for promotion in Cincinnati above his job on the docks.

One night after work, he met a steamboat crew drinking beer in a riverside tavern. They had been down the Ohio River to St. Louis and ferried passengers and cargo north and south on the Mississippi. "St. Paul, Minnesota," said the riverboat captain, "is the fastest growing town in America. Next spring, when the Upper Mississippi rises with snow runoff and rainfall, we're going back. Everybody is making money in St. Paul."

Then and there, Heinrich decided to go west. He resumed his old job in a new location, St. Paul's lower levee, and started looking for something better. Before long, he found more than he had bargained for. The young man met and fell in love with Hildegard Bauer, another German immigrant. The following spring, Heinrich and Hilde, ages twenty-three and twenty-one, were married in their German Catholic church.

In 1858, when Minnesota attained statehood, the young couple toiled and saved. Heinrich labored on the docks and did extra jobs delivering wagon loads of goods from the levee to homes and businesses in St. Paul, now the state capitol. Hilde was an excellent seamstress. She took in extra laundry, mostly from single male dockworkers, and mended worn clothing for an additional fee. With both working, their nest egg grew, as did the family. Their daughter Johanna was born the following year.

Heinrich and Hilde believed they could successfully operate a hardware store in their rapidly growing city, where building supplies were in demand. In 1859, they borrowed enough money from the bank to buy a two-story building in downtown St. Paul. They made their home upstairs and invested almost all of their savings to stock the street-level store with merchandise.

Meier Hardware was an immediate success! Heinrich was an astute business manager, and Hilde continued to take in laundry and mending. The young couple was respected and well-liked when their second daughter, Emelia, was born the following year.

However, misfortune came in 1861. After Abraham Lincoln became President, eleven southern states seceded from the Union to form a separate nation—the Confederate States of America. Lincoln asked northern states to provide 75,000 troops, and Minnesota Governor Alexander Ramsey was the first to pledge a regiment.

St. Paul had its own well-organized volunteer militia, the Pioneer Guard. As an officer among those citizen soldiers, Heinrich considered it his duty to join Ramsey's regiment. He was twenty-seven years of age, physically fit, and a leader in his church and the business community. Furthermore, like most "Forty-Eighters" in America, Heinrich was an outspoken critic of slavery. He and Hilde debated his enlistment, which meant leaving her to care for Johanna, Emelia and the hardware store. Yet everyone agreed that hostilities would last only a few months or less, and she would be fine until his quick return.

It wasn't quick. A month after their June departure via steamboat, Union forces were defeated at the Battle of Bull Run, and the First Minnesota regiment suffered twenty percent casualties. More than a year later, they won a critical victory at Antietam, but Heinrich was among the many casualties. A musket ball shattered his right elbow, and his arm was amputated at the bicep. After recovery in a Washington, DC, hospital, he arrived home in October of 1862, and the little Meier family celebrated a somber Christmas that winter.

Heinrich grew stronger the following spring, and so did the hardware store. A third daughter, Katharina, arrived in 1865 when the Civil War ended. The conflict's end sparked a renewed economic and population boom in St. Paul. The capital city, which had doubled in size since Heinrich's arrival, doubled again during the

1860s to twenty thousand people. St. Paul's population would top one hundred thousand within two more decades.

The Meiers moved their young family from above the downtown store into a residential neighborhood on Dayton's Bluff. The area, east of downtown St. Paul, had once been owned by Lyman Dayton, the Lake Superior and Mississippi Railroad president and land speculator. Heinrich and Hilde chose a homesite on the crest of a hill, where the scenic Mississippi Valley could be seen in the distance. They occupied one of two spacious upstairs bedrooms, and the other was shared by their three girls, lovingly nicknamed Jo, Emmy and Kat.

The growing city offered Heinrich an opportunity to enlarge his enterprise. Expansion into the lumber business was natural for his hardware store, which already sold building supplies. Meier Lumber was located near the railroad tracks, a few blocks from Meier Hardware. In addition to boards, the lumberyard contained stacks of doors, windows and shingles. Metal supplies, such as nails, screws, knobs and hinges, were stocked inside a building where Heinrich maintained an office. This structure is where the fire ignited.

* * *

Weaving among the crowd of onlookers, Emelia could see no flames, but heavy clouds of smoke billowed through the roof of the lumberyard office. When she emerged through the front row of people, the girl saw her father in an agitated conversation with fire chief Ben Williams. Emelia recognized Mr. Williams because her father had been a chief of volunteer firefighters before their family moved to Dayton's Bluff. During Heinrich's tenure with the St. Paul Hose Company, the city had purchased the steam engine that was now pumping water into the smoldering building. A pair of dapple-gray horses that had pulled the engine to this location was tied a safe distance from the action.

Emelia heard a bystander say, "The building was full of flames when the fire engine got here. It really sizzled when they began the spray of water." She detected no sizzling now, but it was a noisy spectacle. The *thrum* of the engine pump and *hiss* of escaping steam were louder than the *whoosh* of cascading water. Above it all were the occasional shouts of volunteer firefighters, warning spectators to stay back and redirecting the water hose spray.

While that chorus of noises bombarded her ears, Emelia's nose inhaled a mixture of pungent odors. Most noticeable was the bitter stench of smoke. However, when the night's gentle breeze swirled the soot in a different direction, she caught the musky smell of mud. The showering water hose splashed the ground around the office, and an aroma of wet earth was carried in the rising mist. Still, the lumberyard's everlasting tangy fragrance of pine sap persisted beneath it all. Sure enough, when she pivoted away from the office, Emelia could see all the stacks of fresh, clean boards untouched by the fire.

She raced straight to Heinrich and threw both arms around his waist. "Father, the boards are safe."

He looked down, caught off guard and confused. "Emmy, where did you come from?"

Instead of answering the question, she swung one arm around to point at the stacks of lumber. "The boards are safe," she repeated.

Heinrich gave a nod of appreciation to Chief Williams, then walked hand-in-hand with his daughter toward the rows of boards, shingles, doors and windows. He encircled Emelia's waist with his single left arm and nimbly lifted her to sit upon the edge of a neat stack of two-by-fours. The girl's face was level with his, and he looked her sternly in the eye. "What are you doing here?"

A moment of silence passed between them. Slowly, a mischievous smile began to turn up the corners of Emelia's mouth. "I jumped on the back of the buggy."

"Emmy," he exhaled, "you could have been badly hurt."

"I wanted to help." She was fearless and eager.

Heinrich looked down, exasperated but unable to be angry with the girl. He raised his eyes to hers and gripped her knee. "You're my *best* helper. I need to keep you safe." Then he took a half-step back, offered his steady hand, and assisted her jump to the ground.

Water Wheels

She is my best helper, Heinrich thought as they turned back toward the smoldering office. At age eleven, Emelia hurried from school to the hardware store each afternoon. Her math skills were already good enough to execute flawless accounting of bills and receipts. Plus, she had an uncanny organizational ability to categorize store merchandise and knew the location of everything.

As they returned toward Mr. Williams, Emelia noticed their family carriage approach on the street. Her mother yanked the horse to a stop and jumped out while Johanna and Katharina remained aboard. Hildegard ran to them and enveloped Emelia in her arms. "Thank God you're safe." Yet after a moment, she separated from the girl, and her demeanor switched from relief to anger. "You naughty girl! You scared us half to death."

Heinrich stepped beside his wife. "Everything is all right now," he soothed. "You girls should go home and try to get some sleep." He quickly kissed Hilde's cheek. "When it's safe to go inside the office, I will assess the damage and then return myself. I promise to be home for breakfast."

* * *

No one in the Meier family had slept very much, but the mood around their breakfast table was surprisingly bright. "Our only significant loss was paperwork," Heinrich explained. "The metal merchandise—nails, screws, knobs, hinges and most of the tools—will merely need to be rinsed off."

"Should we come and help with that?" asked Johanna.

"No, we'll be closed today," he answered. "Our lumberyard crew can do that job. I'll take you girls to school as usual. Then you can walk to the hardware store this afternoon."

Hilde asked, "When do you think the lumberyard will reopen?"

"Tomorrow," Heinrich responded. "We can operate out of a tent if we have to." After a pause, he announced, "I intend to enlarge the office. That existing building has been cramped with our growing volume of business."

"Perhaps the fire was a blessing in disguise," wondered Hilde.

"The damaged roof and two walls will need to be replaced anyway," Heinrich stated. "The entire expansion can be done with shingles and boards we already have in stock."

Emelia changed the subject. "What caused the fire, Father?"

"Chief Williams and I think it started on the roof. Perhaps a glowing ember from the smokestack of a passing train."

"So, nobody did it on purpose?" she surmised.

Heinrich and Hilde exchanged glances. They had hardware and lumber business competitors, but no one Heinrich suspected of arson. "No," he said finally.

* * *

Jo and Emmy washed the breakfast dishes while Hilde readied six-year-old Kat for school. Heinrich fed and watered their horse before harnessing him to the family carriage. They didn't need a horse when they lived above the downtown store. Thus, they bought the bay gelding when the Meiers built their new house. The liveryman had recommended the three-year-old Morgan as gentle enough to serve a young family and strong enough to manage the hills of Dayton's Bluff. The girls had named him, appropriately, Morgan.

Heinrich drove the carriage, sitting next to his wife in the front seat. The three girls crammed into the back seat with Kat stuck in the middle. He stopped first at the hardware store, where Hilde got out and unlocked the front door to open for business. While she waved goodbye, Johanna moved alongside her father, leaving more room for her younger sisters in the back.

Several blocks beyond was Assumption Church, where the girls went to school. While they scampered into the building, Heinrich swiveled on the seat, looking two blocks south to where their massive new church would be built. The growing number of German Catholics in St. Paul had outgrown the little chapel on West Ninth Street. This new structure, designed by a German architect, would feature twin spires rising more than two hundred feet tall.

Heinrich could see their young priest, John Ireland, pacing about the construction site. The two men were well-acquainted.

Water Wheels

Ireland had lived in St. Paul since the age of thirteen. His first assignment as a priest was to accompany Minnesota soldiers to the Civil War battlefront. The men who marched with the young chaplain bragged about his inspiration, tender kindness, good humor and unfailing optimism. He had become rector for the entire St. Paul diocese in 1867 and was an enthusiastic booster for the new Church of the Assumption.

Heinrich circled around to greet the priest. "Good morning."

"Mr. Meier," Ireland acknowledged, "I hear you had a fire last night."

Heinrich chuckled. "It is well known that you're an early riser who never misses morning mass. I dare say you hear St. Paul's daily news before the rooster crows."

"Ha ha," the priest laughed as Heinrich jumped down from the carriage. Both in their early thirties, the men liked and admired each other well enough to enjoy some mutual teasing. The slender German extended his lanky left arm. The barrel-chested Irishman smiled and grasped the hand in his own powerful grip.

"We were lucky," Meier admitted. "Very little damage." Then, slipping into business mode, "I can assure you, there will be no interruption of hardware or lumber for the construction of this church." They shared a mutually beneficial financial arrangement. Ireland appreciated that his Catholic diocese received construction materials at bargain prices because of Meier's loyalty to Assumption Church. Heinrich appreciated the priest's loyalty to him as a member of his parish.

Now, it was Ireland's turn to tease. "How much trust should a humble Irishman place in the honesty of a ruthless German capitalist?" After sharing a snicker, the priest asked, "How is your beautiful family?"

"Hildegard is good. She's at the store. I just dropped off the girls at school."

"I commend your decision to educate those young women," Ireland affirmed. "It's good, too, that they are receiving guidance in our faith and morality in addition to academic instruction."

"Thank you," Heinrich accepted. "In Germany, it's normal for girls to attend school into their middle teens. We always expected them to be educated as well as the boys."

"I came here to check on the construction progress, but I think I'll visit the children before moving on." The priest waved goodbye. "God bless you."

Heinrich climbed back into the carriage seat and watched Ireland walk away with his typical dynamic strides. The priest's bold gait was the same as his leadership of the parish, Meier thought. St. Paul's Catholic diocese was growing as fast as the city. In addition to the old cathedral, five new churches were recently built or under construction. St. Mary's in Lowertown and St. Michael's on the West Side were attended primarily by Irish patrons. The Church of St. Louis at Tenth Street and Cedar was built to serve Catholics of French ancestry. Now, simultaneous with the construction of this new Assumption Church, Eastern European immigrants were erecting St. Stanislaus at Western and Goodhue. Heinrich wondered how all these new churches would be paid for. However, Father Ireland seemed to simply assume that the money would appear by divine providence.

* * *

Emelia was writing multiplication problems on a handheld slate in chalk, all the single-digit multiples of the number seven: *1 x 7 = 7, 2 x 7 = 14*, all the way through *9 x 7 = 63*. She was impatiently waiting for Sister Genevieve to check her work. Emelia knew all her math calculations were correct, but the nun required that every student's work be approved by the teacher. Only then could she erase her slate and proceed to the multiples of eight. As usual, Emelia was nearly done with her math problems, while other children in the age group worked more slowly. Sister Genevieve was patiently assisting other children. So, as often happened, Emelia put down her slate and moved along the bench to where she could help some struggling classmates decipher their numbers.

After a few moments, a disturbance began in the rear of the church. Emelia stood up and looked to see Father Ireland coming through the main entrance. Bouncing loudly and happily alongside was the youngest group of pupils, including her sister Katharina. Some children clung to his arms and legs while the muscular young priest grinned and plowed down the center aisle toward the altar. Before long, all the students had joined him near the sanctuary, where he sat down on a step. The little ones circled him on the floor while the older kids like Emelia and Johanna sat in the first rows of pews. Their teachers, the Sisters from St. Joseph of Carondelet, stood quietly to the sides.

He spent a few minutes in lighthearted banter with the children, asking about their favorite activities and subjects in school. Suddenly, a little boy from Kat's class blurted, "My father says you're an Irishman." There was an awkward moment of silence except for quiet gasps from the nuns. Emelia turned quickly to see Sister Genevieve nervously cover her mouth.

"Ha-ha-ha-ha!" Out of the lull boomed the priest's boisterous laugh. "Your father is right," he confirmed with a merry grin. Then, pointing a playful finger at the boy, he teased, "I'll bet you're a German." The lad bobbed his head up and down in confirmation. The boy's expression brightened from glum to glee in response to the priest's jolly face and growing giggles from his fellow students.

When the laughter subsided, Ireland assumed a more thoughtful demeanor. "The *more* important thing is that we are all Americans," he asserted. "Regardless of the land our parents came from, we are lucky to live in the United States where everyone is free to think and speak and worship as we believe." The priest spread out his arms, creating the image of a circle around the entire group. "And the *most* important thing is that we are all children of God." His gaze rotated full circle, seeming to connect with the eyes of every child.

* * *

In mid-afternoon, when school ended, the three Meier girls walked several blocks east to the hardware store. Their roles within the family business were mutually understood through months of routine. Johanna usually worked with customers in the aisles. Tall and slender like Heinrich, she was a pretty girl who felt comfortable greeting and communicating with shoppers. Her height and social skills made Jo seem more mature than her thirteen years. She was good at understanding what people wanted, and her customers frequently left the store with something more than intended when they entered.

Johanna also had an eye for style. A colorful scarf or sash often accented her simple dresses. She helped her mother assemble the store's window displays, presenting fashionable new merchandise in eye-catching arrangements. Likewise, she was attentive to the appearance of merchandise on the shelves, often readjusting items after shoppers handled them.

Emelia's talents lay more in the background. She was often upstairs, where the Meiers' former living quarters had been converted into warehouse space. When the family moved to Dayton's Bluff, Emelia helped organize the vacant residence into separate stock rooms. Work clothes were stored in one former bedroom, garden tools and supplies in the other. Kitchen goods were accordingly located in that area, and household hardware was neatly arranged around their previous living space. She knew what inventory they had and where it was located. She commonly restocked the store shelves and kept a list of items that needed to be replenished.

Downstairs, Emelia's place was behind the counter. She operated the cash register and gave each customer a handwritten receipt. Heinrich and Hilde had double-checked her accounting when the girl began to handle exchanges of money, but that was more than a year ago. The thoroughness and accuracy of her receipts were never mistaken. The balance of money in the cash register was never incorrect. Contrary to her talkative older sister, Emelia's verbal exchanges with customers were brief and matter-of-fact, but the girl was completely trustworthy.

In the early years of Meier Hardware, husband and wife were the only staff. Eventually, when they added Meier Lumber, Heinrich operated the lumberyard while Hilde managed the hardware store. However, their daughters were ages seven, five and newborn. She needed help. A series of clerks assisted her, as had been the case when Heinrich marched off to war.

Presently, their clerk was Rudolph Gottfried, a kindhearted bachelor from their church who went by the nickname Dolf. Heinrich had worked on the steamboat levee with Dolf years before. However, the man was in his fifties now, too old for the backbreaking labor experienced by dock workers. He worked half-days with Hilde from when the door opened each morning until the girls arrived in the afternoon.

Six-year-old Kat was too young for an independent job in the store. She was expected to shadow her mother or occasionally one of her sisters. Nowadays, Hilde can usually keep one eye on her youngest while managing the business. Jo and Emmy were fully capable of performing the routine daily tasks.

Ting-a-ling. The front door opened, jangling a small bell above the entrance, which signaled the entry of a customer. The Meier girls all turned to see a good-looking young man step inside. Johanna welcomed him with a smile and offered, "What can we help you with today?"

The youth was dressed in work clothes and wore a short-brimmed flat cap. Seemingly surprised to encounter a teenage girl, he whipped off the cap and stammered, "I-I-I'm looking for a wheelbarrow."

"Hmmm," Jo hesitated. She pivoted to ask her mother, but Emelia overheard the conversation from behind the counter.

"Wheelbarrows are at the lumberyard," she shouted.

He glanced nervously back and forth between Johanna, in front of him, and toward the voice from the back of the store belonging to a girl he couldn't see. "Where's the lumberyard?"

"Well, it's closed today," Jo explained. "We had a fire last night." The young man put his hat back on and began to turn away. "Wait," she stopped him. "The lumberyard is only a few blocks away, and our father is there. My younger sister can run down there and roll a wheelbarrow back here." She turned to the back of the store, but Emilia stubbornly refused to acknowledge the suggestion.

"Yes, she can," Hilde's firm, deliberate voice broke the silence.

Slowly, Emelia came out from behind the counter. She walked past her sister and the boy without a word. *Ting-a-ling.* The bell jingled as she went out the door and turned down the street.

Arriving at Meier Lumber, Emelia saw that much of the damaged office roof was already removed. Alfred Kohler and another man were standing in the rafters, prying off scorched boards and shingles, which they tossed to the ground. Both men had removed their shirts, revealing filthy arms and torsos smeared with sweat and soot. Her father held a rake in his single left arm, pulling the discarded pieces of wood into mounds.

"Hello, Father," she called, advancing toward him.

"Whoa, Emmy," Heinrich dropped the rake and held up the palm of his one hand. "Some of these roof boards and shingles have nails sticking out."

"What are you doing?" she asked.

"I'm raking them into piles," he pointed. "One we can reuse and this other heap for firewood kindling." Bending to pick up the rake, he countered, "What are *you* doing?"

"Oh, a customer at the hardware store wants a wheelbarrow. We knew you were closed, so Mother sent me down here to get one."

Heinrich nodded toward an undamaged aisle beyond the office. "Beside the ladders," he told her. "Be careful walking over there."

Rounding a stack of fence posts, she noticed Dolf rinsing some tools in a big tub of water. "Hello, Mr. Gottfried."

"Miss Emelia," he looked up and smiled. "Your father needed some extra help here today." Dolf was dunking tools into the tub and wiping them clean of soot and ashes. He arranged neat stacks of hammers, saws, wrenches, screwdrivers and the like on nearby planks.

She selected a wheelbarrow and began to roll it away when Dolf called out, "I hear you took a wild ride last night."

Emelia stopped and looked over her shoulder to see a mischievous grin on the man's face. He glanced up to the roof and confessed, "Alfred told me."

Water Wheels

She smiled at his warmhearted teasing before turning to depart. *"Heh-hee-hee."* She could hear him giggle as she strode away.

Back at Meier Hardware, Emelia parked the wheelbarrow outside the front door and entered. *Ting-a-ling.* The young man stood at the back counter near her mother and two sisters. Upon approach, she could see he was holding a brand-new shovel. Johanna announced, "Tim decided he needed a shovel to go with his new wheelbarrow."

Her flirtatious sister had talked him into it, Emmy suspected.

Hilde interrupted from behind the cash register, "This is Timothy McGowan. His family is new to St. Paul." Nodding toward Emmy, she introduced her, "This is our middle daughter, Emelia."

"Pleased to meet you," he offered.

"How much do these things cost?" asked Hilde.

Emelia reached for the receipt book and pulled a pencil from her pocket. "Five dollars for the wheelbarrow, and this shovel is two-fifty."

* * *

John Ireland (1838–1918) was the most famous religious leader in Minnesota history without question.

Michael Barnes

Born in Ireland, he immigrated with his family, settling in St. Paul at the age of thirteen.[10] Ireland soon entered the seminary and was ordained a priest in 1861 at the outbreak of the Civil War. He served as a chaplain on the battlefront, where he earned the lifelong friendship and admiration of many Minnesota soldiers across lines of ethnic background and religious belief.[11]

A charismatic personality, dynamic orator and energetic leader, Ireland became a bishop when he was thirty-six. During fifty years at the helm of his Catholic diocese, he oversaw the construction of hundreds of Catholic churches, including the St. Paul Cathedral and the Basilica of St. Mary in Minneapolis.[12]

Ireland was an advisor to US presidents, most famously William McKinley and Theodore Roosevelt. A well-known patriot for "Americanism," he consistently praised the country's religious freedom and public education. Some controversial causes were passionately boosted by Archbishop Ireland, including the modernization of the Catholic Church, colonial settlement of poor Irish immigrants, and prohibition of alcohol.[13]

Chapter 4
Blizzard
1873

Thunk. Halvor awakened to the familiar pre-dawn sound of his father knocking snow off his boots by kicking his feet against the squared log wall just outside their front door. *Thunk.* The boy's bed was in the upper half-story above that door, and the wall vibrated with the kick of each boot.

Halvor closed his eyes. It was a cold January morning, still dark outside. He wanted to drowse under his blanket for a few more minutes.

Whish-whump. The door opened and closed when Goran stepped across the threshold, probably carrying a bundle of firewood in one arm. *Clomp-clomp.* The man let both of his boots drop beside the entry. Then Halvor heard his father's stockinged feet *whuff-whuff-whuff-whuff* across the kitchen floor to their large iron stove. *Squeak.* The metal stove door swung open.

None of the Dahl children were stirring. Their beds were built end-to-end under the west-side eave of the loft, and the shelves that held their clothes and personal belongings stretched beneath the opposite eave. Perhaps Halvor's brothers and sisters were still asleep. More likely, they, too, were listening and hoping the morning fire would warm the house before they swung their bare feet out from under the covers.

Scritch. Their father struck a match and ignited the slender sticks of kindling. *Clank.* He closed the stove door. The small house would warm quickly. Its thick log walls were tightly chinked to eliminate air leaks. No heat would escape through the low-peaked ceiling, covered by six inches of sod above several layers of birch bark. The traditional Scandinavian turf roof was picturesque in summer, especially when wildflowers bloomed amid the green grass. However, its primary value was insulation in the winter.

Creak. The sections of tall, bare stovepipe began to expand with heat as they channeled smoke from the fire up through the roof peak. *Creak.* The heat from the stove's center location would soon flow throughout the house. There was a large opening in the main floor ceiling, approximately eight feet square. Surrounded by an upstairs railing, the opening was directly above the stove and the open staircase to access the loft.

Before long, Halvor listened to Ingrid shuffle into the kitchen, followed by her quiet morning greeting for Goran, "*God morgen, min kjaere.*" The air was beginning to warm, and Mathilde was the first child to venture downstairs. Directly, he heard his mother and sister exit by the front door, headed for the outhouse. It was time to get up.

* * *

Each member of the Dahl family had morning chores to perform, except for three-year-old Thorvald. Ingrid needed to manage him in addition to her preparation of breakfast. Mathilde and Astrid oversaw the chickens, gathering eggs, feeding and returning them to their coop at night.

"It's warm out there," Mathilde told Halvor. She had returned from the outhouse and was hanging her coat on a hook beside the door while he was putting his on.

"Of course, 'warm' is a relative term during January in Minnesota," Ingrid interjected.

"Especially," Mathilde giggled, "when your naked butt makes contact with the outhouse seat." The two females laughed, but Halvor just shook his head and turned right out the door.

Water Wheels

The outhouse was thirty paces west of their house. Halfway there, the boy agreed that the temperature was relatively mild. *Close to twenty degrees,* he thought. Normal midwinter temperatures were in the single digits at six o'clock in the morning.

Halvor looked up to see thousands of twinkling stars in the cloudless pre-dawn sky. The half-moon had already dropped beneath the horizon, while the eastern sunrise was still an hour away. January 7 would have just nine hours of daylight rather than the fifteen hours of midsummer. *At least Minnesota is better than Norway*, he thought. A January day in the northern latitude of his former homeland is only one-third the length of a day in June.

After leaving the outhouse, Halvor retraced his steps past the front door and continued a similar distance onward to the barn. The Dahl family homesite was on gently sloping ground, from Wolf Creek on his right to a higher ridge along his left. Both the house and barn faced the creek and were built into the slope so that most of the northern walls were buried underground. When the two-story barn was originally built, dirt was excavated to create a level floor and transferred onto the slope. Thus, an earthen ramp covered the lower north wall of the barn and provided entry into the upper level. Weight-bearing beams in the lower level also supported stalls where cows and horses sheltered overnight. Additionally, the barn roof extended several feet beyond both side walls to cover a space for a pigsty on the east, plus a chicken coop and firewood supply on the west.

It was Halvor's job to feed the livestock before breakfast. He angled past the chicken coop and curved up the earthen ramp to enter the top floor. This upper level provided a loft to stack large quantities of hay and straw. In one nearby corner, horse harness equipment was neatly hung. The boy turned in the opposite direction to where the livestock feed was stored in wooden cabinets. Halvor scooped oats into one wooden bucket and filled another with grain ground from corn. He carried these buckets down around the corner to the pigsty. The boar and sow were already snuffling in their feed trough, where he dumped half the pail of grain. *Uh oh*, Halvor thought, noticing their frozen water basin. *I'll have to refill that.*

He continued into the barn's lower level, dimly illuminated by an oil lantern hanging where his father was milking one of their two Jersey dairy cows. As usual, it was a little warmer inside this central portion of the barn. The cattle and horses generated some of their own body heat, which was retained by the foundation walls partially encased by earth. Halvor noticed that his father and brother had both removed their winter coats.

Erik's unpleasant task this morning was shoveling manure-soiled straw out of the stalls. Once the barn floor was cleared, he would use a pitchfork to toss new dry and clean straw into those spaces from the hayloft in the barn's upper level. "Can you feed the horses outside," asked Erik, "while I clean their stalls?"

"Sure," Halvor answered. He emptied the remainder of the grain into the cows' feed boxes and divided the oats evenly between his two buckets. The boy opened Harald's stall and led the big Belgian out of the barn, where he lowered one bucket in front of the stallion's nose. He repeated the process with Ragnhild and set the other pail down for her. By the time Halvor came for Haakon, the colt anxiously whinnied and kicked a sideboard to register his impatience.

Outside the barn, Haakon approached Harald's bucket. *Chomp!* The older sire bared his teeth and warned his four-year-old offspring that no oats would be shared. When Haakon turned and tried to stick his nose into Ragnhild's bucket, she jostled to defend it. The pail was knocked over, and oats strewn across the ground. "Oh no," Halvor moaned. He bent forward, intending to sweep the food back into the bucket. However, both horses muscled over the scattered seeds and hastily licked them off the snow-packed ground. "I give up," the boy shrugged. He picked up the pail, turned it upside down and pounded his hand on the bottom to dislodge any remaining oats.

Halvor strode to their well, located between the house and barn. He lifted a large, insulated barrel that surrounded the iron pump to prevent it from freezing. Levering the pump handle up and down, he soon produced a flow of water into his pail, which he carried to the pigsty. Ice had to be removed from the frozen water basin, which the boy accomplished by banging it upside down on top of a fence post. He refilled it for the thirsty hogs and returned to keep an eye on Haakon.

The barn door opened, and clumps of dung and damp straw began flying out from Erik's wide, flat shovel. Steam rose from the pile of waste, and as the vapor dissipated, Halvor could smell the dank aroma of moist manure. "Phew!"

"How about some help?" his brother requested. "You could go up to the loft and toss down a couple of straw bales."

Halvor checked to make sure the horses remained calm before he consented to Erik's appeal. Entering the loft, he became conscious of its dry and dusty air. The scent of hay and straw brought back memories of the harvest and a hot, sunny afternoon, quite a contrast to the steaming stench piled on the icy ground outside. He dropped two bales into the lower level, and Erik spread fresh straw among the stalls.

The morning chores were complete, with cows milked and horses back inside a clean stable. Father and sons walked side-by-side to the house for breakfast. The first rays of morning sunshine peeked over the eastern horizon and cast a glow on their backs. "One more job," interrupted Ingrid, meeting them outside the door. She thrust an empty bucket into Goran's hands. "I need another pail of water in the kitchen." Then, pivoting with a grin, she placed an arm on each of her sons' shoulders and steered them inside. "I'll bet you boys are hungry."

* * *

Each family member washed their hands and face in a basin of water Ingrid had heated on the stove. One by one, they moved into their usual chairs around the breakfast table. Goran was the last to wipe his face, after which he tossed the dirty water outside. He replaced the basin onto the stove and refilled it with water, which would heat to wash the dishes.

Bowls of *havregrot*, a hearty Norwegian oatmeal, were served to everyone. In the middle of the table were three plates. One was heaped with warm, crusty *kneippbrod* rolls. A block of brown *brunost* cheese sat upon another. The third plate held a scant portion of wild raspberry preserves.

The cheese and fruit had been retrieved from their cellar, where perishable foods were stored. The Dahls had a unique cellar where they could access it from inside the house. Ingrid's pantry was behind the staircase. Through there and beyond was a heavy door built into the north wall that was underground. Goran had dug a short stairway beneath that earthen slope, leading to a beam-supported room that maintained a cool year-round temperature.

Ingrid began to pour a cup of milk for each of the children, but Erik stood and got himself a coffee mug. Mother and father exchanged a gaze of silent understanding while their fifteen-year-old son filled his mug with the strong brew from the stovetop percolator. The previous year had been a year of change for Erik. After finishing his eighth-grade year of schooling, he decided, with his parent's consent, to become a full-time farmer. The Wolf Creek fields yielded bumper crops during the summer and fall. The family's succession of financially successful years enabled them to purchase an additional quarter-section of land adjacent to their original claim.

Expectations of more work and greater responsibility were placed upon Erik, which he accepted without complaint. He and Goran used many long summer evenings to clear the 160 acres of rocks and stumps, aided by the power of Harald and Ragnhild. They decided to breed the mare for a new foal in the spring of 1873. Haakon would be five years of age, ready for the burdens of a fully functional draft horse. Someday, Erik imagined, he might inherit the new ground and a new horse. Secretly, he hoped to build a new house where he could live with a new bride—Kjerstin Lund.

"After breakfast," Goran snapped the young farmer out of his daydream, "you can shovel that manure and some dung from the pigsty onto our flatbed wagon. It can be scattered across the east field to provide fertilizer for next season."

Later, Mathilde and Astrid washed the breakfast dishes before heading off to school with Halvor. The boy led Haakon from his stall up along the barn's north wall, where their sleigh was parked. He draped a harness onto Haakon, backed the horse between the sleigh shafts, and strapped him into the traces. The big colt was familiar with this routine and pulled the vehicle down beside the house with ease. It was lightly constructed, and the twin oak runners were smooth and fast.

Halvor went inside to collect his schoolbooks. The girls pulled on their coats, and all three bid goodbye to their parents. Before climbing onto the single bench seat of the sleigh, Mathilde folded their blanket into a seating pad. "No need to cover our legs with this," she declared. "It's plenty warm today."

* * *

The children were seated in the church pews at school from front to back, according to their age and grade level. Five-year-old Astrid was in the front row, as this was her very first year. She could identify numbers and was pretty good at counting. Astrid could recite the alphabet and write her own name.

Ten-year-old Mathilde sat five rows back. Most of the pews contained a few children, all members of this Norwegian Lutheran Church. However, the row in front of Mathilde was empty, as there were no nine-year-olds. She was reading small books and could write a simple paragraph. Mathilde was good with maps and could locate all thirty-seven US states. On this Tuesday morning, the teacher, Mrs. Eva Lund, was moving back and forth among the ten-year-olds, working on math problems. All of them could add and subtract. Most could multiply and divide. Mrs. Lund had Mathilde convert fractions to decimals and vice-versa.

There were no students behind Halvor. He and fourteen-year-old Jorgen Jensen were in the last row. Jorgen was a quiet, kindhearted boy who was friendly with Halvor, but the two were not close companions. Though a year younger, Halvor was a better student. His essays were better written. He was quicker and more accurate with geometry and algebra. This week, he studied the US Constitution and memorized its basic principles.

Technically, Kjerstin Lund was the oldest student in the class. However, she spent more time as her mother's teaching assistant than as a student. This morning, she was helping the youngest children write the alphabet, A to Z, and verbalize the sounds of the letters.

When the clock reached eleven-thirty, Mrs. Lund announced the lunch break. Mathilde had packed three ham sandwiches before they left home. Now she pulled them out of a cloth sack, and the Dahl siblings sat together on a pew.

Within a minute, Kjerstin Lund came to stand in the empty row before them. She held a small bowl containing raw-cut carrots, beans and squash. With her fingers, the young woman delicately plucked pieces out of the bowl and ate them one at a time. Looking at Mathilde, she asked, "How is your brother Erik?"

"He's working hard. Father needs his extra help now that we have more land."

"We miss him here at school," Kjerstin sighed. "But I suppose he's becoming a man now, with grown-up responsibilities."

Halvor looked at Mathilde, who did not respond. He guessed that she, like him, had never thought of Erik as a grown man. He wondered if Kjerstin thought of herself as a grown woman. Awkwardly, the boy stood up with his ham sandwich and headed for the door, leaving the girls to continue their conversation.

Stepping outside, Halvor could feel the temperature had become even warmer, perhaps approaching thirty degrees. However, half the sky was now shrouded by clouds that looked progressively darker from the west. He walked across the trampled snow to where Haakon was tied near their sleigh and unfastened the colt's halter from his rope. "Get up," the boy said, directing his horse to exercise its legs. Other children came outside to race and play games, but Halvor walked with Haakon. The colt found a clump of tall prairie grass poking through the snow and cropped it off for a noontime snack.

At twelve o'clock, Mrs. Lund appeared on the steps to call everyone back inside the church. Halvor reattached Haakon to his hitching post and stroked the horse's neck. Turning toward the doorway, he felt a gust of cooler air against his face. He looked up and saw the darkening clouds nearly stretched across the entire sky.

During the afternoon, Mrs. Lund produced a book of short stories written by American author Washington Irving. She turned to a story titled *Rip Van Winkle* and began to read aloud for the entire class. It was a tale about a man who lay down for a nap in the woods, only to reawaken after a sleep of twenty years. The students enjoyed the entertaining story, and the teacher believed it was an exposure to good literature that included a bit of American history.

After reading the first page, Mrs. Lund handed the book to Kjerstin, who read page two. She then delivered the hardcover edition to Jorgen Jensen, who quietly read the third page before passing it on to Halvor. After finishing his page, Halvor stepped around the pew, handing the book to the next younger student.

Returning to his place, the boy noticed droplets of melting snowflakes on a side window. Pausing to look outside, he could see the weather was quickly changing. The snow was falling from clouds, which appeared lower and more ominous. Moreover, the flakes were being driven almost sideways by a western wind that was now blowing in earnest. He looked at the clock—only half an hour until the school day would end.

The church clock was mounted on the back wall above the main entrance, where the preacher or teacher could easily see it. It was a beautiful timepiece housed inside a three-foot-tall cabinet of carved wood and glass. Behind its narrow window hung the brass pendulum, which consistently swung back and forth the exact same distance in the exact same time.

At two o'clock, Mrs. Lund announced dismissal. Halvor hurried outside to check on Haakon's condition. Wet snow stuck to the horse's body, but temperatures were dropping fast. The colder flakes were dry, but fierce wind propelled the snow pellets and stung his face. Halvor feared the wind chill might be nearing zero.

He went to the sleigh and snatched up their blanket, which had blown off the seat onto the ground. Whipping most of the snow out of it, the boy began furiously rubbing the blanket over Haakon's body, attempting to dry his hair as much as possible.

"When can we leave?" Halvor's sisters had come up behind him. Mathilde was shouting to be heard through the wind.

"Go back inside," he yelled. "I'll come get you after I hitch the sleigh." As the girls hurried the short distance to the church doorway, their forms blurred as he watched through the snow. When they went in, Halvor saw Jorgen Jensen come out with his sister Siri, who was two years younger. They were bundled in warm coats and began trudging homeward through the blizzard. Brother and sister disappeared quickly, swallowed within the swirling whiteout. The Jensens' farm was also along Wolf Creek but in the opposite direction from the Dahls. *Jorgen will make his way to the creek and follow it home*, Halvor thought. *That's exactly what I'll do.*

After drying Haakon as best he could, the boy harnessed his horse in front of the sleigh. He drove it near the church door and bounded inside. He could see worry on his sisters' faces and in the expressions of every other person huddled in the building. "We're going to wait until family members come to get us," asserted Mrs. Lund. "I won't go home with Lars until all of the children have been collected."

Halvor could see that some of the younger students had put on their coats. It seemed cold inside the room, although it was difficult to tell since he had just been outside. There appeared to be a low flame inside the church's wood-burning stove, but he could see the stack of available firewood was too low to last through the evening. "I'll bring in some more firewood," he stated.

"I'll join you," added Kjerstin as she threw on her coat.

Halvor was glad to find a good supply of logs neatly stacked along the west wall. Some were split and ready to burn. However, most of the wood was still in short cylinder form, not yet split. He packed several chunks of wood into Kjerstin's arms and scooped a heap for himself. They carried their loads inside and piled them next to the stove. Kjerstin kneeled to open the hatch and quickly thrust two fresh lengths onto the flickering fire.

Water Wheels

Halvor turned toward the door. "Mother and Father will be worried about us. Time to go home."

Mathilde and Astrid were next, followed by wishes from their classmates, "Good luck."

* * *

Halvor sat in the middle of the sleigh bench, flanked by his sisters. They covered their legs with the blanket, now decorated by horsehair and icy with frozen moisture from Haakon's back. Still, it would provide a partial windbreak.

Before driving away, the boy looked over his shoulder at the church. He wanted to get started on an angle of departure that would intersect with Wolf Creek. "Get up," he yelled and flicked the reins to urge Haakon forward. Halvor shouted his intended route to the girls so they would understand his strategy for finding their way home. After a few seconds, he glanced back at the church to confirm his direction. The structure was already disappearing beyond a flying curtain of snowflakes.

Several minutes later, Halvor was worried. He thought that by now, they should have intersected the tree-lined waterway. His mind raced, *Was the creek further than he remembered? Were the deepening drifts slowing Haakon more than he realized? Had they mistakenly curved from his planned route? If so, which way?*

"Whoa," after another minute, Halvor pulled on the reins. His heart was pounding, and he was afraid. Nonetheless, he tried to display a calm expression and speak with a confident voice. "We're going back to the church."

"Where is the creek?" Mathilde shouted.

"I don't know," Halvor admitted. He saw a look of terror flash into his sister's eyes. "But if we get lost out here, we could freeze. By turning around now, we can follow our tracks back to the church."

Mathilde nodded, and Halvor got Haakon circled around, retracing sleigh tracks in the snow. The driving sleet, which had been somewhat behind them, was now quartering into their faces. The girls raised mittened hands to shield themselves. Tiny frozen particles needled into the boy's exposed skin and hindered his vision. Gripping the reins in one hand, he pulled the brim of his hat down halfway over his eyes.

Now keenly aware of their angle into the wind, Halvor resolved to maintain this direction if he lost sight of the sleigh trail. That was becoming a very real possibility. The snow was falling heavily and blowing across the dual grooves, which had been sliced by sled runners only minutes before. Occasionally, only one channel was visible. As time elapsed, both tracks intermittently disappeared through spaces of drifting flurries but reappeared ahead. More and more, his ability to see the trail became sporadic.

Abruptly, Haakon stopped. *What's wrong?* Halvor wondered. "Get up!" he yelled, desperate to keep moving in his chosen direction. He furiously snapped the reins, but the horse refused to budge.

The girls peeked out from behind their mittens, and Astrid suddenly pointed off to her side and said, "Look!" They all peered through the tempest to see a pair of dim, glowing rectangles—church windows.

"You did it!" Mathilde gasped.

Haakon did it, Halvor thought. If the colt had not stopped, they likely would have driven right past the building. The girls jumped down and ran inside while their brother unhitched the sleigh. He wrapped the blanket around Haakon's torso, hoping to hold it in place by fastening part of the harness on top of the cloth. The blanket blew out of position two or three times while his numb fingers fumbled with the task. The gusting gale was not letting up, and Halvor could tell the temperature was continuing to plummet.

"I'm so glad you came back," Mrs. Lund hugged Halvor when he whished through the door. "Your sisters have told us how you saved them."

"Haakon saved us," he motioned outside.

"Oh, your horse," the teacher realized. "Bring him in."

The boy looked around, trying to visualize his big Belgian inside the sanctuary.

Water Wheels

"We'll create a stall by rearranging pews here in back," the teacher insisted. She pointed through a window and asserted, "If we leave him out there, he will die."

They needed to open both double doors, and Haakon had to duck his giant head as Halvor led the colt inside. The children had already cleared ample space, and they stared with wide eyes when his heavy hooves clomped loudly on the wooden floor. Instinctively, they scooted backward as Halvor turned the horse around in a rear corner. Haakon simply blinked his eyes and stood calmly as if this were a perfectly normal place for him.

* * *

As the clock ticked toward five o'clock, Halvor looked at his sisters and wondered about his brothers and parents at home. It was time to do evening chores before supper. The boy walked to a window and tried to peer through the thickening frost. He felt useless and imprisoned by the storm. Halvor grabbed his coat and announced, "I'm going to chop some more firewood."

"We have plenty to get through the night," Mrs. Lund protested.

"I know," he acknowledged, "but I have to do something. Besides, a lot of the wood in our pile still needs to be split." When he was outside, he looked up. The sky was totally dark now that sunset had passed. Whatever illumination had dimly penetrated the storm clouds an hour earlier was completely gone.

However, around the corner where wood was stacked, it was brighter. Lantern light, which shined faintly out the windows, twinkled off the swirling snowflakes to cast a fuzzy glow about the space. Halvor dragged a large, heavy stump block into the center of the light and stood one of the stove-length logs vertically on the stump. He picked up the axe and raised it powerfully above his shoulder. *Thwock!* The blade penetrated half the log's length and stuck. He lifted the axe again, now embedded into the log, and bashed it down on the stump once more. *Thwack!* The log cracked in two halves, which he quickly split into quarters and flipped aside.

Three or four logs later, two of his younger classmates appeared at the edge of light. "We volunteered to carry your firewood," one of the boys reported. Halvor pointed to the heap of quartered chunks and helped to stack them into each set of eager arms. After they scurried away, he returned to his axe. Twice more, the young men repeated this routine. With more than enough firewood inside, Halvor piled the last pieces on the stack outside.

When they reentered the church, he noted that another hour had passed. Mrs. Lund and Kjerstin had helped the students to assemble a circle of makeshift beds on the floor near the altar, making use of every bit of soft material available inside the church. Next, they lined everybody up for a commute to the outhouse, two by two. When that duty was done, the women settled the children onto their improvised pallets and began to tell bedtime stories.

Halvor heard his stomach growl and remembered that he had had nothing to eat since lunch. No one had. Nor would they, until at least the following morning. Still, not a word of complaint was heard. *Perhaps*, he thought, *story time will distract them from their hunger.*

Just then, a snort erupted from behind him, and Halvor was distracted by his horse. The youth retreated to Haakon's temporary stall and stroked the big colt's neck. "Easy boy," he spoke softly. "Take it easy. You have earned a rest." Halvor did not consider himself particularly tired, but he stretched out on one of the pews that formed Haakon's stall. Continuing whispers to the horse, he closed his eyes.

* * *

Sound and fury startled Halvor out of his sleep—the sound of the church door bursting open and stomping feet at the entry. A fury of frigid cold air whooshed through the opening, blasting in a squall of snow crystals. The boy sat bolt upright on the pew, looking into the bewildered eyes of a man who was frosted from head to toe. They shared a speechless moment before hearing a child's frightened peep from across the sanctuary. Mrs. Lund stood up.

Water Wheels

"Who are you?" stammered Halvor at the same instant Haakon's heavy hooves repositioned loudly in the corner.

The man pivoted in surprise to see the massive draft horse. Whereupon he suddenly realized the church door was standing open and slammed it shut. Turning back around, he stole a nervous sideways glance at Haakon. "Stalder," he gasped, "Bill Stalder. I'm a conductor for the St. Paul and Sioux City Railroad."

"What?" Halvor was thoroughly confused. He could think of no connection between the man's occupation and his appearance during this furious blizzard.

Mrs. Lund stepped up beside them. "Come nearer the stove, sir, and please sit down."

"Thank you," he replied, starting to catch his breath as she led him by the elbow. He sat in a pew and said, "Our train got stuck in a snow drift somewhere south of here. I don't know how far." Stalder loosened a scarf from around his face and neck and began unbuttoning his coat. "There are nineteen passengers stranded on the train. I'm backtracking the rails, hoping to recruit a rescue party from the nearest town. At least I was until I saw light in your windows."

"I don't know how you could see anything out there," Halvor was astonished.

"I know!" the conductor agreed, "I've seen nothing but the tracks for miles. Then there was a hesitation, like the wind paused to switch directions, and up on this hill was your church. It's a miracle."

"Thank God you're safe," breathed Mrs. Lund. "But we have nothing to help your passengers." She motioned to where Kjerstin huddled with the curious students. "We don't even have food for these children."

Halvor scanned the faces of his younger classmates then turned to see the clock had ticked past midnight. Amazingly, he had slept on the pew for hours.

Stalder asked, "Will it be all right if I get warmed and rested here before going farther up the tracks?"

"No!" Mrs. Lund exclaimed, causing the conductor to sit back in surprise.

Halvor smiled. "She means 'no' you cannot go farther up the tracks," he explained. "The storm is too dangerous. You must stay here through the night, Mr. Stalder. I'll go with you tomorrow."

They stayed awake another half hour, planning for the ensuing morning. Then Halvor fed more wood onto the weakening embers inside the stove. When Stalder lay down near the fire, he was quickly overcome by its warmth and his exhaustion. *What a coincidence*, the boy thought, *it sounds like a locomotive when this train conductor snores!*

* * *

Dawn arrived, but sunrise did not. Thick clouds extended darkness for an additional hour. Snow was still falling, and the wind continued to howl. Though Bill Stalder was impatient to get going, Mrs. Lund convinced him to wait until visibility improved. Finally, at about nine o'clock, the sun rose high enough to penetrate the cloud cover and illuminate the landscape below. Peering through the west-side windows, they could see the slender, swaying, shelter belt trees that had been planted two years before.

Halvor led Haakon to the sleigh, where the conductor helped with the harness. Once underway, they soon located tree-lined Wolf Creek, and the boy wondered, *Where was it last night?* Heading east, Haakon made steady progress, powering through numerous snow drifts until they intersected the railroad tracks.

Halvor steered his big Belgian colt alongside the rails facing north and hollered, "Whoa." He jumped to the ground and asked Mr. Stalder to do likewise. Together, they hoisted the right-side runner of the sleigh over one of the iron rails. This way, Haakon would be able to tramp straight down the tracks. Climbing back onto the bench seat, the boy declared, "The railroad ties provide a good level surface for him to walk on."

"Yes," the conductor affirmed, "and most of the snow seems to have blown across the tracks. It's not as deep on the higher railroad bed."

Water Wheels

"We should make good time," Halvor predicted. "Northfield is a little more than four miles up the track. We could be there in less than an hour."

He was right. They pulled up beside the town's train depot before lunchtime. Mr. Stalder went inside the depot and requested a telegram be sent to St. Paul and Sioux City Railroad headquarters. He wanted the company to know about the plight of their nineteen stranded passengers and what he was doing to help them.

A small cafe was open near the depot—D. E. Jeft's Diner. Pointing in that direction, Mr. Stalder proposed, "Let's get something to eat."

Halvor hesitated and instinctively touched his empty pockets. "I don't... "

"Forget about paying," the conductor interrupted. "The railroad will pick up our tab. And if they won't, I'll pay for your meal out of my own pocket. I owe you that and more."

Man and boy were consuming two hearty breakfasts when the train depot's telegraph operator hurried into Jeft's Diner. "Mr. Stalder," he approached the table, catching his breath, "Headquarters responded to your telegram." He lifted the transcribed message and read, "Rescue train coming from St. Paul. Stop. Shovelers and food on board. Stop. Report when mission accomplished. Stop."

"Thank you," the conductor accepted the telegram. Then he turned to Halvor and slid a coin across the tabletop. "Take your horse to the local stable and feed him. We are indebted to that big colt."

By mid-afternoon, re-nourished Haakon had pulled the sleigh back to where a small railroad bridge crossed over Wolf Creek. The wind persisted, so it was hard to tell if more snow was falling or simply blowing across the landscape. Halvor thought the storm had weakened a little, but it was still cold, and he knew temperatures would plummet as evening approached.

"Gee!" The boy turned Haakon to the right and had passed about one acre westward when a locomotive could be heard rumbling behind them. He looked over his shoulder to see the engine pushing one passenger car down the tracks, the rescue train. "Good luck, Mr.

Stalder," Halvor murmured to himself just as a whistle pierced the air. *Toot-toot!*

* * *

Boy and horse swerved uphill to the church, where tracks of many other horses and people crisscrossed the yard. When Halvor ventured inside, the building was empty and cold. He saw a few faint embers still glowing in the wood stove but guessed that families had retrieved all their children hours before.

Before the dim glow of day was gone, they crested a hill on the Dahl family farm and headed for home. Halvor parked the sleigh beside the barn, unharnessed Haakon, and led him into his familiar stall. Ragnhild tossed her mane with a head bob and neighed "welcome home" from mare to colt.

When the boy stepped through the front door, he was greeted by a hug from Ingrid. "*Velkommen hjem,*" she whispered into his shoulder. A warm fire was burning in their stove, and the entire family smiled at him from around the room.

Before long, vegetables and venison were being chopped in preparation for a stew. The Dahls gathered around the table to share separate stories from the previous day and a half. Mathilde described their stay overnight in the church. Halvor reported his account of the trip to Northfield with Mr. Stalder.

"We are so thankful you made it safely home," his mother sighed. "We pray for the Jensen children."

"Jorgen and Siri?" Halvor asked.

Ingrid looked to Goran, and their father solemnly spoke, "They froze to death." He paused while the family sat in silence. "They must have been blinded by the blizzard. They were found near the creek, but beyond their house from the church."

Halvor and Mathilde shot a knowing glance at each other, remembering how they had become lost trying to find their way home in the storm.

"Mr. Jensen went to retrieve them from school this morning," Goran continued. "When Eva Lund told him Jorgen and Siri had left yesterday afternoon, he began searching along the stream. They were together, frozen in the snow."

With that, Goran stood up. "It is time to do evening chores." He reached for his coat, hanging on a peg beside the door. "Mother's stew will be ready by the time we are done."

Indeed, the smell of freshly baked bread and simmering stew was already spreading through the house. However, it could not lift the gloom over the Jensens' tragic loss. The Dahl children sat motionless for a few moments more. Erik was next to stand, and one by one, they followed silently out the door.

* * *

Blizzard of 1873 (January 7–9, 1873)

One of the worst winter storms in Minnesota history, the blizzard raged for three days. It was particularly deadly in southern and western rural counties where it suddenly arrived. Tuesday, January 7, began with clear skies and unseasonably warm temperatures, prompting many area farmers to venture from home and turn livestock out into the fields. However, by late afternoon, heavy snow was falling, a northwest wind was gusting to seventy miles per hour, and temperatures dropped to forty degrees below zero.[14]

Snow driven by gale-force winds caused enormous drifts and blinded many travelers. Multiple trains were halted on the tracks by mounds of packed snow. Nineteen passengers aboard a southbound St. Paul and Sioux City Railroad route were stranded overnight near the town of St. Peter. The train conductor attempted a rescue effort on foot, whereupon he encountered a teacher and students trapped in their schoolhouse. All the passengers were saved with the help of supplies provided by a horse-drawn sleigh.[15]

Dozens of people and hundreds of livestock died in the blizzard. A Nicollet County doctor who survived his harrowing journey home from a house call reported snow blindness so bad that he occasionally lost sight of the horses pulling his carriage. Among the dead were a teenage brother and sister, Robert and Sarah Foster, who wandered for miles trying to find their way home along a stream. Their frozen bodies were found two months later.[16]

Chapter 5
Panic
1873

It was a beautiful October morning on Dayton's Bluff. The Meier family was riding to school and work in their horse-drawn carriage. Green leaves were turning yellow, orange and red on the ash, maple and oak trees that lined the street. The calm, crisp air felt cool on their faces as their bay gelding, Morgan, trotted briskly along. The day promised to get warm, however, once the sun climbed higher into a clear blue sky.

Morgan's hooves clattered loudly on the plank bridge over Phalen Creek, and soon they were downtown, nearing the Meier Hardware store. Normally, Hilde opened the store by herself, but today, Heinrich jumped down to enter with her. As their eldest daughter moved to the carriage's front seat, he told her, "Jo, I need to transfer some rope and chain from here to the lumber yard. Just hold the reins until I come back," and he handed her the leather lines.

At that instant, Emelia glimpsed a flash of sunlight from the corner of her eye. Her head snapped in that direction to see a glass bottle arcing down from the sky. *Crash!* The bottle smashed down on the wooden boardwalk, shattering into pieces that ricocheted against the wall and into the street.

Morgan jumped sideways from the explosion and reared on his hind legs. When the gelding's forefeet hit the ground, he bolted forward, the carriage lurching behind. The horse whinnied with fright, and Johanna shrieked as the reins were jerked out of her grasp. Emelia grabbed an armrest with one hand and reached for Kat with the other. All three girls floundered on the benches but stayed aboard.

Suddenly, Emelia saw a powerfully built man appear on the dirt street. He was standing directly in front of Morgan with arms outstretched. The horse did not stop but dodged and slightly stumbled around the man. Dressed in a dark business suit, the fellow latched onto the harness and threw one arm around Morgan's neck. Bracing the heels of his skidding boots against the ground, he gradually wrestled the horse to a stop. The gelding continued to quiver, still wide-eyed and frightened. The man gripped his halter in one strong hand and stroked his neck with the other, speaking in a firm, quiet voice.

Emelia spun on her seat to look back into the sky from where the bottle had come. Nothing was there, but she instantly visualized an arc through the air, which might have originated from a narrow alley between adjacent buildings.

Her father came running up and immediately recognized the man in the street as his friend James J. Hill. "Jim," he shouted, "thank goodness you were here." Heinrich was surprised by Hill's presence but not by his actions. Several years earlier, when both men worked on the steamboat docks, he had seen Hill dive into the Mississippi River to rescue an eleven-year-old boy.

"Hello, Heinrich," Hill grinned. "What a coincidence. I was coming this way to speak with you."

Heinrich looked over one shoulder to appraise the condition of his three daughters. They looked excited but safe and sound. Pivoting back to Hill, "Give me some time to deliver my girls to school at Assumption and then open the lumberyard. Where will you be later this morning?"

"I'm going to check on the warehouse now. Could you meet at my office between ten and ten-thirty?"

"Good, Jim. I'll see you then."

* * *

74

Water Wheels

James J. Hill was a well-educated Canadian who landed on the St. Paul levee in 1856, the same year as Heinrich Meier. Both had been volunteer firefighters and members of the Pioneer Guard militia. Now, they were happily married fathers in their late thirties. Each had become an entrepreneur. Meier opened the hardware and lumber businesses; Hill built a waterfront warehouse where he stocked bargain-priced goods to be sold for profit.

An odd similarity between the two men was Heinrich's one good arm and Jim's one good eye. At age nine, in his native Rockwood, Ontario, the youthful Hill crafted a self-made archery bow and proceeded to accidentally blind his own right eye. The wound became almost unnoticeable, and he continued to be a voracious one-eyed reader for the remainder of his life.

Upon entry into Hill's office, Heinrich observed that the room matched its occupant—efficient, not fancy. The man was known as a workaholic perfectionist who toiled long hours, attending to every detail. Meier was not surprised when he got straight to the point. "I want to speak with you about this financial panic which has plunged the country into economic recession."

"I am not a financial expert," Heinrich confessed.

"No, but you're a good businessman," Hill insisted. "This panic was caused by bad businessmen who borrowed too much money and couldn't pay it back."

"Unfortunately," Meier lamented, "a lot of good people are being hurt by their mistakes. Banks have collapsed, hundreds of businesses driven into bankruptcy, and thousands of hard-working people have lost their jobs."

"Exactly!" Hill's fist thumped on his desk. "But that won't be us!" He continued with resolve, "Timid merchants who cut back to reduce their losses will wither under this recession. Now is the time to boldly seize opportunity."

"What opportunity are you suggesting?" Heinrich had heard a rumor that his host was entering the railroad business. "I'm not prepared to buy a train."

Hill smirked. He was amused but not surprised that Meier had heard the rumor. "The St. Paul and Pacific Railroad has gone bankrupt. Norm Kittson and I can buy it for pennies on the dollar. We'll finish laying tracks to the Red River and monopolize trade between here and Winnipeg. However, that is not the opportunity I invited you here to discuss." The man leaned his barrel chest forward and said, "We're starting our own bank."

"Who is '*we*'?"

"Fellow St. Paul businessmen John Merriam and Albert Scheffer, among others."

Heinrich nodded in recognition. He knew them both as former Civil War officers, now successful entrepreneurs. Scheffer was a fellow German immigrant in the newspaper business. Merriam had made money in transportation, first with horse-drawn wagons and stagecoaches, now with trains. Also a politician, he had recently been Speaker of the Minnesota House of Representatives.

Hill continued, "This panic has resulted in a tight money supply and high interest rates, which make it nearly impossible to borrow. Owning our own bank will provide St. Paul businessmen with a source of funds to invest in the future." He snarled, "The Washburns and the Pillsburys are doing the same thing in Minneapolis."

Hill stopped, waiting for a response. Heinrich mulled over the idea before inquiring, "How much would it cost?"

"That's your decision," came the answer. "The bigger your stake, the greater your share of the profits. We're calling it the First National Bank of Minnesota."

Heinrich was interested. He knew it was a solid idea, and James J. Hill's involvement made the venture even more inviting. Still, he worried if his family could afford the investment. "I can't decide right now," he conceded. "I'll have to talk it over with Hilde and get back to you."

"Certainly," Hill affirmed, with the caveat, "Just don't wait too long." Then he snapped his fingers. "Oh, one more thing. Our oldest daughter, Mamie, has reached school age. My wife Mary and

Water Wheels

I have arranged with Father Ireland and our friends, the McQuillans to start a new Catholic school for girls. It's called Visitation Convent Academy, and the teachers are nuns who recently arrived from St. Louis. You should enroll your daughters."

"We're pretty happy with Assumption."

"I know you are members there, but this will be a better school. If you don't believe me, ask the priest."

* * *

Later that day, after the Meier girls had come to the hardware store from school, Emmy saw Marie Giesen walk in. The well-dressed woman approached Hildegard with a smile, and they shared a warm-hearted hug. Hilde dwarfed Marie in height and girth, but they had much in common. Both were German immigrants and nearly identical in age at thirty-seven. They shared membership in the Catholic Church of the Assumption, and both were married to successful St. Paul businessmen. Each was a young mother, though Marie had four boys to Hilde's three girls.

The two became friends years before when both were sewing to make a living. Hilde had done laundry and mended worn clothing, mostly for unmarried men who worked on the waterfront with Heinrich. Marie, on the other hand, was primarily a garment maker who designed fine clothing for St. Paul's wealthier residents. Her husband Peter was a bookbinder who gained exclusive rights to print lawbooks for the prosperous West Publishing Company. Peter, also a German immigrant, was well-known for his fine singing voice. He played the lead in numerous musical performances and spearheaded the construction of Mozart Hall, which contained a theater in addition to dining facilities.

Marie had begun making costumes for plays and operas on a volunteer basis. However, within the previous year, she launched her own business, Giesen's Costumers. Now, in addition to theatrical wardrobes, she produced formal wear, pageant apparel and masquerade attire. Most of the outfits were rented and returned to Marie's expanding business closet.

From behind the hardware store's rear counter, Emelia heard Mrs. Giesen say to her mother, "I need your help."

"What is it?" asked Hilde.

"You're the best seamstress I know," stated Marie, "and I'm overwhelmed with orders for costumes. People are requesting masquerade attire for the upcoming All Hallows' Eve party at Mozart Hall."

"Yes, we received an invitation from Peter," Hilde confirmed before expressing frustration, "I have no idea what kind of disguise Heinrich will be willing to wear."

Marie exhaled a knowing chuckle and then begged, "Please help me sew some of the costumes other people have ordered." She added, "I will pay you handsomely."

Hilde paused after the latter statement but assured her friend, "Of course, I'll try to help."

"Thank you," Marie grasped one of Hilde's hands in both of hers.

"It's just," Hilde hesitated, "with our girls, and the housework, and this store… " Her words trailed off as she scanned the hardware shelves. "I don't know how I'll find much time."

Mrs. Giesen suggested, "Maybe your girls could do more."

The room fell silent. Each of the Meier females looked into the eyes of the others while contemplating their personal interpretation of that word, 'more.'

* * *

Evening supper at the Meier household was pork sausages baked in sauerkraut. Some of Hilde's excellent German potato salad was served alongside carrots and green beans. The girls were drinking milk, but mother had a glass of red wine and father a stein of beer. Heinrich lifted his beverage and announced, "We have some important family decisions to discuss."

Prior to supper, Mr. and Mrs. Meier had spoken privately in their bedroom. Now, their mother sat knowingly while Johanna, Emelia and Katharina listened to their father. "This panic, which has fallen upon the entire United States economy, is making it difficult for our businesses to thrive. We must operate the lumberyard and the hardware store as efficiently as possible. Still, this economic recession might offer unique openings to greater prosperity in the future."

The girls tried to interpret his meaning when Heinrich proceeded, "By coincidence, your mother and I have received two intriguing proposals today from different trustworthy friends." He motioned across the table. "You were all in the store when Mrs. Giesen offered to hire your mother to sew for her costume business." Jo, Emmy and Kat nodded. "In fact," he continued, "Mrs. Giesen has invited Hilde to continue sewing professionally on a part-time basis into the future."

Heinrich took a sip of his beer. "The other proposal came from Mr. Hill after he wrangled Morgan to a stop in the street this morning. I spoke with him in his office, where he offered us a partnership in forming a new bank." Heinrich lowered his stein to the table. "I would not be involved in day-to-day management of the bank, nor will most of the investors," he explained. "Our share of earnings would be determined by the size of our investment, assuming the bank becomes profitable."

"Will the bank make a profit?" Emmy blurted out the question.

"Well," he responded slowly, "some banks have been ruined by the panic. However, Mr. Hill has joined some of St. Paul's most astute businessmen in what they're calling the First National Bank of Minnesota. Your mother and I have confidence in these partners."

The girls looked to Hilde, who nodded in agreement.

"Furthermore," Heinrich added, "negotiating a loan during this panic has become almost impossible. By investing in our own bank, we can expect to receive preferential treatment if we want to borrow money in the future." He leaned back and rested his single left hand beside his dinner plate.

Johanna broke the brief silence. "What does this mean for us?"

"To begin with," Hilde responded, "I will create a sewing workshop by rearranging some of the storage space above the

hardware store. That way, I will always be nearby if you need me."
With eyes fixed on Jo, she took a deep breath. "Your father and I
have decided to let you quit school and work full-time in the store."

"That's what I want!" the girl exclaimed.

"We know," Hilde spoke calmly and raised a hand to check
her oldest daughter's enthusiasm. "You have had enough schooling
to operate our store and have proven yourself worthy of the job.
We have complete confidence that you and Dolf can manage the
business during the mornings while I sew for Mrs. Giesen."

Johanna's face beamed with pride and joy as she pictured
herself in this new capacity.

Hilde turned her eyes to the youngest daughter. "Kat, you're
eight years old now. Old enough to start behaving like a young
woman... "

"I *am* a young woman!"

"Settle down," her mother cautioned. "We are impressed by
the maturity you are beginning to demonstrate. You don't need, or
want, to be under my wing all day." The cocky tilt of Kat's chin
proved the truth of that statement. "We know you're capable of
doing more work around the store, and your growing independence
is another reason why your father and I believe this plan can be
successful."

Emelia sat wondering if the plan involved a change for her.

Heinrich addressed her. "Emmy, we believe you should
continue your education. In fact, we are enrolling you in a new
school."

Her face wrinkled with puzzlement.

"Father Ireland has started a new school, especially for girls,
named Visitation Convent Academy. The teachers are a group of
nuns who recently arrived from St. Louis."

"What's wrong with Assumption?" Emelia asked.

"Nothing is wrong with Assumption," Heinrich replied. "But
these sisters are more highly educated. Your mother and I believe
that a girl with your academic ability should be thinking about
higher education as well."

Water Wheels

Academic ability? Higher education? While Emmy wondered about the meaning of her father's words, he forged ahead.

"Visitation is farther away than Assumption, so I'm going to teach you to drive the carriage." When her eyes got big, he offered reassurance. "You're a natural teamster. After we drop Mother and Jo at the store each morning, I'll get off at the lumberyard. Then you and Kat can drive to school. There's a stable at the convent where Morgan can rest until the school day is done."

Heinrich lifted his beer and drank the last few gulps before lowering the empty stein onto the table with a thud. Emelia thought he looked like a judge, banging down his gavel to end a session in court. *We have reached a decision*, she concluded to herself.

* * *

Two weeks later, Emelia sat in her mother's new workshop above the hardware store. She watched Hilde's skillful fingers stitch together a masquerade party garment. "Why do people wear costumes on All Hallows' Eve?" she asked.

"I don't know," the seamstress admitted without interrupting the rhythm of her needlework. "Long ago, I think some people wore costumes to imitate the saints. Maybe others disguised themselves so they wouldn't be recognized by ghosts returning from the spirit world."

Emmy raised an eyebrow. "Saints and ghosts?"

"Well," Hilde tried to explain, "All Hallows' Eve was originally a European holiday, but here in America, the occasion has become a unique conglomeration of religious rituals and autumn traditions." Her daughter's perplexed expression led to a more thorough description. "On the first day of November, Christians celebrate All Saints' Day, sometimes called All Hallows' Day. The purpose of the celebration is to honor and remember people from history who are recognized as saints by the Catholic church. Over time, people have begun to memorialize their own family ancestors on All Saints' Day."

"All Hallows' Eve is the night before?"

"Yes, the last night of October became a time to spiritually connect with the souls of deceased saints and loved ones. Worshippers dedicate prayers to the dead. They sometimes light candles, lanterns, or bonfires to illuminate a path of welcome between heaven and earth."

"And we have parties?"

"We do," Hilde nodded. "In America, feasts are held on All Hallows' Eve to capitalize on the autumn harvest and traditional hunting season. Wild game is frequently served as a main course. Fruits and vegetables grown in Minnesota, like apples, nuts, corn and squash, are common menu items here."

The seamstress tied off her last stitch and stood up. She hung the finished garment on a hanger and placed it alongside others in a closet. "Now," she turned to Emelia, "I need your help. Bring Morgan around to the back of the store. We'll load these outfits into our carriage and transport them to Marie's shop."

Minutes later, Emmy reined her horse to a stop in the rear alley. Hilde carried the costumes out the back door and laid them carefully upon the carriage's back seat. Katharina appeared with a blanket and length of rope, which her mother used to cover and safely secure the garments. "Thank you, Kat," she said. "Tell Jo we will return within the hour."

"Gittyup," Emelia barked to Morgan, and her sister waved them goodbye. After two weeks, the gelding was used to the girl's voice and touch on the reins. He quickly emerged from the alley, turned the corner and trotted down the dirt street to Giesen's Costumers.

Marie was thrilled with the creations. "These are beautiful," she gushed. "My customers will be elated." She stepped forward and shook Hilde's hand. "Thank you."

Emmy saw pride in her mother's face, but she also saw confidence. At that moment, it dawned on the girl that she was witnessing a business deal between professional women. She was reminded of Caroline Hall, the young Grange delegate she had met years before. All three women were smart and capable. They stood and spoke with proud, self-assured confidence.

Water Wheels

Emmy looked at her mother from a new and different perspective. For her entire life, the girl had simply seen Hilde as her mother. Of course, she was the hardware store manager, but she always seemed second in command to Heinrich. Not now. Hilde was an independent, skilled artisan in this financial endeavor with Marie Giesen.

This is my destiny, Emmy resolved to herself. *Someday I will be a successful professional woman.*

Marie snapped Emelia out of her private thoughts by slapping her hand down on the counter, where a copy of the St. Paul Press daily newspaper lay. "What is your opinion about the Susan B. Anthony trial?"

A women's rights advocate, the fifty-three-year-old woman had been arrested for voting in New York's 1872 election. "I think the trial was a sham," answered Hilde. "The judge silenced her by ruling that no woman is qualified to testify in her own defense." She continued, her voice rising with indignation, "Then he ordered the all-male jury to find her guilty before they even had a chance to vote."

"I know," Marie moaned. "I had been hopeful, with the recently passed Fourteenth Amendment, that women's rights of citizenship might be extended into the voting booth." Ratified after the Civil War, that constitutional amendment granted citizenship to all persons born or naturalized in the United States and guaranteed equal rights to every citizen.

"Her punishment is a fine of one hundred dollars," said Hilde.

"Yes," chuckled Marie, "but she refuses to pay, and they don't have the guts to put her in jail."

Hilde reached over to touch Emelia's arm and said, "Maybe someday my daughters will gain the right to vote in America." Little did they know that dream would come true, but not until Emelia was sixty years old.

* * *

Upon returning to the hardware store, Emelia tied Morgan to a hitching rail in the back alley. Her mother walked up beside the horse's neck and produced a pair of scissors from her pocket. She snipped a lock of black hair from the gelding's mane and quickly entered the building. Emmy followed upstairs to the sewing workshop, where they both removed their coats.

"Why did you cut that hair from Morgan's mane?" the girl inquired.

Instead of answering, Hilde stepped to a nearby table where Heinrich's red hunting cap and jacket lay. Picking up the jacket with one hand, she turned to face Emelia and displayed it against her own torso. With her other hand, the woman draped the horse hairs across her upper lip, where they formed a bushy mustache. Her mouth spread into a mischievous grin.

Emmy laughed. "You're going to be a hunter at the All Hallows' Eve party." The girl snatched Heinrich's cap off the table and placed it on her mother's head before stepping back to admire the disguise.

"And," Hilde declared, "I'm going to carry your father's rifle."

"What will his outfit be?" Emmy asked.

Her mother nodded to a tan-colored jacket slung over a chair beside the table. The girl picked up the plain garment. *Hardly a costume*, she thought.

Hilde dropped the hunter's disguise upon her sewing desk and spun back around, lifting a paper-mache helmet onto her head.

"It's a deer," Emelia exclaimed. Antlers extended up from the crown of the helmet alongside a pair of pointed ears. The entire mask covered the top half of her head, with eyeholes to see through and a snout extending several inches out from the nose. The girl lifted the jacket up in front of her mother to see the color was perfectly matched with the painted paper-mache. "Does father know that he will be dressed as your prey?" she asked.

"Not yet," Hilde said, removing the helmet to reveal a twinkle in her eye. "But he will on All Hallows' Eve."

* * *

Marie Dreis Giesen (1836–1923)

The Dreis family immigrated from Germany to Chicago in 1850 when Marie was fourteen years old. Four years later, they moved to St. Paul, where she met Peter J. Giesen, also a German immigrant. The two were married in 1860 and raised a family of four sons.[17]

Peter established a successful book-binding company best known for printing law books. Marie started Giesen's Costumers, which flourished as a family-operated St. Paul enterprise for eighty-eight years. She founded the business in 1872 when she was a rare female entrepreneur. Marie ran the costume shop with independent creativity until, at the age of sixty-seven, she turned it over to her youngest son, Martin.[18]

Marie and Peter were both active in St. Paul's theater scene, which offered a performance on all fifty-two Sundays of 1873. She provided the wardrobe, and he took the stage as an actor and singer.

They became owners of Mozart Hall, which housed a bar and formal dining restaurant, in addition to the theater, also used as a ballroom.[19]

The couple built a well-known Queen Anne-style home atop a hill on Dayton's Bluff. The red brick and sandstone mansion is listed in the National Register of Historic Places.[20]

Chapter 6
Lumberjack Pony
1874

Halvor sat at the kitchen table, alone with his parents. He was apprehensive about the situation because it had never happened before. His brothers and sisters were sent to remove weeds from the vegetable garden with hoes and spades while he was asked to remain in the house. *Was he in trouble?* Halvor wondered.

Goran sat in his regular chair, and Ingrid settled into hers, looking at her husband to begin the conversation. "We want to talk about your future," he said.

Halvor glanced nervously back and forth between the two.

"We want you to go to college," Ingrid declared.

"But not right away," interrupted Goran.

After a moment of silence, Halvor said, "We cannot afford it."

His father slowly inhaled and said, "Let's back up. To begin with, you are a smart young man…"

"Very smart," his mother exclaimed, leaning forward.

Goran took another deep breath, and Ingrid eased back. "As I was saying, you're a smart young man…"

"Mrs. Lund says you already know more than she does," Ingrid couldn't help herself from butting in. "She says it would be a terrible shame if you didn't go to college."

After a pause, Goran continued, "You are correct, Halvor. We cannot afford to pay college tuition, especially during this financial panic. Farm prices are so low this year that we will barely be able to sell the crops for more than we paid to plant them."

Halvor looked down at his hands on the tabletop.

His father proceeded, "So rather than return to our schoolhouse this fall, we want you to get a job."

"There aren't any jobs around here," the boy lamented.

"You're right," Goran said, "but the lumber camps are hiring. After the harvest, you can take Harald and Haakon up north. Teamsters with their own horses can make a lot of money in the winter, hauling trees out of the pine forest."

"What about my chores?"

Ingrid answered, "Erik is nearly a grown man. The farm partly belongs to him now, and someday he will own it all." She acknowledged a nod of confirmation from Goran. "So, after the harvest this autumn, your job will be to start earning your own way in the world."

"Ragnhild can handle our farm work through the winter," his father assured. "And Mathilde will be able to drive Sophia back and forth to school." Sophia, named after another Norwegian queen, was the family's new two-year-old filly. Ragnhild had given birth to a female foal the previous spring. After weaning, that foal was exchanged for Sophia with a farmer named Eugene Schrader from Hastings, Minnesota, who also raised Belgian draft horses. Both he and Goran knew it was wise to mix genetic bloodlines of animals on any farm.

"Mr. Schrader has rented horses to lumber camps in the past," said Goran. "He will connect you with a reputable logging company, where Harald and Haakon will be well-treated, and you will be well-paid."

"I would like to attend college," Halvor admitted, "if it's possible."

Ingrid reached across the table to touch Halvor's arm. "This will probably take more than one winter," she cautioned. "You will be expected to come home next spring and help tend our crops."

Water Wheels

"Plus, we'll need the horses for planting and harvest," Goran added. "Then, with another year in the woods, you may earn enough to attend the university when you're sixteen."

* * *

The Dahl family pushed to finish their autumn harvest by mid-October. As expected, prices were low, but they had grown bumper crops, which enabled them to earn a small profit. Soon after, it came time for Halvor to leave.

The boy packed most of his warm winter clothes into a cloth sack, which could also be used as a pillow. Then he climbed onto Haakon's back and attempted to lead Harald, leashed to the end of a rope. However, the sire refused to tolerate being led by his colt. The stallion jerked furiously at the tether and continuously tried to barge ahead rather than alongside. So Halvor reversed the roles and mounted Harald instead. The older horse seemed content with this new arrangement and began trotting along with ease.

Their destination on this first day of travel was Eugene Schrader's farm. The route was simple to follow from Wolf Creek, through Northfield and along a well-traveled road straight to Hastings. However, the thirty-mile trip would take all day, so Halvor was expected to stay overnight at the Schraders' home. The elderly couple was waiting for his arrival near dusk. Eugene Schrader helped the boy find stable space for Harald and Haakon and provided grain to feed them.

"Thank you, Mr. Schrader," said Halvor as they closed the barn door and walked toward the house.

"Call me Gene," the man insisted, gesturing toward his wife on the porch, "and she's Joyce."

"Supper's ready," the woman called to them. "Come sit down after you wash up."

While dining on roast beef and mashed potatoes, Gene said he would guide Halvor to Stillwater the next day, despite the boy's insistence that he could navigate the twenty-three-mile journey on his own.

"I'm not worried about you finding the way," Schrader explained. "I intend to discuss some business with Mr. Isaac Staples."

"Do you know him?"

"Hah, I worked for the old Scotsman," Gene chuckled. "My winters in the lumber camps are long past, but I have rented horses to the man for many years."

Halvor glanced at the wiry muscles in Schrader's compact arms and could easily imagine the teamster's command of a draft horse team.

Gene continued, "I have two young Belgians, not as seasoned as your pair. Duke is three years old, and Daisy is four. They're not ready to pull a fully loaded log sled, but each of them can drag a few logs out of the forest for five dollars a month."

"How much can I earn with Harald and Haakon?"

"That's just it," blurted Schrader. "I don't want him to cheat you—or me."

Halvor had not eaten since breakfast, and he enjoyed two helpings of Joyce's delicious meal. His stomach was full, but he couldn't resist when she offered *krumkake* for dessert. The traditional Norwegian cookies were baked on a waffle iron then rolled up sweet and crispy.

"I grew up German and married a Norwegian," Gene laughed, using both hands to pat his belly, where a smattering of *krumkake* crumbs had fallen. "I've been spoiled by good cooks my whole life."

Joyce smiled and turned from her husband to Halvor. The merry twinkle in her eye changed to a look of motherly concern. "I believe our young guest is worn out," she said. "Show him up to the bed I prepared in the boys' room."

Mr. Schrader led the way upstairs, where there were two large rooms, both containing beds. "We raised two boys and three girls in this house," he said. "They're all moved away now."

Halvor dropped his pillowcase full of clothes on a bare mattress and sat on the next bed, which was made with sheets and blankets.

"That's a pretty small bundle you've got there," said Gene, nodding at the pillowcase. "Do you mind if I take a look at your supply of winter clothing?"

Water Wheels

"I know it's not much," admitted the boy. "I thought I might buy more from the lumber camp store when I find out what I need." He dumped the contents out on the mattress.

"Experience tells me what you need," the old lumberjack declared. "You don't have nearly enough socks or an adequate hat."

Halvor watched Gene walk two strides to a battered chest at the foot of the bed. The man kneeled, threw back the lid, and reached inside. "Take these wool socks," he said, tossing three pairs beside Halvor's few things. "They'll be warmer and dryer than what you've got."

"I shouldn't take your clothes," the boy protested.

"You need 'em more than I do," said Schrader. He bent and dug deeper into the trunk, producing a fur-covered cap with ear flaps. "Try that on," he ordered.

Halvor did as he was told, detecting a mixture of old smells in the cap: musk, sweat and maybe a hint of pine.

"That'll keep you warmer than your stocking cap," the man declared. "Your coat looks good, but we're gonna have to get a better pair of boots."

"The coat belonged to my father… "

Gene barged ahead, "And you're not gonna buy 'em from Isaac Staples's camp store! We'll find better boots for less money here in Hastings."

Halvor was speechless.

"Have a good night's sleep," said Schrader, and he disappeared down the stairs.

* * *

Halvor did have a restful sleep but awakened early, as usual. He and Gene did morning chores together before sitting down to Joyce's hearty breakfast. Soon after, they bid her farewell and started down the road. Halvor again mounted Harald, leading Haakon by the rope. Schrader drove a one-horse carriage with Duke and Daisy tethered behind, side by side. He would need the carriage to return the following day.

Where the road was wide enough, Halvor rode abreast of the carriage. Gene called over to the boy, "We're going to stop at the trading post in Hastings. Old Alexis Bailly was the first fur trader to locate a post here on the Mississippi River. He was crooked as a dog's leg, but he bought and sold quality merchandise. Bailly and his wife were both of mixed blood, Native and white. They founded this town in 1850 when Minnesota became a territory. Their two sons opened a hotel and tavern, started printing a newspaper and became active in politics. They're dead now, but the store is still there, with good boots for sale."

"I don't have any money for boots," Halvor protested.

"But you need 'em," Schrader insisted. "So, here's what we're gonna do. First, I'll buy these boots for you. It's a loan."

"I'll pay you back."

"Darn right you will," the man pointed a gnarled finger at Halvor. "I expect you to take good care of Duke and Daisy up there in the north woods. See that they're well fed and brush 'em dry every night. For that, I'll split their rent money with you, fifty-fifty. Then bring 'em back to me when the winter's over and we'll settle up."

"That's fair."

"Fair enough."

* * *

Halvor had to admit his new boots felt good.

"Rub oil into the leather every so often," Gene advised. "It'll make 'em more flexible and help to keep the moisture from soaking through to your feet."

Down the street from Bailly's trading post, they approached the ferry landing to cross the Mississippi River. The ferry operator's eyes got big when he saw the five big draft horses, which probably weighed a total of nine thousand pounds.

"Don't worry," Schrader shouted out to him. "We'll split 'em up apart for two trips."

The wooden ferry raft was plenty large, about eight feet wide by twenty feet long, with a railing on each side. Halvor joined Gene with his carriage, plus Duke and Daisy, to make the first crossing. They both helped propel the raft by pulling it along the cable stretched across the river. The two trips back and forth used more than an hour of their time, but the boy considered it an exciting adventure. The ferry ride was a unique experience for Harald and Haakon as well, but true to their Belgian nature, they stood placidly calm on the moving ferry.

Back on the road to Stillwater, Halvor asked about Isaac Staples.

"The man has been in the lumber business for more than twenty years," Gene began. "He's outsmarted and outlasted several of his competitors."

"Outsmarted how?"

"Well, several ways." Schrader poked one finger in the air. "First, he buys the best forestland and," raising another finger, "pays the lowest price." The third and fourth digits flipped up. "He modernized his sawmill with steam power and more efficient saw blades. Then he established a boom on the St. Croix River."

"A boom?" Halvor tilted his head in curiosity.

"It's a wide, gathering spot on a river where floating logs from multiple logging camps are collected. Each log gets identified and steered to its own sawmill, but the owner of the boom, Isaac Staples, collects a fee for this service," Schrader's thumb popped up.

Halvor's expression widened at the growing explanation.

"That's not all." Gene switched the reins to his opposite hand and started lifting other fingers. "He provides food to his camps from his own farms and flour mill, and he sells supplies to his own loggers from over-priced Staples company stores."

"Which is why we bought my boots in Hastings," Halvor said.

Schrader smiled and wiggled his fingers in the air. "Plus, he is president of the Lumberman's National Bank."

They entered Stillwater as the sun lowered toward the bluffs of the St. Croix River. Gene pointed to a mansion above. "There is Isaac Staples's house. His office will be at the sawmill."

Halvor could smell fresh-cut pine and hear automated saws buzzing through logs. As they approached the sprawling factory, he read a large sign with "St. Croix Mill" painted above the main entrance. They entered and asked to see the proprietor.

"Who are you?" inquired a suspicious clerk.

Gene stood to his full five feet, four inches and loudly announced, "I am Eugene Schrader, the best teamster Isaac Staples ever hired."

Almost immediately, a bald, barrel-chested man appeared in an adjacent doorway. With a grin spreading across his face, the man remarked sarcastically, "An inferior teamster with superior horses."

"Well, you're in luck," Schrader declared. "I have brought you some superior horses."

The two men converged to shake hands, and Halvor was introduced to the lumber baron. "My pleasure to meet you, sir."

"It's late," Gene said. "We're hungry and need to find lodging for ourselves and our horses. Come on outside, where you can see the animals, and let's negotiate a deal."

"These are good-looking Belgians," Staples agreed, reaching out a hand to stroke Harald's strong shoulder. "They will each be worth five dollars a month."

"Plus, you provide daily rations of grain," Schrader added.

"That goes without saying," assented Staples.

"Okay," Gene said with a nod toward Halvor, "What about my teamster?"

The lumberman took a step back to appraise Halvor. "He's pretty young. I normally pay inexperienced teamsters thirty dollars a month."

"He has enough skill and experience that I trust him with my own horses," Gene insisted. "What would you pay *me*?"

"But he's not you," Staples hesitated. "Maybe I could go to thirty-five."

Gene did not hesitate. Instead, he climbed up into the carriage seat and said to Halvor, "Come on, let's go. There are nine sawmills in this valley. We will find someone who's willing to pay us what we're worth."

Water Wheels

Staples watched the four powerful draft horses start to turn away and weakened. "Darn you, Schrader. Thirty-seven fifty."

Gene lifted the reins, ready to drive away, and stated with finality, "Forty dollars a month."

Staples planted his hands on his hips and exchanged a lengthy stare with Schrader before relenting, "Forty it is."

Gene turned to the boy with a nod of approval. "Seal the deal," he said.

Fourteen-year-old Halvor Dahl stepped forward and shook hands with fifty-eight-year-old Isaac Staples, the most powerful lumber baron in the St. Croix valley.

* * *

Halvor started north from Stillwater the following morning, riding Harald and leading the three younger Belgians single file along an extended rope. He followed a wagon road that hugged the St. Croix River's western shore, bound for Taylors Falls thirty miles away. His first job as an Isaac Staples employee would begin in that town. The boy was to pick up a wagonload of supplies and haul it to his assigned lumber camp on the Snake River.

The journey would have been easy were it not for a cold autumn rain that fell steadily from the low gray sky. The road became muddy and slick, so Halvor kept the horses to a walking pace, guiding them onto surer footing in the grass wherever possible. He was soaked and shivering when they reached Staples's supply depot in Taylors Falls near dark.

Thankfully, the stable accommodations were excellent. Halvor spread dry straw beneath each horse in the snug barn. He found ample grain and hay to feed them. Finally, he found some empty feed sacks to rub the cold moisture out of their chestnut-colored coats.

Food for humans was scarcer when Halvor finally found the bunkhouse kitchen, long after other Staples employees had eaten supper. He was shown an empty cot to lay on, and his eyes did not open until he heard clattering breakfast dishes. The boy quickly claimed a seat at the table because he wasn't going to miss another meal. The breakfast was hot and brown, and there was a lot of it. He filled up.

By the time Halvor finished morning chores with the horses, he found a young man already stacking supplies onto his assigned wagon. Most of the load appeared to be food, but a pair of sturdily framed windows were lying on their edges behind the wagon seat. He could see numerous bags of beans, peas, flour, sugar, coffee and tea. There was a canister of molasses beside a barrel of apples and two barrels of potatoes.

"Hello," the boy offered a friendly greeting at Halvor's approach. "Are you the teamster?"

"I am if this wagon is going to a Staples lumber camp on the Snake River."

"It is, and I'm coming with you. My name is Emil Lindstrom. Hired on as a chore-boy to the camp cook."

Halvor judged Emil to be near his own age. The boy was slender with shaggy blonde hair, and he spoke with a Swedish accent. "Glad to have your company," Halvor expressed.

"The wagon is just about loaded," Emil said. "You can bring your horses and hitch 'em up."

Within twenty minutes, Harald and Haakon were harnessed in front of the wagon while Duke and Daisy were tied to the back. Halvor was happy to see only a few clouds remaining in the distant eastern sky. They were illuminated pink and golden by the rising sun.

Emil hopped onto the wagon seat beside him and announced, "I know the way. I've made this trip before."

"Get up," Halvor bid to the horses, and away they rolled. He turned to his fellow traveler and asked, "What is a chore-boy?"

"I do whatever the cook tells me to do," Emil responded with a cheerful laugh, "and I better do it quick." Then, he proceeded with a more thorough job description. "My entire day revolves around breakfast at six a.m. and supper at six p.m." He lifted his hands about shoulder-width apart to visually frame the day. "So, I wake up at four-thirty to get a fire going in the wood stove and help the cook make breakfast until we serve at six o'clock. Then there are dishes to wash."

Halvor nodded his head in understanding.

"Through the day I perform odd jobs like cleaning the kitchen and chopping wood." Emil hesitated. "Unless it's my turn to deliver the lunch. If so, I pull the snack sled out to wherever the men are felling trees. They eat lunch at noon." Halvor kept listening. "By late afternoon, it's time to start peeling potatoes or some other supper chore. We serve the meal at six, and then it's time to wash dishes again." Now, he reached his arms out wide. "A fifteen-hour day."

Most of their wagon ride continued in that fashion. Halvor would ask a short question, and Emil would respond with a long answer. They were a well-suited pair. Halvor was a good listener, and Emil was a good talker.

"Are you a Swede?" Halvor asked.

"Almost all of us who live around here are Swedes." Emil swept his arm from east to west. "I understand there are three hundred farms of Swedish immigrant families between the St. Croix and Mississippi rivers."

"It's pretty country," Halvor said, observing the thick forests, "but it doesn't look like farmland to me."

"My parents say it looks like our homeland with all of the lakes and trees," Emil said. "The ground may not be as fertile as yours in southern Minnesota, but we don't need to make a profit. Our people just want to produce enough food for a happy life: grains, vegetables, livestock and dairy."

"So then, why are you going to work fifteen hours a day in a logging camp?"

"Most Swedish men from the Chisago County lakes area become lumberjacks in the wintertime. Especially young men who want to buy their own farmland. In fact, many of our people have purchased acres of ground from logging companies after the trees were removed. They're willing to sell it cheap when the pines are gone."

After a long day on the wagon seat, Halvor and Emil arrived at the pioneer village of Pine City. The young town was growing here at the intersection of the Snake River and new train tracks. The Lake Superior and Mississippi Railroad was completed in 1870 to provide daily transportation between St. Paul and Duluth.

They were to wait for the next morning's train, which would deliver perishable food from one of Isaac Staples's farms. After evaluating the evening weather conditions, they agreed to forego the costs of a hotel and livery stable. The boys found a grassy spot along the river where they allowed the horses to graze, and they laid down on the ground beneath the wagon. Halvor realized Emil was asleep when his companion finally stopped talking.

* * *

The boys were waiting beside the Pine City depot when the train arrived. They unloaded two large hog carcasses packed in ice and rearranged the wagon to pile them aboard.

"This is a lot of ham and bacon," commented Halvor.

"The meat will still be fresh when we get to camp," Emil said. "It's less than a couple of hours from here."

They traveled a narrow road westward along the Snake River, past a large lake that Emil called Pokegama. The land on both sides of the river had been logged in previous winters. Young saplings of aspen and spruce were sprouting from the acres near town where pines had been harvested a few years before. However, as they traveled upstream to more recently logged acres, only dead, discarded tree limbs lay strewn across the ground. Halvor observed the brown and brittle branches and said, "This looks like a fire hazard."

"The slash will rot and decompose after several years," Emil replied, "unless somebody buys this land. If so, they will rake the brush together with the stumps and burn it."

Then, miles ahead, Halvor saw a wall of towering green pines. He pointed and asked, "Is that where we're going?"

"Yes, that will be this year's cut."

Water Wheels

Rolling into the standing trees, they entered a completely different domain. Halvor's eyes perceived a darker scene beneath the lofty canopy of branches. His skin felt cooler near the shaded forest floor. His nose inhaled the unmistakable scent of pine sap. He could hear a breeze rustling through the treetops, but the surrounding stockade of timber contained them in a sanctuary of calm.

Rat-a-tat. Rat-tat-tat-tat-tat. A hammering woodpecker broke the quiet, and Halvor looked up to find it high among the trees. He spied a large black bird with bright red and white markings on its head. "That's the biggest woodpecker I've ever seen."

"It's a pileated woodpecker," Emil said. "They can peck out holes big enough for families to nest inside."

The bird's beak was shaped like a dagger, about two inches long. The wedge of red hair that crested its head stuck up like a flame, and two black stripes extended back from its eyes and beak. Halvor thought the stripes looked like a thin mask and mustache, prompting him to say, "He looks like a bandit."

Suddenly, the bird launched from the tree and screeched a staccato cry that sounded like a rapidly spinning squeaky wheel. The wings extended twelve inches on each side, and both had an arc of white feathers on their leading edge. It was an undulating flight, with powerful wing flaps initiating each swoop.

"I guess he didn't appreciate being called a bandit," Emil chuckled. Then he nudged Halvor with his elbow and pointed through the trees. "Our camp is over there."

They approached a collection of three log buildings, where he could see a handful of men working. When one of them stepped forward to meet the wagon, Emil called out, "Hi, Boss."

"Welcome back, Emil," said the man. Then, turning to Halvor, "Hello, I'm Bill Boston, the foreman of this camp."

"My pleasure to meet you, sir."

"You can forget the 'sir.' Everybody calls me 'Boss.'" The foreman pivoted and gestured toward the largest structure. "Pull your wagon over beside the shanty. The cook will help Emil unload supplies so you can unhitch your team and take care of the horses. I'll show you to the stable."

While Halvor was busy releasing Harald and Haakon from the harness, Boss untied Duke and Daisy. He led them toward a side building and swung open a wide door. They led the horses into separate stalls, and Halvor used a pitchfork to provide each one a ration of hay.

Boss stepped outside to scoop water from a rain barrel and returned to fill four drinking pails. He said, "Mr. Staples sent a message to tell me that you were pretty young."

Halvor stood to face the man after lowering a water bucket inside Haakon's stall. The foreman added, "But he says you come with a trustworthy recommendation and four reliable animals."

"I'm grateful for this job, and I'll do my best to earn your confidence." Halvor cleared his throat. "I especially appreciate being hired during this economic recession when others are looking for work."

"The panic has hurt our business a little, but people still need lumber," Boss said. "Minnesota's population has doubled since the Civil War. All those people need houses and furniture and barns and fences. The towns are building stores and boardwalks and bridges. The demand for these pine trees has not slowed very much."

While they walked away from the stable, Boss gave a quick description of the camp. "All three of these buildings are two-in-one." He hiked a thumb back toward the stable. "The other half of that barn is a workshop. The carpenter is using it now, and it will be the blacksmith shop when we start logging next month."

The man pointed to the opposite side of camp. "There's the office and store. The backside of that building has sleeping quarters for our four top hands."

"Who are the top hands?"

"The cook, blacksmith, top loader, and me. We also draw the highest wages and stand first in line at mealtime." They stopped beside the wagon, which Emil and a burly man were unloading into the largest log structure. It stretched fifty feet long, with a middle doorway through which the burly man emerged. "Cookee," Boss said, "meet our new teamster, Halvor Dahl."

While the cook sized him up and down, the boy said, "My pleasure to meet you, sir."

"'Pony,'" the cook blurted out. "At this age and height, you're not a full-grown teamster. Your name is Pony."

"Ha-ha," the foreman laughed. "It didn't take Cookee long to hang a handle on you."

"A handle?"

"Yes, Cookee gives everybody a nickname. You're one of the boys now... Pony."

At that moment, another man walked up and smiled when he saw the pair of framed windows on the wagon. "I'll get busy with those this afternoon," he said.

Boss offered an introduction, "Pony, this is Hammer, our carpenter." The foreman pointed to both ends of the long log building. "He's going to install windows on either end of the shanty."

Each framed window was big and heavy, so Halvor offered to carry one. "I get it," he said to the carpenter. "Hammer?"

"I'm lucky," the man grimaced. "At first, Cookee called me 'Hammerhead.' Now I'm just Hammer."

Before returning to the shanty, Halvor asked, "Is there an outhouse?"

Hammer smiled and pointed thirty paces back into the trees. "Built it myself."

It was the most spacious latrine Halvor had ever seen. Six feet wide, with three holes to sit on. He chose one of the side locations and hoped nobody else would enter before he finished. The wood surface around each hole was sanded smooth, and the entire structure was rock solid. Walking back to the shanty, Halvor murmured to himself. "Hammer does good work."

He was about to see more evidence to support that conclusion. The boy entered the large central building and paused inside, allowing his eyes to adjust to the darkness. A few kerosene lanterns provided dim light, so Halvor could see why they were excited about new windows. A gigantic wood-burning cookstove was located near the center of the structure. Open rafters above would allow heat to radiate throughout the building on cold winter days and nights.

Between the doorway and the stove stood a large metal washtub. Beyond the stove was a kitchen with dozens of pots, pans and utensils suspended on hooks from overhead beams. Emil was busy in a storage area behind the kitchen. To Halvor's right was a cafeteria area with three long tables and benches to seat two dozen people or more. Between the cafeteria and kitchen was a buffet counter, where loggers' plates would be filled from serving platters and bowls.

To the left was a large dormitory area, with upper and lower bunks lining all three walls, enough to sleep twenty bodies by Halvor's quick count. He could see storage space beneath each bunk and under benches that were aligned parallel to every bed.

"Take the upper bunk next to mine," Emil said. "I'm right next to the kitchen. The top bunks are warmer in the winter."

Over the next couple of weeks, Pony got used to his new nickname. He and Emil made two more supply runs to Taylors Falls. They had beautiful weather for the first round trip but returned through a snowstorm on the second one.

Boss was happy with the blizzard. "We want frozen, snow-covered ground for logging," he said. "Our entire crew should be here by mid-November, with two additional draft horses." He was right, and a large contingent of the lumberjacks were Swedes from Emil's home region near the Chisago Lakes. They were experienced woodsmen, having been seasonal loggers in previous years.

Emil explained, "This is pure profit for young farmers. Harvest season is over, and they will not be able to plant crops until May. They can take free food and lodging from Isaac Staples through the winter and collect their wages come springtime."

It soon became evident why Cookee was considered a top hand. Good meals were important to lumberjacks, and many of them chose their camp based on the quality of food. Foremen like Boss understood that they needed to hire a good cook if they wanted to attract good loggers. So Cookee was highly paid and treated with great respect.

The Chisago County men were friendly with Emil, and they quickly grew fond of his Norwegian friend. Both boys were early risers, Pony to do pre-dawn chores with the horses and Emil to help prepare breakfast. Cookee often served generous slices of bacon with mountains of delicious pancakes, and the Swedes were particularly fond of his strong coffee.

* * *

The tallest white pine stood at the edge of this year's cut. It had sprouted from the ground two centuries earlier when European immigrants started to settle America's thirteen original colonies. It grew slowly at first, requiring five years to reach one foot and ten years to become five feet tall, but then spurted three feet per year to reach its towering mature height of one hundred fifty feet.

A sticky, fragrant resin seeped from beneath the white pine's scales of gray bark. High overhead, horizontal branches were decorated with evergreen foliage in clumps of five wispy needles. At twenty-five years of age, the tree had begun producing slender pinecones that turned from green to brown before dispensing their seeds but then germinated once every three to five years.

The Iroquois Confederacy symbolically identified white pines as their "tree of peace." The British navy treasured the tall, straight trunks that stand as masts in their sailing ships. Now, American lumber companies found tremendous value in the light, buoyant wood of these magnificent pines.

Today, this Staples logging crew trudged into the woods at twilight, when the sun cast soft, diffused light up into the eastern sky from just beneath the horizon. Boss selected the progression of trees to be felled and marked them with his axe. Halvor saw his foreman chop a notch near the base of the tallest white pine, designating the direction he wanted it to fall.

Ax men once felled pines, but Staples crews used two-man crosscut saws, six feet long with handles on both ends. One sawyer pushed the blade while his partner pulled from the opposite side of the tree, back and forth. These modern saws were less likely to stick under a tree's immense weight because they had alternating teeth that cut and removed pulp with each stroke. The sawyers' ability to aim falling pines was amazingly accurate. Nonetheless, when a tree began to lean, they yelled "timber" at the top of their lungs to warn everybody that a mighty giant was coming down.

Squeak, creak, whoosh, boom! When the colossal pine crashed to earth, it shook the ground with a vibration the loggers could feel through their boots. Nonetheless, a pair of swampers were quickly beside it with their hatchets, chopping branches away from the tree trunk. Needle-covered boughs, which minutes before had whistled through the air, were sliced away and dragged aside.

Then, other sawyers converged on the remaining tree trunk, which was four feet in diameter at its base, gradually tapering toward the top. The sawyers crosscut the cylinder into sixteen-foot lengths. This typical white pine would yield nine enormous logs.

Now, the Belgians were put to task. Workers, who were called groundhogs, chained logs behind Duke and Daisy, who dragged the timbers, one at a time, to a loading area known as a skidway. Halvor was waiting there with Harald and Haakon harnessed beside a sturdy sled, capable of holding thirty to forty logs, depending on their thickness.

The top loader, nicknamed "Topper," oversaw this tricky and dangerous process. He stood on a platform above the sled, guiding a rope through a heavy-duty pulley. One end of the rope was hooked to each log by one of the groundhogs. The opposite end of the rope was hitched behind Harald and Haakon. Topper directed Pony to walk the Belgians forward and backward, to raise and then lower each log into place on the sled. When each capacity load was complete, Topper secured the timbers with heavy chains.

Next, Pony moved Harald and Haakon to the front of the loaded sled, which might weigh fifty thousand pounds. However, the powerful draft horses were able to pull this massive sled because its runners glided through icy ruts maintained by a crew of workers called road monkeys. The ice road was strategically routed to the river, down a gradual decline, without any sharp turns. The road monkeys kept this road smooth and slippery by adding snow and water when necessary. They were also constantly alert to remove debris from the road, typically chips of tree bark and horse manure.

The big white pine on the sled came to rest alongside the river. Its valuable logs rolled off when the heavy chain restraints were released. The stamper supervised this dangerous maneuver and also marked the logs. He swung a heavy hammer against both ends of every timber, which stamped the imprint of Isaac Staples's logo into the wood. All the lumber companies used this system to identify their trees because they were likely to get intermingled during the spring log drive. Melting snow would raise the river levels, enabling these logs to float downstream to the sawmills.

Come sundown, everyone headed back to camp, but Pony's work was not done, nor was that of the blacksmith. Cookee's nickname for the blacksmith was "Doc," like a dentist, because he sharpened each tooth on all the saws every night. Axes and hatchets were also sharpened every night, but most of the lumberjacks cared for their own blades.

Pony's salary as a teamster included responsibility for horse care. He gave them food and water when they returned to the stable. He frequently raked soiled straw out of their stalls and replaced it with clean bedding. Then, he massaged each animal with a towel to get them warm and dry. Running his hands over their legs and bodies was soothing for the horses, plus it also helped Pony discover any sore spots that needed his attention.

The busiest evening workers, however, were Cookee and Emil, who were preparing supper when the weary lumberjacks marched in through the entry door. The warm shanty atmosphere was thick with cooking aromas of baking bread, roasting pork, simmering beans, mashed potatoes and applesauce. "Smells wonderful in here," one of the swampers hungrily proclaimed.

Cookee snarled a response in mock anger. "It smelled good until you got back." He was only partially kidding. Body odors from twenty sweaty loggers began to filter through the air. The men removed perspiration-stained hats from their oily hair, stomped snow from moist leather boots and wriggled their feet out of wet wool socks. This combination of fragrant foods and musky bodies resulted in a strange smell unique to a lumberjack shanty. They were familiar with the pungent perfume.

* * *

Isaac Staples (1816–1898)

In 1853, when Isaac Staples arrived in Minnesota at the age of thirty-seven, he was already a veteran of the New England lumber industry. Relying on that experience, he built the biggest timber operation in the St. Croix River Valley, harvested the most trees and sold the most lumber.[21]

Water Wheels

Staples instituted a system of vertical integration and modernized every step in the process of his organization, from the natural resources to the delivery of the finished products. He bought forestland at bargain prices and hired his own logging crews, who were supplied from his own hardware stores and fed from his own farms and commercial fisheries. Staples transported logs to his own boom, produced boards in his own sawmill, and shipped them on his own trains. The Lumberman's National Bank, of which he was president, financed the entire operation.[22]

Both physically and mentally powerful, Staples hired hundreds of employees, including the famous cruiser Lyman Ayer. Known as the "Timber Wolf," Ayer surveyed forestland for Staples over more than three decades. The well-educated son of pioneer missionaries, he used a compass and amazing endurance to find the most profitable acres of timber in northern Minnesota.[23]

Staples and his wife, Olivia, moved from Maine with three young children and increased that number to five in Minnesota. When he reached age seventy-one, the couple retired to their magnificent three-story brick mansion on a bluff overlooking Stillwater.[24]

Chapter 7
Wolves in the Woods
1875

By the middle of March, snow was melting in the north woods, and logging season ended. The winter yielded a good timber harvest, and Halvor reached a handshake agreement with Boss to return the next year. On the way home, he returned Duke and Daisy to the Schrader farm near Hastings, where he spent the night and enjoyed another delicious meal.

Halvor settled finances with Eugene the next morning, splitting money earned by the man's two young draft horses and paying him back for the cost of the now-cherished leather boots. The boy rode home with slightly more than two hundred and fifty dollars in his pocket. That amount would pay for one year's tuition at the University of Minnesota. Unfortunately, Halvor knew that college attendance would include the cost of books, lodging, food and miscellaneous expenses he could not yet afford. Furthermore, he expected another year of maturity would make him more at ease among a college population.

Arriving home to the farm on Wolf Creek was a happy occasion. Halvor resumed his comfortable role within the family after a few nights in his old bed and a few days of familiar chores around the barn. However, his siblings seemed slightly more grown up, especially Erik. His older brother was trying to encourage a sparse patch of blonde whiskers to sprout on his cheeks and upper lip. Light in color, the hairs were invisible unless you were within a few feet. But the young man had assumed a more serious demeanor. He was *acting* like an adult.

With the clearing of Erik's new quarter-section, the Dahl family had twice the acreage to grow crops this year. Halvor's help was valuable, but the truly essential workers were the horses to plow, plant, cultivate and harvest. Harald and Haakon were teamed to do the heaviest jobs. Ragnhild became a training partner for three-year-old Sophia, and the mares combined to perform less strenuous work.

Ironically, the grasshopper plague that devastated grain fields in western Minnesota was an economic boon for eastern farmers like the Dahls, who were lucky enough to escape the insects. A reduced supply of crops from across midwestern America resulted in higher prices for successfully harvested plants. After the Panic of 1873, two consecutive years of financial recovery were welcome.

* * *

With the October harvest over, Halvor left the farm to spend his second season as a logging teamster. Again, he stayed one night with the Schraders and picked up Duke and Daisy. This year, Gene remained at home while Halvor traveled alone to Stillwater. He was proud to learn from Isaac Staples that Boss had vouched for an increase in his wages of five additional dollars per month. The boy harnessed Harald and Haakon to a wagonload of supplies in Taylors Falls, hauling them to Rush City before stopping to rest. Finally, on the fifth day, his journey ended at the relocated Snake River lumber camp.

Several miles farther upriver, this year's camp looked remarkably familiar. Sure enough, Emil Lindstrom's friendly face emerged out of the shanty to greet him. The two youngsters shook hands and noticed that each other had grown during the year, with more muscular and manly features. Emil began unloading the wagon cargo while Halvor stabled the four Belgians, providing them with water and feed.

Water Wheels

"Welcome, Pony!" the boy smiled in recognition of his lumberjack nickname upon entry to the shanty. He observed a circle of men seated around one of the cafeteria tables: Boss, Cookee, Hammer and a stranger with a long, white beard.

"We have the honor of a legend in our midst," said Cookee. "Meet the Timber Wolf."

The stranger stood politely and extended his hand. "The name is Lyman Ayer. I'm a cruiser for Mr. Staples." The man's voice was precise, with a New England accent. His posture was ramrod straight, and his clothes were unusually neat for a lumberjack shanty.

"Pony is our teamster," Boss interjected. "I know he looks like a schoolboy, but this kid can really handle horses, and his Belgians are first-rate animals."

Halvor's face blushed at the compliment. He hoped it didn't show in the shanty's dim light. Boss explained that a logging cruiser's job was to survey forestland, looking for the most profitable stands of trees.

Ayer elaborated, "The pine land on both sides of this valley is valuable. There are many trees per acre, with an average height and diameter, to produce a bounty of lumber. Your camp can be readily supplied from nearby towns, and the Snake River is an excellent tributary to float logs to sawmills on the St. Croix."

Boss had a question, "What about the railroad?"

"Trains are becoming a factor," Ayer said. "More so every year. Mr. Staples would prefer to drive logs down the rivers because it is free. But sometimes the logs get hung up on shallow rapids or jammed into narrow bottlenecks." He paused. "Trains cost money, but they are reliable in every season of every year. Plus, tracks can be laid to bountiful stands of pine that are more distant from navigable rivers."

"We're going deeper and deeper into the forests every year," said Boss.

"Let me tell you a cruiser's story about a distant forest," Ayer smiled, "the Lost Forty. I'm told that a northern Minnesota surveyor lost his bearings while trying to navigate through a mess of swamps miles away from the nearest river. He incorrectly drew a logging map that located a forty-acre lake in the wrong spot by half a mile. So, the lumberjack crews were not directed to harvest trees from that location. It seems the loggers could see the trees but assumed some other crew was assigned to cut them down." He laughed. "Those pines are still standing there. They've been standing there for centuries!"

"Lucky for those trees," Cookee remarked, "they didn't get cruised by the Timber Wolf."

* * *

The next day, Pony and Hammer rode the wagon back to Pine City, where the carpenter needed some supplies from the lumberyard. Along the way, Hammer shared some of his knowledge about Lyman Ayer. "The Timber Wolf is a teetotaler—no alcohol, no tobacco, no profanity. His family came from New England and settled on the Canadian border. He grew up among the Ojibwe and can speak their language. Before Ayer started cruising for Isaac Staples, he was a fur trader who also carried dispatches between Fort Snelling and Fort Garry up by Winnipeg. I also understand the Northern Pacific Railroad hired him to chart a route to lay their tracks from Lake Superior through the Red River Valley."

Halvor changed the subject. "The new camp you have built looks great."

"It's about half new and half old," the carpenter said. "We took last year's buildings apart and moved a lot of the pieces to our new location—bunks, tables, shingles, doors and windows. We saved all the metal equipment—stoves, pipes, latches, hinges and knobs. The outhouse is on skids, so we just dragged it over in one piece."

"Who are 'we'?"

"Lefty Jackson is my primary helper," Hammer answered. "You remember he was a groundhog on last winter's crew. Lefty is a year-round employee for the Staples Lumber Company. He's a river pig for the spring log drive, works at the Stillwater sawmill during the summer, and then comes to assist me in the fall."

Water Wheels

"I remember him," Halvor said. "Lefty's a hard worker."

"Yeah, not a great thinker," Hammer admitted, "but he's a cheerful soul who does his best every day. He'll be waiting for us at the lumber yard in Pine City."

Sure enough, Lefty was there, and he helped load lumber and equipment onto the wagon. Heading back toward camp, their first stop was four miles west of town, where the Snake River made a hairpin turn. When Hammer walked from the road down to the riverbank, Halvor could see a temporary wooden dam with a large gate in the middle. The carpenter returned to the wagon, tied a big tool belt around his waist and asked Lefty to bring a long, sturdy board. The pair of them spent the next two hours repairing the dam gate by replacing broken boards and missing hardware.

When they were back on the wagon, Hammer explained to Halvor. "This is a splash gate. We build them at spots in the river where logs would likely snag if the water were too shallow. This dam will hold spring runoff at a high-water level until a collection of logs is ready to be released. When the gate is opened, a surge of water will carry the logs through the dam and far downstream."

"They work," said Lefty. "We drove logs through this splash gate last May."

"We've got time to check another one this afternoon," Hammer declared, and he directed Pony to drive four miles further upstream to the next wooden dam. Luckily, it required only minor repairs, and they arrived back at camp well before supper time.

* * *

Two weeks later, the ground was freezing solid, and the Staples camp was ready for winter. When snow flurries appeared, so did the crew of lumberjacks. On the first Sunday of December, the Swedes lit an Advent candle in the shanty, marking four weeks until Christmas. On Sunday, December 19, they lit the third one. This was the brink of winter solstice, the shortest day and longest night of the year.

Topper and Doc, leaders of the Chisago County Swedes, sat down with Boss. Doc said, "Tonight, our families will celebrate

Saint Lucia. Our girls will carry candles and wear their prettiest white dresses, with wreaths in their hair."

Boss nodded.

Topper picked up where Doc left off, "Next weekend, we're going home for Christmas Eve and Christmas Day. We'll come back to work a full day on Sunday, our usual day off."

Boss did not object. It was a fair exchange, and he could see their minds were set.

The happy crew worked extra hard in the days leading up to their two-day vacation. Emil invited Halvor to come home with him, a plan to which the boys agreed after Lefty Jackson consented to care for the horses overnight.

On the morning of Christmas Eve, everyone ate breakfast in the shanty before the Swedes walked to the Pine City railroad depot. Topper spoke to the ticket agent and negotiated a bargain fare for the forty-mile ride to Chisago County. Then, they all piled into a boxcar on the southbound Lake Superior and Mississippi train.

After unloading, the happy lumberjacks scattered toward their homes amid the dozens of small lakes in the area. Emil pointed east, and the boys commenced at a lively pace bound for the Lindstrom family farm. "We will get home in time for the julbord feast," he raised his voice and spread his arms out wide. "Food will be spread all over the table: glazed ham, meatballs, smoked fish, bread, cheese, and we'll have rice pudding for dessert."

The Swedish boy was welcomed home by his loving family, and they offered every hospitality to his Norwegian friend. Emil's parents were quiet and kindhearted, but his two younger sisters—twins—were full of energy. They bounded around the house and were constantly jabbering at the same time.

Late that night, Halvor reclined on a mattress stuffed with straw and pine boughs. His belly was full from the smorgasbord, which offered delights as delicious and bountiful as Emil had described. He pictured the Lindstrom family and, upon closing his eyes, imagined a happy vision of his own parents and siblings in their Cannon Valley home. This holiday visit would last only one day, from the time of their arrival until tomorrow's departure, but it was worth the journey. He drifted into a restful slumber.

On Christmas morning, both boys helped with farm chores before a hearty breakfast. Leftover meat, bread and cheese from the julbord feast was just as tasty as the day before. Halvor attended a Christmas morning church service with the Lindstroms. Then, the family relaxed in conversation until early afternoon, when it was time to leave, and everyone wished each other well. Emil decided to strap on his cross-country skis, which he wore to meet the train that would take them back to Pine City. Halvor trudged through the snow by the most direct route while Emil glided near and far in joyful loops. The Swede gracefully lifted his knees forward in alternating cadence while simultaneously thrusting the poles with his opposite hands. Halvor heard his voice pierce through the brisk winter wind, "Hurrah!"

* * *

With the new year—1876—came a stretch of extremely cold weather. Halvor took extra caution to protect the horses from illness or injury. He dried them thoroughly at the end of each day, checked every hoof for signs of ice damage, and gave them extra feed to sustain their strength. After supper on the coldest nights, he maintained a fire in the blacksmith's stove, which was under the same open rafters adjoining the stable.

One evening after completing this task, Halvor detoured up the outhouse path before returning to the shanty. The squeak of his boots on the crunchy snow indicated a temperature well below zero. That cold fact was confirmed moments later when his naked rump met the frigid toilet seat. "Yeow," he gasped to himself, "that stings."

Leaving the outhouse, Halvor could clearly see the entire camp. The half-moon's reflected luster off the snow-covered ground illuminated every building. Suddenly, a haunting howl made the hair stand up on the back of his neck. The wolf's call was echoed by a chorus of yips and yelps from several of its canine mates. The boy hustled nearer the shanty and paused for a few moments, listening to the pack of predators before going inside.

Stepping inside, Halvor saw that Emil was still at work washing the supper dishes. Around the dormitory to his left, some men relaxed on their bunks while others hung wet stockings to dry from the clothesline that circled the room. To his right, a few others sat at the cafeteria tables. One of the sawyers was writing a letter, and two road monkeys were playing a game of checkers. Halvor said, "A pack of wolves are howling out there. They sound really close."

A road monkey looked up from the checkerboard. "We've seen them near the ice road," he commented. "Lack of prey and this cold weather has made them desperate enough to come near the camp."

"Maybe they're hunting for Babe the Blue Ox," laughed Topper. "The legend says he was turned blue by a winter as cold as this."

Boss joined in the folk tale merriment. "Don't worry, Pony. Paul Bunyan won't let those wolves get after Babe or your Belgians. If he can fell a giant pine tree with one swing of his axe, I imagine he could chop up a few mangy wolves."

Now Cookee toured around the room with a hot coffee pot, refilling the mugs of men who were still enjoying an after-supper sip. He stopped beside the letter-writing sawyer. "Paul Bunyan could be distracted by his girlfriend," the cook teased. "Maybe he's writing a love letter to Lucette Kensack, like Whipsaw here."

Laughter echoed around the shanty, and Lefty joined in, "If Paul Bunyan were around, we wouldn't be needing you swampers. Babe the Blue Ox would just eat the branches off all the downed trees."

One of the swampers shot back, "Then I wouldn't have to worry about gashing my leg or foot with a hatchet." He turned to Boss. "Maybe the foreman would give me a safe job like one of you loafers."

"Be careful what you wish for," Boss cautioned. "Everybody on a logging crew has a risky task. In addition to our sharp saws and axes, we need to be careful around those big logs. Topper could get rolled off the sled or love-sick Whipsaw could get smashed by the kickback of a falling tree." He motioned toward Halvor. "Don't get too distracted by Pony's howling wolves. Concentrate on your jobs."

Water Wheels

Stamper swung his feet over the side of his top bunk and sat on the edge of his bed. He produced a harmonica and blew one rising crescendo of notes before declaring, "Enough dreary talk. How 'bout some merry music? Cookee, get your fiddle. Let's play 'The Shanty Man's Life.'"

The screeching tone produced by the cook's fiddle would never be welcome in an orchestra hall. It only slightly harmonized with Stamper's melody. But the tune was jaunty, and he stomped one foot so loudly that everyone could sing in time with the beat.

Then here's to the lumberjack, bad or good,
Who toils in the depth of the dark green wood.
Though rough of dress, of visage grim,
Beneath it all there's a heart in him.

After a few more songs, Halvor saw Emil return from the wood pile and stoke the stove that would keep the shanty warm into the night. It was the final task of the chore boy's fifteen-hour workday. Boss rose to dim a lantern and declare, "Lights out, boys."

* * *

The next morning, Emil was back on the job. He rekindled glowing embers in the stove and helped to make breakfast. The young Swede heated a large kettle of brown beans and mixed a big stockpot of pancake batter while Cookee prepared a hash by shredding ham into fried potatoes. They fed the crew, and then, again, there were dishes to wash.

After the loggers were gone, Cookee ordered Emil to split more firewood. They were burning a lot of it in this subzero weather. The woodpile was heaped with logs the sawyers had cut into cylinders about a foot and a half in length. Emil's job was to divide these chunks lengthwise by splitting them with an axe. He chopped some of them into extra-thin pieces of kindling that would burn fast and hot.

The hard physical work warmed the boy up despite the frigid temperature. After a while, he could feel perspiration under his clothes, so he removed his outer coat and continued chopping. He guessed that two hours had passed when he split the last cylinder and carried an armload of kindling into the shanty. "Our entire woodpile is split," he told Cookee.

"Good work," the man said. "Let's remind the groundhogs to drag in another couple of trees tomorrow."

"I thought I smelled doughnuts." Emil's face brightened as he pointed to a countertop covered with fat rings of pastry.

"Yeah, I thought the boys could use a treat on this especially cold day." The cook smiled. "You have probably earned one or two of 'em with your axe."

Emil did indeed eat a couple of doughnuts. Then after they had cooled and dried, he stacked them like a telescope by poking a narrow wooden stick, three feet long, through their center holes. This is how the doughnuts would be served to the lumberjacks so each man could slide one off when the stick was extended in his direction.

At eleven o'clock, Emil pulled the lunch sled to just outside the shanty door. He and Cookee filled it up with food for a noon snack to be served at the crew's work site. Usually, the snack consisted of leftover food from breakfast, which the men called flaggins. Today's addition of doughnuts would be a special treat.

Emil positioned himself in front of the sled and climbed into a custom-made harness of two belts that crisscrossed in front of his chest and over each shoulder. Then he clamped on his cross-country skis and picked up his poles. Cookee waved goodbye, and the young Swede strode away, pulling the lunch sled down the icy trail.

Emil got a kick out of using his skis to deliver the noonday meal. They made a gentle clattering sound on the crusty path, packed and glazed by the daily boot traffic of the lumberjacks coming and going. The men were working just two miles from camp, and he was halfway there in fifteen minutes. He leaned forward and pulled with extra exertion to climb a short, gradual incline.

When he lifted his eyes near the top of the rise, he confronted a sight that stopped him. A wolf stood motionless in the path, facing squarely at him from no more than twenty feet away. It was light silver, almost white, like the vapor of breath that puffed from its nostrils. The frigid, cloudy air was windless and silent. Now Emil could just barely hear chopping axes and a shout from the logging crew another mile ahead.

The wolf's unblinking eyes sparkled sky blue, the only shining objects in this overcast scene. Emil froze with fear, his heart pounding in his chest. By comparison, the wolf seemed completely relaxed as it patiently observed the boy, seemingly without a worry in the world.

A sound surprised Emil from behind. He spun around to find a semicircle of wolves in his wake. He quickly counted four of them in various shades of gray. Not stationary, like the white wolf, they were approaching rapidly and surrounding him. He heard a snarl, and two of them were baring their teeth. Emil awkwardly clambered around on his skis, instinctively raising the poles like makeshift swords. Unfortunately, one of the poles tangled in his harness of belts, and he struggled to wiggle it free. *Oof!* A sudden impact into his back forcefully expelled breath from the boy's lungs and smashed his face onto the icy path.

* * *

Lefty Jackson led Daisy through the snow to where the young Belgian mare pulled a sixteen-foot log beside the skidway. Swampers had trimmed branches from the freshly cut pine, so it was clean and ready to be loaded upon the sled where a layer of similar timbers was already placed. Topper stood on his platform above the sled, watching the groundhog and Daisy approach while Halvor waited on the opposite side with Harald and Haakon. Topper grasped a heavy rope that ran through an overhead pulley from a hitch behind Pony's horses. The top loader swung the other end of the rope to Lefty, who fastened it onto both ends of the log with sturdy iron hooks.

The groundhog stepped back and gave Topper a thumbs-up signal to lift the timber. The top loader, in turn, gestured for Pony to begin walking his horses away, hoisting the log up above the sled. *Thwang!* Just as the timber lifted off the skidway, one of the iron hooks slipped free and whiplashed up toward the pulley. Topper ducked to avoid it, and Halvor immediately yelled, "Whoa!" to stop Harald and Haakon.

One end of the log crashed down and rolled crazily off the skidway directly at Lefty. He tried to jump out of the way, but there was nowhere to go. The timber hit Lefty in the knee, knocking him to the ground, and rolled up onto his pelvis where it came to a stop. The helpless groundhog was pinned into the snow.

Topper and Halvor both scrambled to his side. Lefty was conscious, but his face was scrunched into a grimace that revealed severe pain. "Can you breathe?" Topper asked.

Lefty gave a nod of confirmation but didn't speak or open his clenched eyes. He had one arm braced against the five-hundred-pound timber, although it wasn't going to move.

Topper turned to Pony. "We'll need your horses to lift this log."

Halvor noticed a nasty gash across Topper's cheekbone. "You're bleeding," said the boy.

The top loader wiped a mitten over his wounded face, revealing a little blood. "I'm fine. We've got to get this log off Lefty." Then he hurried to refasten the iron hooks to each end of the timber while Pony moved his Belgians back into position. Other crew members were now running toward the skidway in response to the accident.

When Topper shouted instructions, Pony slowly guided Harald and Haakon forward, carefully raising the log upward. Lefty winced at the initial movement, then seemed to sink limply onto the snow as the enormous weight was lifted away. Fellow lumberjacks grasped the victim under each armpit and dragged him backward to a safe distance. Lefty's right leg appeared completely unstable. The boot was turned sideways, and his lower leg wobbled unnaturally as if held in place by nothing but his pant leg. The frightened loggers didn't know whether to touch the leg or not.

Just then, Boss arrived and kneeled beside the prone groundhog. "Lefty, can you hear me?"

Lefty nodded but kept his eyes clamped shut.

Water Wheels

"Can you talk?" Boss placed one hand on the man's chest where he could feel Lefty's thumping heart and the rise of his ribcage when he gasped for a breath.

"My leg," the groundhog whispered through clenched teeth, and his eyes fluttered open. He viewed the foreman's reassuring face and lifted his right hand to point at the source of pain.

Boss reached down to gently squeeze Lefty's thigh. The man's entire body jerked in agony, and once again, his eyes clamped shut. Slowly, Boss massaged upward toward the hip, which had borne the log's weight. Lefty held his breath, and every muscle in his body seemed tense. Next, when Boss's fingers explored downward toward the injured knee, Lefty shuddered and inhaled a desperate gasp. When Boss touched the man's shin, there was no response. He reached to straighten the wayward right foot, but it flopped back sideways when he let it go.

The foreman readjusted himself and began to investigate the other leg. Lefty relaxed a little, and Boss asked, "Can you feel my hands?"

"Yes," came the answer, "that leg doesn't hurt as much."

Boss examined Lefty's upper body for other injuries, pressing on ribs and squeezing both arms. Thankfully, the man seemed otherwise unharmed.

Topper spoke up, "Let's get this sled unloaded. We'll lay Lefty on there so Pony can transport him back to camp." The flatbed was quickly cleared, and six loggers placed their hands under Lefty's body, three on each side, to carry their injured comrade to the temporary ambulance. Several men took off their coats to pack around the victim, two to immobilize his injured leg and the others as blankets to provide warmth against a possible shock reaction.

Boss told Topper, "You're in charge for the rest of the day. Don't work too long or these men without coats will suffer from exposure. Just collect the next full load of logs here beside the skidway, and Pony can haul them to the river first thing tomorrow morning." Then the foreman climbed on board the sled and sat astride Lefty to hold him in place.

"Let's go, teamster," he shouted.

Michael Barnes

* * *

"Aieeow!" Emil shrieked from the shocking pain of powerful canine teeth piercing into the collarbone between his neck and shoulder. He spun onto his back, and the white wolf was momentarily tossed aside. Luckily, the boy's thick coat collar had prevented the animal's jaws from a fatal lock onto his neck. In an instant, the wolf was on its feet and lunging at Emil's face. Somehow, the boy thrust a ski pole in front of the beast and braced it sideways with both hands. The predator's glistening teeth snapped the pole in half, which blunted the advance of its mouth but not its feet. Wicked claws extending from rugged forepaws raked into the cheek and neck of its prey.

The wolf coiled upon the boy's chest and curled back lips to expose its deadly fangs. The beast pounced on Emil's head and sank its teeth into his face. Instinctively, the Swede struck back, stabbing his broken ski pole into the wolf's neck. The severed wooden stub had a sharp, jagged point that punctured through his attacker's throat. The surprised creature yelped in pain and bounced back from Emil in confusion.

In that moment of hesitation, the wolf noticed its flurrying pack mates. The other four hunters had toppled the lunch sled, spilling the flaggins onto the ground. They were fighting each other for the food, scattering hash and beans and doughnuts across the snow-packed path. In a flash, the white wolf joined the fracas. It was a snarling, gobbling free-for-all. Suddenly ignored, Emil took the opportunity to quickly free his feet from their ski bindings.

On the other side of the knoll, one hundred yards away, came the sled that carried Lefty Jackson. Harald and Haakon began displaying signals of apprehension that caught Halvor's attention. They both lifted their heads, with ears pricked forward. Haakon raised his tail like a warning flag, and Harald snorted air through flared nostrils, smelling trouble.

When Halvor caught a glimpse of chaotic movement ahead, he could tell it was different from Emil's usual lunch sled delivery.

Water Wheels

"Something is happening on the trail," he called over his shoulder. Then Harald planted his forelegs far apart and balked at Pony's command to "Get up." Suddenly, Haakon reared on his hind legs and bolted forward when his front feet hit the ground. Both horses galloped up the rise, totally out of Halvor's control. He hoped that Boss was hanging on to the sled and Lefty. Emil stood up and turned to hear his friend yelling.

"Emil!" Pony shouted just as he and the Belgians saw the swirling pack of wolves. Harald and Haakon swerved to avoid them, bouncing the sled up and over the snowbank at the edge of the trail. Halvor couldn't stop his terrified team, but they were slowed by the sled, now plowing through the deeper snow.

Emil angled sideways in front of the charging horses, hoping to intersect their course. With each lunging stride, the Swede lifted his feet and tried to hurdle over the snow rather than through it. Pony pulled on the reins with all his might, trying to slow the frantic stallions, but his efforts were futile. Harald and Haakon were oblivious to everything except the snarling wolves, from whom they were desperately attempting to run.

Emil could not grab the harness when the horses stampeded past, nor could he reach the hand that Halvor tried in vain to extend. But with one more bound and a desperate dive, he landed halfway onto the sled. Halvor twisted around to see the boy's snow-covered mittens failing to get a grip on the flatbed while his legs dangled off the edge. However, a sturdy vertical post extended up from each corner of the sled, and Emil managed to hook his armpit around a rear one. Halvor was relieved to see Boss still on the sled, clinging to one of the front posts with his left hand. His right hand gripped a fistful of Lefty's coat, and the foreman's legs remained wrapped around the groundhog's torso.

As he turned back to his team, Pony saw they were pulling away from the overturned lunch sled. Evidently the wolves were preoccupied with fighting each other for the remaining morsels of food because none of them were chasing the horses. In fact, none of them were even watching their getaway.

Gradually, Harald and Haakon slowed down. Halvor didn't know if they sensed the danger had passed or if they were simply exhausted. He didn't care. He was just glad to have them under control again. He glanced back to see Emil finally struggle to drag his entire body onto the sled. The Swede slumped over on the flatbed, apparently drained of his strength. Halvor guided the Belgians back onto the trail, frequently glancing back to see if the wolves were pursuing. He dared not stop to check on his passengers fearing that the horses would panic again and gallop away without him.

Within minutes, they arrived back at the camp. "Cookee," Pony yelled, stopping in front of the shanty. "Cookee!"

The cook rushed out the door, hearing the urgency in Halvor's voice. He arrived just in time to see Emil sit up on the sled, his face a bloody mess. "My God," Cookee lamented as he glanced back and forth from his wounded chore boy to Lefty's limp body, "Who should I help first?"

"I can walk," Emil declared. "Let me wash my face," and he headed for the shanty door.

Boss eased off the flatbed and told Cookee, "Help us with Lefty." Then, the foreman looked up at his young teamster on the sled seat. "Pony, help us carry Lefty inside. Then you can check on your friend and care for your horses."

Boss stepped forward to press his belly against the edge of the sled, right beside where Lefty lay. The foreman directed Cookee and Pony to flank him shoulder-to-shoulder so all three men could slip their hands under the injured man's body. "Are you listening to me, Lefty?" Boss asked.

The groundhog nodded his head.

Boss gently wedged his forearms, one under Lefty's back, the other beneath his butt. Cookee supported the man's head and shoulders. Halvor got one arm beneath Lefty's thighs and the other under his calves. He could feel the leg muscles tense and knew the man was in pain.

Boss gave instructions. "Now we're going to back up together and then side-shuffle through the shanty door. Once inside, we'll lay him on the nearest cafeteria table." He glanced from side to side and asked, "Ready?" They both consented, and he ordered, "Okay, lift."

They hesitated at the door, but Emil opened it up and stood to the side, holding a bloodstained towel to the side of his face. After laying Lefty on the table, Halvor joined his friend at the sink. "I should look at your wounds," he said, "but it's too dark here. Take off your shirt and stand in the lantern light beside the stove." Emil did as he was told while Halvor rinsed the towel in the sink.

The Norwegian boy approached his Swedish friend and dabbed blood away from ugly gashes. "The deepest cuts are on either side of your mouth, here on the left side of your chin and back behind the right side of your jaw."

"My face was inside the wolf's mouth."

Halvor pulled back, looking at Emil with awe. "You're lucky to be alive."

"I stabbed it with my broken ski pole."

Halvor tilted his head and allowed a slight grin before investigating the wounds further. "Your right ear is pretty torn up, and there's a lot of blood matted in your hair there, but most of the bleeding seems to have stopped. These claw scratches on your neck look grisly, but they're not too deep."

"My shoulder hurts worse than my face." Emil reached across and pointed to his left clavicle.

"It's gonna be black and blue," said Halvor, cupping his hand over the top of the Swede's shoulder.

"Ouch!" Emil recoiled in pain.

"That's your collarbone," Halvor told him.

The chore boy lifted both hands and gingerly ran his fingertips sideways along the bone. He held his breath and grimaced. "I think it's broken."

"Well, let me wash you off," suggested the Norwegian. "Then you should lay on your bunk and rest." By the time they were finished, Halvor could feel cold seeping into the shanty, and he remembered his Belgians standing outside. He added a couple chunks of firewood into the stove and headed out the door. Boss and Cookee were still hovering over Lefty Jackson.

Halvor was careful to move smoothly and speak in a calm voice when he approached Harald and Haakon. "Easy, boys." He was worried they might still be jittery after their terrifying encounter with the wolfpack. Rather than mount the sled, he walked to their heads and escorted them to the stable on foot. Halvor took extra time to rub them down and scrutinize every leg for injury, talking quietly all the while. "You lived up to the names of Norwegian kings today," said the boy, and then he fed them like royalty.

Emerging from the stable, Halvor saw the logging crew returning. One of the road monkeys pulled the empty lunch sled. Lefty's groundhog partner led Duke and Daisy, holding halter ropes in both hands. Halvor intercepted the man and relayed the young Belgians to the stable, where he groomed and fed them both.

When the young teamster got back to the shanty, he found it unusually subdued. Lumberjacks were speaking in whispers, with worried expressions on their faces. After removing his coat and boots, Halvor exchanged wet socks for dry ones and then went looking for Emil. He found the young Swede huddled with Cookee and Topper in a back corner of the cafeteria.

Emil lay on his back, upon a dining table, while Cookee stitched the worst of the boy's facial cuts with a needle and thread. Topper was holding a lantern to illuminate Emil's face. The Swede's eyes were shut tight because of the bright light, or the pain, or both.

Topper told Halvor, "Cookee is our doctor."

"I ain't no doctor," the cook snarled. "Keep that lantern shining in the right place."

"Well, you're the best doctor we've got," Topper continued, "and you're doing a right smart sewing job on the chore boy here."

Pony asked, "What about his collarbone?"

"It's busted," Cookee growled. "He'll have to take it easy for a couple weeks. I suppose I'll get stuck choppin' all the firewood for this gosh darn outfit."

Topper grinned at the cook's cranky demeanor. "Relax,

Cookee. We've got a whole camp full of lumberjacks to chop wood for you. Now, you need to adopt a more cheerful attitude before you start stitching on *my* face." Topper turned to show the gash on his cheekbone from the skidway accident.

"How about Lefty?" Halvor asked, pointing at the groundhog who still lay on the cafeteria table, covered by a blanket.

Cookee frowned. "His leg can't be saved. Gonna have to take it off at the knee."

"Amputate?" Halvor asked.

Topper gave a confirming nod. "Boss has given him three glasses of whiskey to deaden the pain. When he's passed out drunk, Cookee will have to saw it off."

"I'll need four strong men to hold him steady while I do the cuttin'," grumbled the cook. "Even with all that whiskey, Lefty might thrash a bit."

Three hours later, Cookee's medical chores were complete, and a late supper had been served. Pony and a few other men had volunteered to substitute for Emil in the kitchen and were washing dishes. Lying in his bunk, Stamper broke the gloomy silence that hung eerily beneath the shanty rafters. Haunting notes flowed forth from his harmonica that soon were joined by Doc's soulful voice.

> *Then here's to the lumberjack, bad or good,*
> *Who toils in the depth of the dark green wood.*
> *Though rough of dress, of visage grim,*
> *Beneath it all there's a heart in him.*

* * *

Michael Barnes

Paul Bunyan and Babe the Blue Ox.

Though a fictional character, Paul Bunyan and his mythical companion Babe the Blue Ox are among Minnesota's most famous historical characters. Hundreds of stories are told about the size, strength and deeds of the man and beast who harvested pine trees from America's northern forests.[25]

The legend portrays Paul as a giant-sized man with immense muscle, energy and sense of humor. His lumberjack skills were extraordinary, as were his ingenious problem-solving schemes. Likewise, Babe's size and power enabled the ox to haul incredibly huge loads of logs. According to legend, Babe's hide was colored during the historically cold "winter of the blue snow," and Minnesota's 10,000 lakes fill the deep depressions made by his giant hooves.[26]

Paul Bunyan folklore began in the late 1800s with stories told in logging camp bunkhouses. Old timers would spin yarns to tease newcomers, or jokesters would try to top each other by telling successively taller tales. Eventually, the fables became popular with a broader audience when they were printed in pamphlets, magazines and books. Paul Bunyan's name is attached to numerous statues, festivals, businesses and tourist attractions throughout Minnesota. Among other public institutions, a state park, scenic highway and snowmobile trail are all named after Paul Bunyan.[27]

Chapter 8
Fourth of July
1876

The Meier family was gathered on the lawn of Rice Park amid a festive sun-splashed crowd of people. The throng awaited St. Paul's Independence Day parade on this especially significant one-hundredth birthday of the United States. The festivities had begun north of downtown, where a series of horse races featured a collection of Minnesota's fastest thoroughbreds and trotters. Some members of this Rice Park crowd were a little richer or poorer from their wagers on those contests.

Boom! A thunderous blast of one hundred guns, one for each American year, echoed from City Hall a few blocks away. That was the signal to begin the parade, and a wave of cheers cascaded along the procession's route. Out front marched an honor guard of Civil War veterans, displaying flags of the United States and Minnesota. Behind them, in order, came soldiers from the state's regiments who had survived battles against the Confederacy a decade earlier. There, in the depleted ranks of Minnesota's first regiment, was Heinrich Meier. He proudly wore his old black hat and Union army jacket buttoned snugly around his stomach, grown slightly rounder and softer. Of course, his empty right sleeve swung limp from below the elbow.

Heinrich's regiment disbanded upon reaching Rice Park, where he joined his wife and daughters to watch the remainder of the parade. Following the Civil War veterans came a band that marched up to the park playing the tune "America," for which everyone stood and sang,

> *My country, 'tis of thee,*
> *Sweet land of liberty,*
> *Of thee I sing.*
> *Land where my fathers died,*
> *Land of the pilgrims' pride,*
> *From every mountain side,*
> *Let freedom ring.*

A series of politicians followed, seated in horse-drawn carriages decorated with red, white and blue streamers. St. Paul's mayor, James Maxfield, was next to the chief of police, Jim King, and escorted by a phalanx of marching officers. The chief of St. Paul's volunteer fire department came, ringing the bell of a steam-powered pump engine and flanked by the board of fire wardens on foot. Next came Samuel J. R. McMillan, newly appointed US senator from his previous position as chief justice of the state supreme court. He was seated next to the outgoing senator, legendary Minnesota statesman Alexander Ramsey, who at sixty-one, was still a power in state and national politics. Finally, the previous and present state governors, Cushman Davis and John Pillsbury, arrived. Since both men were scheduled to deliver speeches in Rice Park, their carriage stopped beside an elevated stage adorned with patriotic pennants. The governors' oratory was preceded by a reading of the Declaration of Independence and followed by the fire chief's announcement that a fireworks show would begin at eight o'clock that night.

The Meier family headed toward Dayton's Bluff after the speeches. But instead of going home, they stopped to enjoy the afternoon in the beer garden attached to Hamm's brewery beside Phalen Creek. Through the door, they walked into the moist tavern air that smelled heavily of cigar smoke and tangy lager beer. Sounds of clinking glasses, creaking bar stools and jolly laughter echoed around the spacious open room. These were familiar sights, sounds and smells for Emelia, who worked as an accountant and secretary for Mrs. Hamm.

Theodore and Louise Hamm, both German immigrants, were married in America in 1855. He became a successful butcher in St. Paul, and Louise was an able co-manager when the couple opened a hotel and then a saloon in the city. Ten years later, they loaned money to a small brewery owner who died unexpectedly, transferring ownership to the Hamms. During the next decade, they developed the struggling brewery into a thriving success. Now, the expanded facility was adjacent to a boardinghouse for their growing number of employees, and the beer garden had gained a reputation for excellent food served in a family atmosphere.

Emelia was hired by Louise Hamm, who managed both the boardinghouse and the beer garden. At sixteen years old, the girl aimed to earn money toward a college education. Emelia kept financial records for both operations under Mrs. Hamm's supervision and occupied the boardinghouse office in the evenings. That way, she could go to school during the day and work at night.

Today, however, was a holiday. The Meiers were just one of many families enjoying the festive atmosphere inside Hamm's beer garden. Most of the customers were of German ancestry, for whom music and lager beer were vital parts of their culture. Theo Hamm saw them enter. With a quick wave, he ushered the family to an open table and sat down beside Heinrich.

"Welcome," Hamm already had a mug of beer in his hand, and almost instantly, a mug of the amber beverage was placed in front of his guest. "*Ein prosit*," the host proposed a German toast, motioning for Meier to join him.

The cold glass glistened with condensation in Heinrich's hand, and the foam-topped guzzle left a froth on his upper lip. "That is refreshing." He plopped the mug back down, and tiny bubbles continued to fizz within the liquid. "You serve the best lager in town."

"I'll take credit for being an able businessman," said Hamm, "but the fine-tasting beer is simply a result of good luck." He explained, "This brewery is built over artesian wells that provide crystal clear water, an essential ingredient. Also, these sandstone bluffs provide the perfect underground caverns where we can age our beer in consistently cool temperatures. However, our best luck is the masterful skill of our brewmaster, Jacob Schmidt." Hamm had known Schmidt in their native Germany, though the brewmaster was nearly twenty years younger. Schmidt was not just an employee but a family friend who lived in the Hamm's household.

"I assumed your water came out of Phalen Creek," Heinrich admitted.

"Well, we do use creek water for cleaning the brewery," Hamm said, "and we have hoses tapped into the stream in case of fire."

"Are your other businesses doing well?"

"Yes," Hamm broke into a broad grin. "The livestock and grain are my areas of expertise." The professional butcher kept herds of cattle and hogs nearby, which he slaughtered to provide meat for local grocery stores and his own beer garden. Additionally, he was part owner of a profitable flour mill adjacent to the Phalen Creek property. "Food for my hogs and cattle are byproducts of both businesses. They eat fresh grain from the flour mill and spent grain that's left over from the brewery."

Hamm clapped Heinrich on the back and stood to greet other customers just as his wife approached the Meiers' table. Louise sat down between Hildegard and Emelia. "Your daughter is a godsend," she said, placing a hand on the girl's shoulder. "She's the best accountant we've ever had."

"Thank you," Hilde responded while Emmy blushed. "But we must express our gratitude for the opportunity you have extended to her. Being able to work in the evenings fits perfectly with her schoolwork."

"Well, that's ideal for me," Louise said. "I need to be with my family through the night." Although the Hamms were nearly a decade older than Heinrich and Hilde, they had more and younger children. William, the only boy, was the oldest at seventeen. Their five girls ranged in age from fifteen down to two. "Louisa and

Minnie can babysit the little ones in the afternoon, but I need to be with them at suppertime and bedtime."

"I remember those years," said Hilde. "But our Kat," she nodded to her youngest, "is eleven now. She's pretty independent." Then, turning to her oldest, "And Jo is eighteen. She could practically manage the hardware store by herself. In fact, sometimes I think she would rather be left alone." Everyone laughed except for Johanna.

"William is our oldest," Louise said. "He's working in the brewery now. Someday, we expect he will take over the business when it's time for Theo to retire."

A band of musicians burst into polka music from their impromptu stage in one corner. A smiling woman bounced in the front and center with an accordion strapped from her shoulders, which she compressed and expanded to produce a wheezing harmony. She was flanked by two men with brass horns, a trumpet to the left and a tuba on her right. Together, they produced a loud enough symphony to make conversation nearly impossible. So, the Meiers simply sat back and enjoyed the music.

* * *

Jesse James stood up from the poker table and watched the two chuckling winners walk toward the exit door with his money. His pockets were empty, but his eyes were full of anger. "Damn Yankee Krauts," he said through clenched teeth.

Jack Chinn, co-owner of St. Paul's Chinn and Morgan Gambling House, immediately appeared close behind Jesse's shoulder. "Settle down, son," Chinn said in a calm but forceful voice. He didn't want violence to erupt in his establishment, and he knew that Jesse James was an impulsively violent young man. During the Civil War fifteen years earlier, Confederate Colonel Jack Chinn had commanded teenage Jesse during Missouri's vicious guerrilla war. They were Bushwackers, southern secessionists who rode in the renegade cavalry known as Quantrill's Raiders.

The James family were slave owners who lived in Missouri's Clay County, known as "Little Dixie" because most residents had southern ancestors. When the Civil War ended, Jesse and his older brother Frank kept fighting. They formed an outlaw gang with neighbors Cole, Jim and Bob Younger that started robbing banks owned by wealthy northerners. After several years, they extended their thievery to trains, targeting those owned by northern railroad tycoons. The James-Younger gang eluded capture by executing their sporadic robberies over a large geographic territory into Missouri's surrounding states. On fast, reliable horses, they returned to their friendly surroundings near home, where sympathetic neighbors refused to reveal their whereabouts.

After a decade of dodging authorities, the gang began to feel the heat of more intense pursuit from law enforcement in the mid-1870s. Higher-priced rewards were offered for their capture, and the nationally known Pinkerton Detective Agency was hired to bring them in, dead or alive. The outlaws laid low for a few months while oldest brothers Frank James and Cole Younger suggested they might move far away, assume new identities and become law-abiding citizens. Frank and Cole were thirty-three and thirty-one years old, respectively.

However, their twenty-something brothers Jesse and Bob would have none of that. They both resented the overbearing authority their older siblings tried to assert. Jesse James and Bob Younger were full of cocky confidence and arrogance in their celebrity bandit reputations. They recklessly accepted an invitation from Minnesota native Bill Stiles to rob a bank in his home state.

Eventually, eight members of the gang agreed to participate. They traveled to Minnesota in pairs and now occupied separate hotels in the Twin Cities. Cole and Jim Younger were at the Nicollet House in Minneapolis, joined by longtime cohorts Clell Miller and Charlie Pitts. Frank and Jesse were lodging at the Merchants Hotel in St. Paul with Bob Younger and Bill Stiles. They were all registered under alias names and claimed phony business occupations. They had plenty of money, so staying in the most expensive hotel accommodations was no problem.

Tonight, the St. Paul group had dined in fashionable McLeod's Restaurant, where they bought a round of drinks for the entire house.

Water Wheels

After supper, Frank suggested they call it a night, but the youngsters were eager to try their luck at the casino. After all, Jack Chinn was an old Confederate friend. They went in opposite directions from the restaurant, up and down Third Street, St. Paul's main thoroughfare. Frank retired to the Merchants Hotel. Jesse, Bob and Bill went to the Chinn and Morgan Gambling House.

The young outlaws ran into misfortune. Jesse lost his luck and his cash. Now he was losing his temper. "Who are those guys?" He glared after the departing poker players who were shoving his loot into their pockets as they headed for the exit.

"Just a couple of German immigrants," answered Jack Chinn. "I think they work at the Hamm's Brewery."

"Where's that?"

"Less than a mile east of here."

"Come on," Jesse beckoned Bob and Bill. "They cheated me."

Younger and Stiles exchanged dubious glances with Chinn. None of them believed that Jesse had been cheated, but he was headed for the door, and his partners were scrambling to follow. Out on the boardwalk, Jesse ordered Bob, "Go get our horses. Bill and I will follow 'em on foot until you catch up."

Judd's Livery Stable was only a block away, but the pedestrians were out of downtown before Bob could get the horses saddled and down the street. They were beyond the streetlamps, into darkness before all three were mounted. The dim silhouettes of two walking figures were barely visible a few blocks ahead. Jesse spurred his horse into a canter, and the others sped up in his wake.

Before Jesse could catch up to the pair of immigrants, they turned left and disappeared off the street. He reined up near the spot where they had veered out of sight. The distinctive smell of the nearby brewery was unmistakable. Slightly uphill from the street, a two-story apartment building loomed in front of them. Other than a faint glow through the center entrance, the boardinghouse was dark. Another light flickered on while the outlaws dismounted and secured their horses to a bush in the yard. The lamplight briefly glimmered from an upper-story window directly above the main entrance.

Bob Younger pointed at the window and whispered, "That must be them."

"Shut up," Jesse snapped. Curtains were quickly drawn to obscure the light while he ascended steps leading up to a front porch. Bob followed Jesse through the front door and Bill Stiles brought up the rear.

The center entry was an open space about eight feet square with hallways that led to first-floor rooms on both sides. Back and to the right, a steep wooden staircase angled up to the second floor. The left rear wall held rows of open mailboxes, a few containing ingoing or outgoing letters. A short counter extended across the back, between the stairway and the mailboxes. Behind this counter was an open door into a small office where a glowing lamp illuminated the face of a dark-haired girl. She stood up from her desk when Jesse's loud boot steps halted in front of the counter.

Stiles saw her from behind Bob Younger's shoulder, and he quickly drew his neck scarf up across the bridge of his nose to mask his face. He recognized Heinrich Meier's middle daughter. He didn't think she could identify him, but the outlaw wasn't taking any chances.

"Two men just came in here," Jesse addressed the girl. "What room are they in?"

Emelia stepped into the office doorway. Her stocky figure was outlined by the office lamp, which cast only dim light onto the men in the entry. All three wore western-style hats, typical of Civil War cavalry riders. She was frightened by the intrusion of these strangers after dark, but she tried to conceal that fear.

Suddenly, a big pistol appeared in Jesse's hand, extended across the counter. The gun was a forty-five caliber Colt revolver, known by its nickname, "the peacemaker." But making peace was obviously not James's immediate intent. His voice burst with impatience. "Where are they?"

Emelia glanced nervously from the threatening gun barrel up at the ceiling. "I thought so," A wicked smile wrinkled Jesse's lips as he, too, looked toward the room above and vaulted up the staircase two steps at a time, pointing the pistol ahead of himself. Younger bolted after James, who commanded sideways, "Bill, you watch the girl."

Now Emelia saw the third man more clearly as he stepped forward from the shadows. He hid his face behind a scarf. He also had a pistol, but rather than being pointed at her, it was seated in a low-slung belt holster. The man's thumbs were loosely hooked on either side of the belt buckle, and he stood with an easy nonchalance.

Emelia was not relaxed. Her eyes darted from the gun to the intruder's masked face, then sideways down the darkened first-floor hallways. Every muscle in her body was tense.

"Calm down, Miss Meier," the man said.

She was startled, first by the stranger's use of her name, then by the sound of a second-story door bursting open.

Her guardian started around the counter and pointed through the office doorway. "In there," he ordered.

Noises of a scuffle and falling bodies came from upstairs. Emelia retreated behind the desk where her accounting ledgers for the Hamm's beer garden and boardinghouse lay open. She gripped the back of the desk chair with one hand to steady herself.

The man stepped halfway through the doorway and looked deliberately around the room's perimeter. Finally, his gaze lifted from the desktop to Emelia's face. "Is there any money in here?"

Another loud thump echoed through the ceiling, and the girl flinched. She held eye contact with the intruder, knowing the proceeds from tonight's beer garden business were in a cashbox under the desk. "No," she lied.

Suddenly, loud boot steps could be heard cascading down the staircase. The masked man swiveled to see his cohorts exit through the entryway before he turned back to threaten Emelia, "Don't you dare leave this room." Then he pulled the office door shut and was gone.

Emelia dropped into the desk chair and finally allowed herself to tremble. Fearfully, she wondered, "How did he know my name?"

* * *

Back at the Merchants Hotel, the outlaws gathered around a whiskey bottle in the room occupied by Stiles and Younger. Frank James heard them from the adjoining room and came over to ask about their fortunes at the casino. He saw Jesse's money loosely piled on the small round table where the three gamblers were seated. Frank smiled. "Looks like you were winners."

Bill and Bob looked nervously at Jesse, who was in the process of pouring whiskey into his shot glass. He initially avoided eye contact with his older brother but slowly set the bottle down and looked up. He suspected that Frank would learn the truth from Jack Chinn anyway. "Not exactly," he said.

Frank's smile turned into a frown. "What did you do?"

Over the next ten minutes, Jesse tried to explain how the money was lost and regained. He admitted that he and Bob had pistol-whipped the brewery workers unconscious but insisted that nobody was murdered.

After Jesse shared his version of the story, Stiles confessed his recognition of the girl. "I know her father from back before the war," he began. "As a teenager, I was a diver on the St. Paul waterfront. Occasionally, while steamboats were being loaded or unloaded, valuable cargo got spilled into the Mississippi River. I got paid a lot of money to swim to the bottom and attach ropes to the sunken items so they could be winched back up to the surface."

"Impressive," said Younger. "I can't swim a lick."

"Even more impressive," Stiles grinned, "to do it at night when you can salvage loot for yourself and sell it on the black market."

Frank James raised his eyebrows. "That's illegal."

"That's what Heinrich Meier said," Stiles continued. "That girl's father was a foreman on the waterfront back then. The goody two-shoes caught me poaching cargo out of the river and reported me to the sheriff. I had to skedaddle out of town to avoid jail, and then nobody would hire me to dive legally or illegally."

"Where did you go?" Jesse asked.

Water Wheels

"Tried my luck in the California gold fields, but that didn't pan out," Stiles answered. "Back here in Minnesota, I found some guys who would buy stolen horses."

"I'm more interested in this Heinrich Meier and his daughter," said Frank. "Could they identify you?"

"The girl wasn't even born when I was diving at the waterfront," Stiles told him. "Plus, I pulled a scarf up over my face tonight. She has no idea who I am."

"What about her old man?"

"Meier is a respectable businessman with family responsibilities. I never go to the kinds of places where he is welcome," Stiles sneered with disdain. "But whenever I'm in St. Paul, I'm on the lookout for a way to get revenge against him. I started his lumber yard on fire a few years ago." He snickered. "Another time, I gave his daughters a wild ride by throwing a bottle that stampeded their horse-drawn carriage."

Frank James gave Stiles a long stare before turning to his own brother. "You three better lay low until Cole and I decide what to do." Jesse and Bob both bristled at the notion that their older siblings were in command of their movements, but in this instance, they held their tongues.

The following afternoon, Cole and Bob Younger arrived in St. Paul for a strategy session. The entire gang agreed it was time to evacuate the Twin Cities and select a rural bank to rob. They had upgraded their weaponry by shopping in local gun stores, including Burkhardt's on Third Street in St. Paul. They had appraised the horses at every livery stable in the area, and now each gang member had a pair of sturdy, speedy mounts.

They decided that half of the outlaws would scout southwest through towns in the Minnesota River valley while the other half toured southeast in the Mississippi River valley. Then, during the first week of September, both groups would reconnoiter and agree upon a target.

Cole Younger led the Minnesota River group, which included his brother Bob, Bill Stiles and Charlie Pitts. They investigated banks in Chaska, St. Peter, Mankato and farther west to Madelia. Cole was a big man and a natural leader at six feet and four inches tall. During the war, he had commanded a three-hundred-man cavalry of Quantrill's Raiders. Charlie Pitts was a heavily muscled man with a thick black beard and a profane vocabulary. He had an ornery personality but respected Cole and would follow him anywhere.

Frank and Jesse James went southeast with Jim Younger and Clell Miller. Frank was thinner and lighter-haired than Jesse. A well-educated man, he often carried copies of Shakespeare and a Bible with his belongings. Where Jesse was reckless and cocky, Frank was more organized and always focused on a plan of escape if things went awry. Between Cole and Bob in age, Jim Younger had moved to California to pursue a peaceful, law-abiding life, but he returned to the gang when they insisted on executing this raid. Clell Miller was young but had idolized Jesse since his teenage years and had ridden on many robberies. He was a daring, skillful horseman and considered by some to be the gang's most accurate pistol shot.

Frank and Jesse's group spent several days scrutinizing a pair of banks in Red Wing but then began to focus on the First National Bank of Northfield. A combination of three factors attracted them to this location, which they believed was fat, soft and evil.

Fat, meaning wealthy. Northfield was a thriving farm community, and the outlaws expected the bank to be full of money during the autumn harvest. Several successful businesses operated in the community, including an iron foundry and a prosperous flour mill. A railroad ran through town and connected with the well-traveled Milwaukee Road, which supported hotels and restaurants in Northfield. The outlaws heard rumors that the bank might hold fifty- to seventy-five thousand dollars in cash.

Soft, because observation of the town convinced gang members that this robbery would be a pushover. Other than Stiles, they were almost four hundred miles from their Missouri homes, so their faces were unknown and unrecognized. Northfield's population was a mere two thousand people, primarily farm and merchant families. The town was located on the border between Rice and Dakota counties, so the nearest sheriff's offices were in the county seats of Faribault or Hastings.

Evil, because two wealthy stockholders in the bank were known to be former Union Civil War generals. Adelbert Ames, owner of the Ames Flour Mill, was a Medal of Honor recipient for heroism at the Battle of Gettysburg. After the war, Ames ruled military occupation in the South as a reconstruction governor before moving to Northfield. His father-in-law was the notorious Benjamin "Beast" Butler, who gained that nickname during the Union army's brutal and corrupt seizure of New Orleans. For the James-Younger Gang, stealing money from these two enemies would be sweet revenge.

Northfield's First National Bank was the perfect target.

* * *

Theodore Hamm (1825–1903)

143

Louise Hamm (1833–1896)

The Hamm's brewery became Minnesota's biggest and America's fifth-largest beer distributor through more than a century of family ownership.[28]

Theo Hamm and Louise Bucholz met in their native Germany before immigrating to America, where they were married in 1855. Theo was a butcher by trade, but together, they owned and operated a St. Paul hotel and tavern.[29]

In 1865, the couple assumed control of a brewery when the previous owner died while indebted to them. The small business was producing five hundred barrels of lager beer per year when the Hamms acquired it. Within a decade, they were brewing five thousand barrels a year, then forty thousand by the end of another decade. Through most of this period, their brewmaster was Jacob Schmidt, who eventually owned his own successful brewery in St. Paul. Schmidt's skillful management of the brewery enabled Theo

Hamm to pursue his more favored side businesses, milling flour and raising hogs and cattle.[30]

All three enterprises flourished along the bank of Phalen Creek. Artesian wells in the area provided excellent water for the brewing process, and the bedrock foundation of sandstone was easily excavated to provide underground caverns where the lager beer was properly aged.[31]

Louise Hamm managed a beer garden attached to the brewery, which gained a reputation for delicious food served in a family atmosphere. She was also in charge of an adjacent boardinghouse that served as a dormitory for unmarried brewery employees. The couple raised six children, all of them born between 1859 and 1874.[32]

William Hamm, the eldest and only son, was assuming the company presidency by 1894 when a massive and ornately decorated new brewery was constructed on the four-acre property. Later in life, the Hamm children built a twenty-room, Queen Anne-style home for their parents. The mansion stood atop a hill overlooking the brewery until it was demolished following a fire in 1954.[33]

Chapter 9
Bank Raid
1876

The James-Younger gang awakened on Thursday morning, September 7, in two separate groups. Half of the outlaws had slept in the Millersburg Inn, about ten miles southwest of Northfield. The other half, posing as horse traders, spent the night as guests of nearby farmer Robert Donaldson. They left eight of their high-priced mounts in Donaldson's corral that morning, promising to return in the afternoon and pay the stable fee and their bill for room and board.

Shortly thereafter, the entire gang assembled in a secluded grove of trees. They were all heavily armed, but the guns were well hidden beneath the duster coats they wore. As the name implies, travelers commonly dressed in these long jackets to prevent road dust from collecting on their clothes. The gang hoped that Northfield residents would not suspect that an arsenal of weapons and ammunition was concealed underneath these dusters.

Cole Younger summarized the plan. "We'll leave here in twos and threes to eliminate the suspicion that might be caused by the arrival of a large group. There are a couple of different restaurants in town, and we'll go about our business peacefully, allowing the townspeople to get comfortable with the presence of a few strangers on the street. At two o'clock, Frank, Bob and Charlie will come from the north and enter the bank. Clell and I will ride in from the south to stand guard outside."

Cole turned to face Jesse James. "You, Jim and Bill will wait beside the Cannon River bridge. That's around the corner, out of sight. If you hear shooting, come charging in with your guns blazing."

Frank James interrupted, "Hopefully, we'll get out of the bank without raising a ruckus. If so, we'll just ride south with the money and meet up with you on the other side of the river."

"Whatever happens," Cole wrapped up, "everybody gallop hard to Donaldson's farm. We'll split up the money there, switch to our fresh mounts, and scatter into several different routes back to Missouri. No posse will find us or catch us."

* * *

A few miles from Millersburg, the wheat harvest was underway for Wolf Creek farm families. Halvor Dahl hoisted himself up onto the wagon seat, and a bead of sweat dripped off the tip of his rounded nose. He paused to remove his straw hat with one hand while wiping the opposite sleeve across his glistening face and forehead. The boy's thatch-colored hair was almost a perfect match with the golden-brown bundles of wheat stalks piled upon the wagon. He replaced the flat-brimmed hat and reached down to his coworker, thirteen-year-old sister Mathilde. She grasped his wrist and almost flew up onto the wagon seat, aided by the lift of her brother's short but muscular arm.

Wheat harvest was a communal family affair in the Wolf Creek valley. Every man, woman and child had a job to perform, and families worked together until everyone's crop was out of the fields. The wheat seeds had been sown in early spring and were among the first plants to ripen in late summer. A period of sunny weather was beneficial at harvest time, and this early September dry spell was helpful.

A year ago, the Dahls, Lunds and two other neighbors had pooled their financial savings to purchase a pair of farm machines: a reaper and a thresher. Before mechanization, wheat stalks were manually sliced down by a person wielding a scythe. However, an inventive Virginia farmer named Cyrus McCormick designed a horse-drawn reaper with a long, low blade and a rolling paddle wheel. Where Goran Dahl had once cut two acres of wheat in an entire day, he now mowed twelve acres behind a draft horse and the mechanical reaper.

Likewise, threshing and winnowing were two steps in the wheat harvest process traditionally done by hand. The nutritious grain heads were threshed off plant stems with a tool called a flail. Then farmers winnowed their wheat from the chaff by hand tossing the seeds through a breeze onto a tarp. However, a single horse-powered threshing machine could perform all these tasks simultaneously.

Last week, the reaper had been used to fell the wheat crop on the Dahl family acres. It was a noisy contraption, but under Goran's steady guidance, Harald, their seventeen-year-old Belgian stallion, had calmly pulled it back and forth across the fields. Other Dahl family members followed in the reaper's wake, Mother Ingrid wielding one rake, Mathilde another. Erik stooped to gather Ingrid's rakings with his arms, arranging the four-foot-tall bundles into vertical cone-shaped stacks. Six-year-old Thorvald quickly tied a strand around each stack to hold it in place where sunlight and air circulation could dry out the wheat stalks. Halvor and Astrid bundled and tied Mathilde's rakings into similar stacks.

This week, the stacks were dry. Goran had moved over to Lund's farm with the reaper, but his family would operate the thresher today. The machine was located outside of the barn entrance, with Ingrid in the center of the process. To one side was the old mare Ragnhild, walking in a circle to power the device. Thorvald was perched on her back, offering encouragement whenever he believed she might be slowing down. Astrid, now eight, handed wheat bundles to her mother one at a time. Ingrid slid those bundles into the jaws of the thresher, which clipped off the stems before dropping the grain heads through a series of shuffling screens. The wheat seeds were threshed and winnowed by the time they dropped from the bottom of the machine.

Meanwhile, Erik worked inside the barn, at the end of a conveyor belt where the headless wheat stems were dumped. This would be their year's supply of straw, and the young man toiled with a pitchfork to pile it higher and higher inside the barn. He was shaded from the sun, but also shielded from any breeze, which made the barn's interior hot like an oven. Erik sweltered without a shirt, and his entire torso was covered by a moist grime of perspiration and grain dust.

Back and forth, Halvor and Mathilde hauled dry wheat stacks with the big flatbed wagon, pulled by the young team of Haakon and Sophia. They deposited each load as near the threshing machine as possible before circling back out to the field. On one such trip, Mathilde pointed across a ridge to where wooden beams formed the framework of a new home under construction. "That's where Erik and Kjerstin will live."

Halvor followed her gaze. Indeed, their brother was betrothed to marry Kjerstin Lund the following spring. He hoped to have the house enclosed with a roof and clapboard siding before winter. On a hillside near the house, several rows of newly planted trees and bushes were visible, which Kjerstin hoped would become her fruit orchard. She had corresponded with Oliver Kelley and Caroline Hall, seeking advice about tree species that might flourish in this northern climate. She settled on three different fruits and bought six bare-root saplings of each variety, which were shipped from a Grange tree nursery. The raspberry bushes and plum trees were native to Minnesota, but the two strains of apple trees had been developed in Russia and Canada.

Though incomplete, the house and orchard seemed to frame a picture of his brother's clear future. It reminded Halvor of his own uncertain destiny. He was enrolled to begin at the university in a few short weeks, but could he succeed there? And if he could, where would that education take him?

"Pretty soon, I'll be the oldest." Mathilde's statement snapped Halvor back from his distant stare at Erik's future home. He blinked at his sister, confused about her meaning. "I'll be the oldest," she

150

repeated. "When Erik is married and you're at college, I will be the oldest child in the family."

Halvor smiled and reached his arm around the girl to give her a hug. "You will be an excellent big sister." Then, after a momentary delay, he added, "But you will always be my little sister."

* * *

Five members of the James-Younger gang settled into D. E. Jeft's Railroad Restaurant around noon. Adjacent to the train depot, this was a common place for out-of-towners. Still, brothers Bob and Jim Younger sat apart from Jesse James, Charlie Pitts and Bill Stiles.

Cole Younger and Frank James were also eating lunch, but they were on Northfield's main avenue at John Tosney's Eating Establishment with Clell Miller. After lunch, they walked across the street into the Exchange Saloon, where they sipped a few leisurely drinks before buying a quart of whiskey to go. The older brothers wanted a closer look at the level of activity in town and to listen for any talk about unusual circumstances. They neither saw nor heard anything out of the ordinary before riding west out of town for one final strategy session with the entire gang.

At two o'clock, Cole and Clell reentered town by crossing the Fifth Street bridge over the Cannon River. They turned down Division Street and saw three of their accomplices approaching on horseback from the opposite direction. The two groups converged in front of the First National Bank in the center of town. Frank, Bob and Charlie entered the bank while Cole and Clell dismounted at the hitching rail. Cole pretended to check the cinch of his horse's saddle. Clell stepped up on the boardwalk and surveyed up and down the quiet, dirt thoroughfare. One young man was sitting across the street in the shade of a drugstore awning. Three others were chatting on a Bridge Square corner only forty feet away.

One of these three men was J. S. Allen, who owned a hardware store just around the corner. Growing suspicious of this collection of strangers gathered about the bank, he walked forward and tried to look through the bank window. Miller grabbed Allen by the shirt

151

collar and dragged him back, ordering the man to "Go away." Allen scrambled down the boardwalk and around the corner, shouting, "Get your guns, boys. They're robbing the bank!"

The young man across the street was Henry Wheeler, son of the drugstore owner and a student at the University of Michigan medical school. He saw Allen flee from the bank and heard the call to arms. Wheeler ran next door through the Dampier Hotel lobby, where he knew a Civil War army carbine was stashed. He ran up to the third floor and scurried to open fire directly across from the bank. Clell Miller was shot dead through the chest.

Jesse heard the shooting and thundered his horse into the fray, flanked by Jim Younger and Bill Stiles. They sprayed bullets in every direction, trying to frighten civilians off the street. However, Anselm Manning fetched his Winchester repeating rifle and began firing from behind the cover of an exterior stairway. He killed Stiles.

Cole Younger shouted to his partners inside the bank. "For God's sake, come out. They are shooting us all to pieces!" But things were going badly in there. The three employees were not cooperating.

Frank James ordered Joseph Lee Heywood to open the safe, but the bookkeeper refused. "It's on a time clock," he lied. "The door can only be unlocked at opening and closing time." Whereupon Frank whacked Heywood in the head with a pistol and dragged him to the vault.

Bob and Charlie confronted the other two bank clerks, Alonzo Bunker and Frank Wilcox. "Empty the money out of the cashier's till," Younger demanded. But Wilcox simply pointed to the change drawer, which contained less than one hundred dollars, mostly coins. A drawer under the counter held three thousand dollars, but it was never opened.

Bunker surprised the distracted robbers by bolting down a narrow hallway out the back door. Pitts gave chase and fired two quick shots, one of which pierced through the bank teller's left shoulder, but he escaped into a rear alley.

Water Wheels

Finally, the frustrated intruders exited the bank empty-handed. Frank James was last out the door after shooting a bullet into the head of bookkeeper Heywood, who died instantly. They emerged into a hail of gunfire. A haphazard swarm of citizens blasted hunting rifles and shotguns at the raiders from storefront windows and doorways.

The outlaws were no longer firing warning shots. They took dead aim at Northfield's defenders, one of whom was recent immigrant Nicolaus Gustavson, who spoke only his native Swedish. Running onto Division Street out of curiosity, he took a bullet to the head, from which he died four days later.

After minutes that seemed like hours, the bandits were remounted, all except Charlie Pitts, whose horse had been downed by Anselm Manning's Winchester. Pitts ran alongside Cole Younger's horse and swung up behind the saddle as the gang galloped south out of town. Every outlaw had at least one bullet wound in an arm or leg. Behind them lay four dead or dying bodies: two slain civilians and a pair of their fallen comrades.

* * *

The Dahl family loaded their bags of wheat onto the big flatbed wagon, and Halvor drove it to the Archibald flour mill in Dundas. The Archibald family—brothers John and Edward, with Cousin George—had come from Canada to settle beside the Cannon River in 1857. The three men farmed eleven hundred acres and built their flour mill using locally quarried limestone. By 1870, they built a second, larger mill with modern improvements, making it a marvel in the Minnesota region. Their new mill enabled them to process harder spring wheat kernels planted in the spring instead of softer kernels of winter wheat, a variety planted in late fall to sprout after the snowmelt. Spring wheat was better suited to Minnesota's northern climate and, with the Archibald's grinding method, produced an even more nutritious flour. In fact, the brothers had just returned from Philadelphia's Centennial Exposition, where their Archibald Extra flour had won a top-quality prize.

Edward "ET" Archibald greeted Halvor's arrival at the mill. "Hello, neighbor. How goes the Dahl family harvest?"

"Good," Halvor said. "We have more bags of wheat than ever."

"Drive your wagon right into the grain elevator," said ET. "We'll weigh the bags, give the wheat a quality score, and provide you with a dollar total before you leave."

Wheat crops are always given a grade based on the size, moisture content and health of the kernels. Healthy wheat is undamaged by tools, insects or fungus and free of dirt and debris. "I'm confident in the value of our spring wheat," Halvor boasted.

"You should be," replied ET. "Your family's grain has always been top quality. Plus, the wheat that comes to us through threshing machines is usually cleaner."

As expected, the Dahl wheat harvest merited a high grade and earned a handsome profit for the family's efforts. The money was not paid in cash; rather, it was credited to their account at the mill for transfer to the First National Bank of Northfield. The Archibalds were major shareholders in the bank.

Halvor said goodbye to ET and told Haakon and Sophia to get up. He steered his wagon uphill out of Dundas and westward toward home. It was quiet in the late afternoon sunlight, so he could easily hear the galloping hoofbeats of several horses pounding up the dirt road from behind. He guided his team to walk closer along the road's right edge so the oncoming riders might have more space to pass. Then, as the boy looked over his shoulder to see who was approaching, he was suddenly surrounded.

The lead rider pulled close beside Haakon, grabbed the rein leading to his halter, and jerked the Belgian to a halt. Halvor was about to protest the rude treatment of his young stallion but got distracted by the unmistakable click of a pistol being cocked beside his head. He turned to his left for a frightfully close view down the barrel of Jesse James's forty-five caliber Colt revolver. "We need your horse," said James.

Halvor was speechless. He saw one of the men slide off the rump of a horse he was riding double and produce a large hunting knife, with which he intended to cut through Haakon's leather traces. "No!" the boy blurted, "I can unhitch him for you."

"Then do it fast," Jesse warned, bending his elbow to lift the gun back a few inches. "We're in a hurry."

Halvor hurried off the wagon seat and nervously stumbled when he landed on the ground. He quickly ducked under Haakon's neck, where he disconnected the neck yoke and unbuckled the reins from his bridle. The boy ran a reassuring hand down Haakon's neck and spoke soothingly under his breath, "E-e-e-easy-y, boy. Everything will be all right."

"That's right," proclaimed the man with the knife. "We're just gonna go for a little joy ride."

Halvor stood beside Haakon's shoulder to unfasten the load straps that would release the horse from the wagon. His fingers could do this task without watching, so Halvor stole a look around the circle of mounted men. They all wore long duster coats, but he could see blood-stained sleeves and pant legs. Some of the men grimaced and slumped in their saddles with discomfort. All the horses were beautiful, long-legged animals built to run. "My draft horse is no match for your thoroughbreds," Halvor said, "and he's not used to having someone on his back."

"We only need your horse for a few more miles," said the man holding the gun. "We've got other mounts nearby, so you can have him back when we're done with him." Then Haakon's passenger climbed awkwardly on top of the harness straps and gripped the neck collar before jabbing his heels into the horse's flanks. Lo and behold, the big Belgian bolted forward, and the other five riders launched after him.

Halvor simply stood and watched them gallop away until only a cloud of road dust could be seen in the distance. Then he picked up the loose harness straps and rearranged the traces so that Sophia might be able to pull the empty wagon home by herself. "I don't know where those men came from," the boy said aloud to the young mare, "but I intend to find out where they're going."

* * *

Over the next two weeks, the wounded outlaws zigzagged in a southwesterly direction, narrowly eluding dozens of posses. It was a disorderly manhunt. Rather than cooperation, most of the search parties competed for glory and reward money. One such group confronted the James-Younger gang but failed to recognize the bandits, who claimed to be hunting for the fugitives themselves.

The gang switched to their fresh mounts upon reaching the Millersburg area farm of Robert Donaldson. The stolen Belgian draft horse was abandoned there and later reunited with the Dahl family. Heavy rain enabled the gang to escape into LeSueur County through a deciduous forest known as the Big Woods. The downpour washed away most of their horses' tracks and kept some of the posses indoors.

A few days later, the outlaws were spotted near Waterville and exchanged gunfire before taking refuge on an island in Lake Elysian. After dark, they created a diversion by swimming their riderless horses to one shoreline while wading onto a different beach on foot. They soon stole new mounts and escaped on horseback again.

The James and Younger brothers agreed to split up one week after the attempted robbery when they reached Rush Lake, five miles beyond Mankato. Frank and Jesse's wounds were less severe than the Youngers'. As a healthier twosome, they figured to travel faster and less conspicuously. So too, they reasoned, with their more notorious names, Frank and Jesse might draw most of their pursuers, giving the other four a better chance to escape.

They were wrong. A large posse tracked Cole, Jim, Bob and Charlie Pitts into the Hanska Slough near Madelia, where they were surrounded. A blazing gun battle ensued. Pitts was killed, and the Youngers were rendered helpless by additional bullet wounds. They were taken captive and jailed for two months while their injuries healed. The brothers were sentenced to life in Stillwater state prison after pleading guilty. Meanwhile, Frank and Jesse got away. They sped west to the Dakota border, circled near Sioux Falls and Sioux

Water Wheels

City, then disappeared into northwestern Iowa.

Back in Northfield, the dead bodies of Clell Miller and Bill Stiles were carried on a different mysterious journey. After burial in the city cemetery, both bodies were dug up. Eventually, Dr. Henry Wheeler admitted to the grave robbery. He had killed Miller and felt a certain entitlement to the victims' remains. With two fellow medical school students, he exhumed the corpses and stashed them into a pair of barrels, which they labeled "paint." When the boys returned by train to the University of Michigan, the paint barrels were transported as cargo. Soon after, the bodies of Miller and Stiles were used as classroom cadavers to be studied by Wheeler and other future doctors.

* * *

James-Younger Gang and the Northfield Bank Raid (September 7, 1876)

Michael Barnes

"The Defeat of Jesse James Days" is an annual celebration held in Northfield, Minnesota, where the notorious James-Younger Gang tried and failed to rob the First National Bank.[34]

Before the Civil War, both the James and Younger families had settled in Missouri after migrating from southern states. They owned slaves and sympathized with the seceded Confederate States. When guerrilla warfare broke out in Missouri and Kansas, the boys took up arms with Quantrill's Raiders on behalf of the Southern cause.[35]

When the war ended, the boys continued fighting, focusing their criminal violence against banks and trains owned by wealthy northerners. They became romantic figures with loyal Southerners during this period. Some people drew Robin Hood comparisons, but there is no evidence these outlaws ever shared their loot with others.[36]

As reward money for their capture grew, pursuit by law enforcement became more intense. During this period, the gang began staging robberies over a larger, less predictable geographic area. When they chose to venture north into Minnesota, the James-Younger gang members ranged in age from twenty-one to thirty-three.[37]

They killed two civilians during the Northfield robbery: Joseph Lee Heywood, a bank clerk who refused to open the safe; and Nicolaus Gustavson, a Swedish immigrant on the city street. However, they failed to steal any of the fifteen thousand dollars in the bank. The gang did steal a horse after one of their mounts was killed during the gunfight in town. They encountered farmer Philip Empey on their escape route and took his draft horse from the harness.[38]

Three bandits died during the raid and attempted getaway: Clell Miller, Bill Stiles and Charlie Pitts. None of the James or Younger brothers were killed. Cole, Jim and Bob Younger were captured in Minnesota and sentenced to life in the Stillwater State Prison. Bob died behind bars, but his brothers were paroled after twenty-five years of good behavior. Frank and Jesse James escaped back home to Missouri, where Frank became a law-abiding citizen. However, Jesse continued a life of crime until he was shot in the back by a fellow gangster who claimed the lucrative reward for his death.[39]

Chapter 10
North Oaks
1876

Halvor Dahl stood at the railing of the Lower Bridge across the Mississippi River, one-quarter mile downstream from St. Anthony Falls. The span was often called the Tenth Avenue Bridge because it extended from Tenth Avenue South in Minneapolis, even though it continued over the river to connect with Sixth Avenue Southeast in St. Anthony. Halvor paused halfway across the wooden plank span to look down at the supporting iron trusses anchored on top of four stone pyramids that stood in the swirling waters of the mighty Mississippi.

The young man lifted his gaze to St. Anthony Falls and the whooshing roar of falling water. A mist exploded from the powerful cascade, and the northwest breeze carried a few droplets of moisture to land on his face. The slate gray November sky stretched from the river's eastern bank, where sawmills dotted the shoreline, to the western bank and its corridor of flour mills. Above the falls was the V-shaped dam that channeled a deeper flow of water to the mills on both sides. Just upriver from there, a brand-new towering suspension bridge was replacing the original span across the Mississippi, which had stood since 1855.

The St. Anthony lumber mills had once been built upon pillars, which allowed them to hover above the falls and more than halfway across the river. However, intrusive excavation of bedrock caused the waterfall to collapse in 1869. Then, after the US Army Corps of Engineers stabilized and fortified the cataract, they forbade the extension of any mills above the river. The lumbermen were hit with another setback in 1870 when fire destroyed an entire row of adjacent sawmills. Nonetheless, the demand for wood was so great that most of them were quickly rebuilt and back in business.

Flour milling on the Minneapolis side was dominated by two families, the Washburns and the Pillsburys. Cadwallader Colden "C.C." Washburn was the builder and owner of the west-side canal, along which all the tall mills were constructed. C.C. had bigger business and political affairs in Wisconsin, so his younger brother William Drew "W.D." Washburn managed their three flour mills in Minneapolis. Coincidentally, C.C. had been elected governor of Wisconsin in 1872, and John Pillsbury became Minnesota's governor in 1876. John was co-owner of five flour mills managed by his nephew Charles Pillsbury.

Halvor, in fact, was on his way to work in Pillsbury's Anchor Mill today. He had attended his classes at the University of Minnesota that morning before returning to the St. Anthony boardinghouse, where he and several other college students rented rooms. He ate a quick lunch, changed into work clothes, and was now walking to his afternoon shift as a part-time Pillsbury employee. They had hired him quickly when Halvor described his thorough knowledge of the Archibald flour milling process.

He was thoroughly enjoying his studies at the university, half of which were in the prep school and half in the college. That was common, especially for new students like Halvor, who were young and from less rigorous rural schools. In fact, more than two hundred of the university's three hundred pupils enrolled in prep school classes.

His favorite upper-level course was in the Agriculture Department, taught by Theophilus Haecker. Halvor enjoyed the challenge of learning alongside the older college students, and he was particularly fascinated by research projects being conducted

Water Wheels

at the university's experimental farm. Thomas Shaw managed the college farm, where he supervised experiments to raise healthier, more productive plants and animals in Minnesota's cold weather climate.

This coming Sunday, Professors Haecker and Shaw were taking their agriculture students on a field trip to North Oaks, a modern farm owned by James J. Hill twelve miles north of St. Paul. Halvor was eagerly looking forward to this trip, partly because Hill's progressive agricultural methods promised to be interesting. Additionally, the boy was anxious to get out of the city. Weeks had passed since he had smelled the fresh air of wide-open spaces.

* * *

Halvor stood with his two professors and a dozen agricultural classmates near a cluster of farm buildings on top of a plateau. They were surrounded by three thousand acres of pastoral beauty that Jim Hill named North Oaks. The sun had risen above the eastern horizon, where thousands of glimmering sparkles reflected off the ripples of Pleasant Lake. Presently, a person emerged from a tree line to their north. Most of the branches were barren by this date in late autumn, but as usual, the burgundy-colored oak leaves were stubbornly clinging to their boughs.

The person was a hunter, evidenced by the shotgun slung over his shoulder and a pointing dog bounding through the tall grass beside him. A canvas jacket covered the hunter's muscular upper body, which seemed incongruously tall above his short legs. Nonetheless, he marched toward the college visitors with a powerful purpose.

"That's him," said Professor Shaw, who stepped forward to offer a handshake. "Hello, Jim."

"Welcome, Professor." Hill doffed his hunting cap, briefly revealing a balding head, and he swiveled to face the students. "Welcome to you all." He leaned sideways to affectionately tousle the floppy ears of his black-and-white speckled English Pointer. "This is Rocky. We've been pursuing partridge this morning. He found one, but I missed." The illustrious host chuckled at his own expense.

161

Shaw introduced Professor Haecker, who expressed appreciation. "Thank you for this invitation, Mr. Hill. We are eager to see your livestock and facilities."

"Well then, let's get started," Hill strode forward with gusto. He proudly pointed to a prize-winning bull inside a nearby corral and expertly praised the animal's outstanding physical traits: square shoulders, thick hindquarters and a wide, flat back. "I have donated dozens of bulls like this, and boar hogs, to farmers along my railroad line into the Red River Valley," he said. "I view that service as a mutually beneficial endeavor. The farmers gain livestock that will help them succeed, and I gain more successful customers who will buy and sell products carried by my trains."

"That leads to a question that has been discussed in our classrooms," said Professor Haecker. "Many Minnesota farmers are devoting most of their acreage to produce wheat, which is profitable when sold to the flour mills. But you are encouraging more diversified farms that grow a variety of crops and raise multiple species of animals. Why?"

"You're right, I do preach diversity," Hill responded. "We know that raising the same plants in the same fields, year after year, is a mistake. Without crop rotation, those fields will become less fertile and infested with weeds and insects that prey upon those particular plants." He began speaking louder and faster. "Furthermore, livestock is a year-round producer, not just at harvest time. Chickens lay eggs in the winter, just like sheep grow wool, hogs make bacon and cows give milk. A diversified farmer can make money during every season of the year and won't be ruined if one crop fails."

A student piped up, "Like the grasshopper plague?"

"Well, that's a little different," Hill conceded. "Those rocky mountain locusts seem to destroy everything in their path and have come back four years in a row." He turned to Shaw and asked, "Do you professors have a scientific solution for the grasshopper problem?"

Shaw shook his head. "Not yet."

Water Wheels

They walked on, past other pens and pastures containing poultry, pigs, sheep and horses. Hill's dog never barked or pestered the animals. Rather, it sauntered along with ease on long, slender legs that stood in sharp contrast to his master's short, stout limbs. On the other hand, the pointer displayed an alert, independent temperament that seemed a perfect character match. Hill paused and casually pointed his shotgun toward a distant grove of young trees on a hillside. "That's part of the forestry," he declared. "I planted various pines and spruces on the property and deciduous varieties of oaks, maples and box elders."

While Halvor stood listening, a black Percheron stallion snorted and stuck its head over a wooden railing to nuzzle his shoulder. Instinctively, the boy turned to scratch under the horse's jaw and stroke its neck. "Good boy," Halvor whispered.

Hill took notice and asked, "Son, are you a horse whisperer?"

Halvor smiled. "We have Belgians, sir."

"Good work horses."

"I have worked ours on the farm and in the pine forest."

Hill cocked his head and gave Halvor a longer look. Then he knowingly nodded before leading the students through several farm buildings: livestock barns, a slaughterhouse, blacksmith shop and icehouse. They spent a lot of time inside the dairy building while the professors quizzed Hill about his modern machinery to separate milk from cream and butter. Again, he answered with attention to detail that affirmed the man's personal involvement in every phase of the operation. He also spoke with a passion that revealed his pride in the farm.

Professor Shaw asked, "We are experimenting with hybrid breeds on our university farm, so I'm curious about your success with dual-purpose cows."

"Yes, our Shorthorns," Hill acknowledged, addressing him and the students. "As you've seen, we have three herd varieties here at North Oaks. Our Angus are exclusively raised for hides and beef, while the Jerseys are primarily dairy cattle. In between, we are trying to develop a Shorthorn herd of cows that produce ample milk and steers that provide plenty of nutritious meat."

Professor Haecker interrupted, "Shaw neglected to mention that he and I disagree on this topic. He is a proponent of the dual-purpose cow idea, while I believe that farmers will be smarter to specialize with separate herds of dairy and beef cattle."

Hill chuckled. "Well, gentlemen, I won't be able to settle your argument. Our Shorthorn breeding program is yet to end in success or failure. But earlier today, I talked about those immigrant farmers in the Red River Valley who live along my railroad route. Many of them are too poor to own more than one herd of cattle, so our breeding of dual-purpose Shorthorns is aimed to serve them and all the other subsistence farm families in the Midwest."

With that, Hill pulled a pocket watch from his vest and excused himself from the tour. "Mary and I are expecting some family friends for Sunday lunch," he said. "Feel free to stay as long as you like and approach any of my farm workers with questions you may have."

"Thank you, Jim," Shaw said. "You've been a generous and informative host. With your permission, we'll eat the picnic lunches we've brought along and then allow our students some individual exploration time before we head back to the university."

* * *

Bells were ringing from the twin spires of Assumption Church when the Meier family departed from Sunday morning service. They climbed aboard their one-horse carriage and began a two-hour drive to spend a relaxing afternoon with friends, the Jim and Mary Hill family. Jim and Heinrich had both arrived in St. Paul twenty years ago, Hill from Canada and Meier from Germany. They each got jobs at the riverfront steamboat landing, served as volunteer firefighters and joined the Pioneer Guard militia.

While the Meier family had prospered in the hardware and lumber business, their financial fortunes paled compared to Hill's accumulated wealth. At thirty-eight years of age, he was already a multimillionaire. Starting with a single warehouse, Hill became a wholesale trader, then a steamboat owner and now a railroad tycoon. After the Panic of 1873, he invited Heinrich to join his group of bank investors. It proved a lucrative venture, and the two men were happy business partners.

Emelia wondered what the Hills' farmhouse would be like. Their family home near downtown St. Paul was a modest two-story structure, though it was recently rebuilt with a modern indoor bathroom. They didn't seem to spend on lavish luxuries; instead, Hill was known to reinvest most of his company profits to make those companies even more profitable.

Upon arrival at North Oaks, Emelia perceived that it was really two properties in one. To the left of the entrance road was an actual working farm with barns, animals, pastures and plowed fields. But curving down to the right was a lakefront home with water and trees as far as her eye could see. Two little girls spilled out of the house to welcome their carriage, and young Mary Hill appeared on the steps behind them. At age thirty, she was a mother of four children, pregnant with a fifth, and destined to have more.

Shortly after the Meiers were welcomed into the house, Jim arrived from the farm, and everyone was seated at a long, large dining table. The men sat down at one end, women at the other, with the kids squeezed in between. A maid helped Mary serve a gigantic roast turkey, along with stuffing, mashed potatoes, corn, beans and gravy. "This is one of our own farm-raised turkeys," Jim proclaimed, "a Mammoth Bronze."

Heinrich raised an eyebrow while he deftly unfolded the napkin with his one good hand. "I can see why they're named Mammoth!" Everyone laughed, and the meal proceeded with genial conversation.

The maid came back to help clear away dishes, but Mary announced that everyone should remain seated for a dessert of pumpkin pie. While they waited, Emelia heard Jim Hill say to her father, "Heinrich, I've got a business deal to discuss with you."

Heinrich smiled. "I thought you came out here to relax." It was a mock surprise. Everyone knew that Jim Hill was a notorious workaholic and that business was never far from his mind.

"I'm sorry," Hill apologized, "but it's true. This place does relax me. It has become our summer home from May through October, and the farm chores are a labor of love for me. Believe it or not, I went partridge hunting this morning." He paused. "Okay, business can wait until after dessert."

After dessert, the two men exited onto a screened porch that extended from one corner of the house. The women moved into the kitchen or the parlor, but Emelia opted to follow her father. She was curious about the business proposal their host had mentioned. When she stepped onto the porch, Hill had a cigar in his teeth and was about to light one for Heinrich. Caught off guard by the girl's presence, he hesitated and looked at her while the match burned perilously close to his fingers. Feeling the heat, he frantically shook out the flame and quickly blew on his fingertips.

"I don't need a cigar," Emelia said.

Hill peered back at the girl and then at her father, who stifled a little giggle. "Emmy's the entrepreneur among my girls," Heinrich said. "No doubt she's here to critique the business deal you promised to discuss."

"I'll leave if you wish," she volunteered.

"No," Hill quickly offered, "it's no secret. I'm merely suggesting a merchandise opportunity for your family's hardware store."

Heinrich inhaled a short breath of cigar smoke and puffed it out into the cool, fresh air that drifted through the mesh screens. "Okay, Jim, what's the opportunity?"

"The future of energy is coal," Hill began. "It's more efficient. Railroad locomotives are switching from firewood to coal. Factories are moving from river-power to coal-powered steam. Before you know it, people will be heating their houses with coal rather than firewood." Jim physically squared himself in front of Heinrich. "You should begin to sell coal-burning furnaces for installation into private homes."

"I could," Heinrich allowed, "but why do you care what's for sale at Meier Hardware?"

"Because," the millionaire announced, "you're looking at the new owner of the Northwestern Fuel Company. I've established a monopoly on all the ore coming north out of the rich coal fields in central Iowa, by steamboat and rail." Hill poked his cigar toward Heinrich. "I'll sell the coal, and you sell the furnaces."

Hill stuck the cigar back into his teeth and waited for a response from Meier. Instead, Heinrich turned to Emelia. "What do you think about this idea?"

"He's right about the future," she said, "and it's not just furnaces. These modern heating systems pump hot water through pipes to radiators located in the rooms throughout houses and buildings."

"Smart girl," the cigar bobbed between Hill's lips as he spoke.

"Yes," Heinrich boasted, "she's working nights as Louise Hamm's accountant and attending the University of Minnesota during the days."

"What a coincidence," said Hill. He lowered the cigar with one hand and pointed toward the farm buildings with his other. "There are a dozen university students here today. They came with their professors to see some of our agricultural advancements at North Oaks. I toured them around the fields and buildings just before lunch."

"I could use some exercise," said Emelia. "With your permission, I'll explore the farm and meet a few of my classmates."

* * *

Emelia emerged from the trees surrounding Hill's lakefront home and walked up a slope to the cluster of farm buildings. She approached from behind a short, broad-shouldered young man feeding a big black horse by extending an apple through a wooden rail fence. "Hello," she said.

The boy spun around in surprise, dropping the apple beyond the fence rail. He had not heard her approaching footsteps. The horse stepped forward and lowered its head to chomp the crisp apple, but the young man seemed frozen, speechless.

"I'm sorry," Emelia apologized, "I didn't mean to startle you."

Halvor recognized her. She was eight years older now and wore a charcoal gray woolen bonnet loosely tied at her neck with a wide

167

black ribbon. Instead of braids, her long dark hair extended from under the bonnet to fall over her shoulders. But the girl's chocolate-brown eyes looked directly at him, the same as before. Her wide face expressed honest curiosity, just as he remembered from Oliver Kelley's farm. "You were the girl at the strawberry picnic."

Now it was Emelia's turn to be speechless. She did not recognize this boy, nor could she remember a strawberry picnic. Her dark eyebrows wrinkled with puzzlement.

Halvor awkwardly extended his hands out to both sides. "It was a long time ago. We were kids. There was a Grange picnic at Oliver Kelley's farm. We were both with our fathers."

She searched her memory while looking at the sturdy blonde youth. His face was not familiar, but the words "Grange" and "farm" brought back the image of Caroline Hall. Emelia vividly remembered that young woman who spoke with impressive confidence and authority.

"You're right," she said. "I was there, but the day was too long ago for me to remember faces." Emelia was too polite to admit that someone else was memorable while this boy was forgettable.

"My family is at North Oaks for Sunday dinner with the Hills," she explained, "but I'm enrolled at the university. When Mr. Hill said there was a group of students here at the farm, I came out to say hello."

"*I'm* a university student," Halvor exclaimed, his face bursting into a gigantic smile.

Emelia had wondered whether he was part of the college field trip or a farm employee. She smiled and extended her hand. "My name is Emelia Meier."

"I'm Halvor Dahl," he eagerly shook her hand. "Maybe you haven't seen me on campus. This is only my first year in the agricultural college, and I work afternoons in Minneapolis. I take some classes in the prep school because my studies weren't too advanced at our country school down in the Cannon River valley." He was nervous, and the words spilled out of his mouth with speed.

Water Wheels

"It's my first year too," Emelia revealed, "but I was lucky. The nuns at Visitation Academy got me ready for college classes. I'm taking history, mathematics, English and German. But I'm not on campus very much either because I have a job in St. Paul and live in my family's house." She paused. "Where do you live?"

"I rent a room in a boardinghouse in St. Anthony," he replied, "but my family lives on a farm southwest of Northfield. Do you know where that is?"

"Well, if I didn't know where it was before the big bank robbery, I do now," she declared. "Believe it or not, that outlaw Jesse James came into the place where I work and pointed a gun at me!"

Halvor's eyes widened in amazement. "I do believe you, but you might not believe this. He pointed a gun at *me!*"

The teenagers exchanged their coincidental dangerous confrontations with Jesse James, Emelia describing the August invasion of Louise Hamm's boardinghouse, and Halvor recounting the theft of Haakon during the gang's escape in September. They both admitted that James was unknown to them during their encounters. Only later did each recognize the notorious outlaw's face in newspaper photographs.

As their stories unfolded, the two unconsciously meandered along a path that overlooked a recently harvested field. Emelia stopped and asked, "Since you're a farmer, I have a question."

"What is it?"

"Well, I work for the Hamm family. They own a big brewery in St. Paul."

"Hamm's beer."

"Yes, it's pretty famous, I guess," she hesitated. "Anyway, they buy huge quantities of farm crops, barley and hops. Do you grow any of that?"

"Sounds like my agricultural field trip is still in session," Halvor grinned. "That's the type of idea that Mr. Hill is proposing."

"Why?"

"He's afraid that Minnesota farmers are too dependent on the single crop of wheat. It's profitable right now, but the price could

169

drop, especially if we produce too much. Plus, crops are seasonal rather than year-round. Mr. Hill believes that farmers should produce diverse products like meat, dairy, eggs and wool and grow different grains and vegetables."

"Do you?"

"My family raises livestock and vegetables to meet our own needs, and we grow oats to feed the animals, but our cash crop is wheat. So, the answer to your question is no, we don't grow barley or hops."

"Maybe you should."

There was that directness. This girl had a way of completely disarming Halvor. But after a moment of consideration, he answered, "I believe Minnesota weather is a little too frigid for hops, although they're grown in the Wisconsin Dells. Barley, on the other hand, is well suited to our soil and climate."

"All I know," Emelia said, "is that the Hamm's brewery buys a lot of it."

They walked along in relative silence, admiring the countryside until the path ended at the shore of Pleasant Lake. Halvor looked at the profile of her face, now illuminated by sunrays reflecting off the low, rolling waves. "I'm glad for this chance to talk with you," he said. "It helps me look at things from a different perspective."

Emelia turned to him and arched an inquisitive eyebrow.

"You're not like the people I'm usually with," he explained. "You're a city girl with German heritage who attends a Catholic church with wealthy friends like Theodore Hamm and James J. Hill. I'm just a country boy from a Norwegian Lutheran church, raised in a sod-roofed house."

They listened to gentle waves lapping at the shoreline for a few moments before Emelia politely disagreed. "We're not so different. You and I are a pair of short, stocky children of immigrants, working our way through college at the same university."

"Yeah," Halvor conceded, "and both of us are survivors of a run-in with Jesse James." They shared a laugh and walked back up the path, her to rejoin her family and him to depart with the field trip.

Water Wheels

* * *

James J. Hill (1838–1916)

Perhaps the wealthiest and most well-known Minnesota resident of all time, Hill became known as the "Empire Builder" after gaining control of a railroad network that served the American Northwest.[40]

Born in Rockwood, Ontario, Hill was the son of Scotch-Irish immigrants. He overcame a childhood bow-and-arrow accident that permanently blinded his right eye and became a brilliant student. A muscular youth, Hill had a particularly powerful upper body. Moving to St. Paul at age seventeen, he worked as a clerk on the busy riverfront, where more than a thousand steamboats per year docked in the late 1850s. Within ten years, Hill built a warehouse and established a company to trade and transport merchandise.[41]

Hill was married in 1867 to twenty-one-year-old Mary Mehegan, an Irish Catholic immigrant, though he was a lifelong

Protestant. The couple raised a family of ten children, but Hill was often absent. He worked long hours, seven days a week, and notoriously micromanaged his many businesses with a perfectionist's attention to detail.[42]

Before age fifty, Hill owned a string of steamboats, a coal company and a bank. He built a railroad monopoly, at the center of which was the Great Northern Railway that crossed the continent to Seattle. He famously reinvested most of his business profits, especially in the trains, pulled by the most efficient modern locomotives, on strong and smooth steel rails over the most flat and straight routes. Hill promoted the livelihood of settlers along his rail lines and, to that end, operated North Oaks, an experimental farm from which he donated hundreds of animals to immigrant farmers. That five-thousand-acre estate became the family home during the warmer half of Minnesota's calendar.[43]

Later in life, Hill built three of the state's structural landmarks: the Lafayette Hotel on Lake Minnetonka, the Stone Arch Bridge across the Mississippi River, and his family mansion in St. Paul. The magnificent house, standing on three Summit Avenue lots, is designated a "national historic landmark" by the US Department of Interior and is operated as a museum by the Minnesota Historical Society.[44]

Chapter 11
Grasshoppers
1877

"Governor Pillsbury, I've got the perfect driver for your tour," declared Professor Shaw. "His name is Halvor Dahl."

The governor was planning a midwinter trip to southwestern Minnesota, where consecutive years of grasshopper devastation had left a wasteland of hunger and poverty for rural families. He wanted an eyewitness look at the catastrophe and an opportunity to speak directly with the victims in his state.

Professor Shaw was not surprised that John Pillsbury came to the University of Minnesota's agriculture department, looking for a driver to accompany this journey. People started calling him the "Father of the University" because of his long service on the board of regents, his fundraising efforts to reopen the doors after the Civil War, and money from his own pocket to carry the college through the Panic of 1873.

"Halvor Dahl is a first-year student," Shaw told the governor, "but he's one of the most natural horsemen I've ever seen. The boy is from a southern Minnesota farm family."

Pillsbury expressed concern about Halvor missing school. "Will he be able to resume his studies after a couple weeks away?"

"He's a smart young man," the professor stated confidently, "and we'll help him catch up when he returns." Shaw cracked a smile. "He will probably learn more from two weeks with you than he would here with us. Furthermore, his classmates will have dozens of questions about the grasshopper-infested area when he comes back to class."

"He might have a part-time job," Pillsbury guessed. "If so, I'll speak to the employer about granting a leave of absence."

"Ha-ha, ho-ho-ho," Shaw laughed. "He works for you in the Anchor flour mill. Your nephew Charles is his boss."

Pillsbury grinned and nodded his head at the coincidence.

The professor added, "If you're as happy with his service as I expect you will be, you might think about paying the kid a bonus. I'm sure his family could use the help."

* * *

Halvor walked the few short blocks from his boardinghouse to John Pillsbury's residence at the intersection of Tenth Avenue and Fifth Street in St. Anthony. He wore his warmest hat and coat, carrying one change of clothes and a few schoolbooks in a haversack slung over his shoulder.

A lightweight buggy with four large, spoked wheels and a black canvas canopy was parked in front of the governor's house. People commonly characterized this style of vehicle as a doctor's buggy. Harnessed in front of the carriage was a beautiful Hackney gelding. The tall, caramel-colored horse anxiously fidgeted his black fetlocked feet and twitched his high-held black mane and tail. Halvor slowly approached the Hackney's head. "Easy, boy," he murmured, gently stroking the animal's neck.

"Good morning," a strong voice called out from the front porch. "You must be Halvor Dahl."

Looking across the Hackney's back, Halvor recognized John Pillsbury's face from newspaper illustrations he had seen. The forty-nine-year-old governor's high forehead was balding while a distinguished, graying mustache and goatee circled his mouth. The man was of moderate height and weight, but his erect posture projected a taller image.

Water Wheels

Pillsbury pointed toward the horse. "I see you have already met Flag." Then he made a beckoning motion. "Come on in. Let's have a hearty breakfast before we get started."

Halvor observed the interior of the governor's home from his chair at the breakfast table while Mrs. Mahala Pillsbury served a generous portion of fried eggs and potatoes. The house and its contents were impressively crafted but without fancy decoration, consistent with the couple's conservative Yankee ancestry.

Once underway, Halvor and Pillsbury drove away from Minneapolis, headed for Old Shakopee Road, which would lead them along the Minnesota River toward the grasshopper-plagued southwestern counties. Alternating between a walk and a trot, the speedy Hackney covered thirty miles per day while the winter weather remained agreeable. Flag's stamina seemed to flourish in the cool temperatures, and when Halvor gave him his head, the gelding pranced away with stylish high knees and his tail flying aloft, an emblem of his name.

Toward the evening of the second day, a jackrabbit spooked from a roadside thicket when Flag trotted by. The hare's explosive initial bound was longer and taller than the buggy, arching through the air with its powerful hind legs stretched nearly a foot behind. The jackrabbit's midwinter fur was snow white. Only the upright four-inch ears held their brownish-gray summer color. Flag flinched when startled by the hare, but just for a moment. Then the jackrabbit landed beside the road, laid those ears back and sped straight ahead. The Hackney tried to keep up, but even he was no match for the hare's forty-mile-per-hour speed.

Conversation between Pillsbury and Halvor was sparing, as neither man was a chatterbox. They might ride in silence for miles, listening to the steady beat of Flag's hooves, watching the prairie landscape and smelling occasional farm-stove smoke. At other times, they exchanged a lively dialogue, asking and answering questions on subjects of mutual interest. One such topic was, of course, the university.

The governor was curious about Halvor's classes and professors in both the prep school and college. "The agriculture courses are my favorites," the boy expressed, enthusiastically describing many experiments being tested at the university farm with livestock and crops.

Halvor asked Pillsbury about his well-known, long-standing support for the school. "I know the value of education," the man responded. "In the near future, your learning will help advance your career. In the distant future, your knowledge will help to improve your community. Eventually, a society of university graduates will help to make Minnesota a better state." The governor told Halvor that his daughter Addie was a first-year student, and he hoped that all four of his children would attend the University of Minnesota.

Pillsbury asked the boy about his farm and family in the Cannon River valley, leading Halvor to describe his parents, brothers and sisters affectionately. He gestured with his arm to depict how Wolf Creek meandered past their wheat fields, then self-consciously turned to face the governor. "We don't take our wheat to a Pillsbury mill," Halvor admitted. "The Archibald Mill is a modern facility, only five miles from our farm."

"You don't have to be embarrassed," Pillsbury smiled. "That mill in Dundas has an outstanding reputation." He leaned back on the buggy seat. "Besides, my nephew Charles is the flour milling expert, and now he's got you working for us."

The travelers reached St. Peter at the end of their second day. Halvor found a livery stable and cared for Flag while Pillsbury checked them into a room at the luxurious Nicollet House. The three-story brick hotel was built in classical style in 1873. By the time Halvor walked into the gracious ground-floor lobby, word of the governor's surprise arrival was spreading. While Pillsbury stowed luggage into their upstairs accommodations, people were scurrying in and out of the elegant restaurant where they would soon be dining. Nobody noticed Halvor.

No sooner were they seated for supper than a young reporter with the *St. Peter Tribune* newspaper approached their table. Halvor considered that a rude intrusion, but Pillsbury politely delayed the young man. "We are weary from the road," he said. "Please allow my driver and me to enjoy a relaxing meal. After dinner, I will gladly entertain whatever questions you may have."

Sure enough, when Halvor left the restaurant, the governor remained for a lengthy interview.

The next morning, they diverted from the Minnesota River and took the overland Traverse des Sioux trail. It was a traditional Native American shortcut to the confluence of the Minnesota and Cottonwood Rivers. A full day's journey would deliver them thirty miles west to the town of New Ulm.

Across a distant plateau, Halvor spied a pine grove, rare in this prairie region with scattered deciduous trees. He raised his arm to point at the green branches. "Those pines remind me of my last two winters in a lumber camp."

Pillsbury's eyes lit up. "Takes me back to my days as a timber cruiser."

"You were a cruiser?" Halvor was surprised. The governor's physical stature seemed inadequate for the north woods. Furthermore, Pillsbury's sophisticated manners did not fit the boy's vision of a typical lumberman.

"I was thirty-five years old," the governor answered Halvor's doubtful reaction. "My body was fifteen years younger," he reminisced. "Congress had just passed the Morrill Act, which granted each state thirty thousand acres per electoral vote to finance agricultural and engineering colleges. We double-dipped to raise money for the university."

"Double-dipped?"

"I surveyed northern Minnesota forest land, which we rented to lumber companies. After the timber was harvested, we sold the acreage separately." Pillsbury slapped his knee with delight. "First, we leased the land and then sold it—a double-dip."

Later, as they passed Swan Lake and approached New Ulm, the governor initiated their one and only discussion of politics. "Is there an active Grange chapter in your community?" he asked.

"There are meetings," Halvor answered, "but they seem to be primarily educational and social rather than political."

"I'm not very popular with the Grange leadership," Pillsbury acknowledged. "My Republican party is more friendly to business than farming, and my family's flour mills are sometimes accused of exploiting farmers."

"I think the Norwegian farmers in our valley are pretty evenly divided, half Republicans and half Democrats," Halvor said. "They are eager to read the Grange publications because they want to keep up with modern agricultural ideas." Pillsbury listened while the boy continued, "Grange meetings are well-attended, but I think folks primarily come for the food, the music and the friendship. It's rare to hear anybody talk about government."

Halvor raised a controversial topic that had been discussed in his college classes. "What about government aid for the grasshopper victims?" The boy knew the governor's predecessor, Cushman Davis, had allocated a modest amount of welfare money for grasshopper plague relief, but Pillsbury was opposed to state handouts.

"Charity should be provided by charitable organizations," Pillsbury declared, "not the taxpayers. That way, people are motivated by compassion to voluntarily help their fellow citizens, not because they are forced to do so by the government."

John and Mahala Pillsbury were among the wealthiest couples in Minnesota, but they were also much admired as among the most generous. While he served a dozen years in the state senate, she helped found Northwestern Hospital. The couple donated large sums of money to the university, to their church, to Minneapolis parks and libraries, to victims of tornadoes and forest fires, and land to preserve a state forest. Furthermore, everybody knew that Pillsbury flour mill employees were the highest-paid laborers in town.

The governor squinted into the late-day sun, its low angle reflecting into their eyes off the fields of snow. "My wife has organized a charitable collection of food, clothing and money for grasshopper plague victims," he said. "We have rented a railroad warehouse where donations from Minnesota churches are being gathered."

"That reminds me," Pillsbury snapped his fingers, "I should send Mahala a telegram from the train depot in New Ulm. She'll be worried about me." Then he turned to Halvor and asked, "What about you, son? Is there a special girl who might be worried about you?"

"No, sir," Halvor shook his head. "There is no special girl back home, and I barely know the one girl I have met at the university." He remembered his awkward feelings in the presence of Emelia Meier. "She's way too smart for me."

Pillsbury gave Halvor a serious look and pointed a finger directly at the young man. "Take my advice, son. Smart girls are worth getting to know."

* * *

Emelia Meier entered the St. Anthony railroad warehouse and scanned the huge open space, looking for Addie Pillsbury. The governor's daughter was seventeen, the same age as Emelia, and a first-year student at the university. Only one-fourth of the college's three hundred enrollees were female, so it was not surprising that many of the girls knew one another. A few of Addie's friends gathered at the warehouse on this midwinter Sunday afternoon, volunteering to help organize donations for grasshopper plague victims.

The relief effort was well known. Governor Pillsbury had written an appeal for charity in an open letter published in many Minnesota newspapers. Posters were displayed around the university asking for volunteers. Churches across the state collected extra food, clothing and money, which was brought to this central location. In fact, just that morning, Emelia had heard her priest encourage people to provide a helping hand during services at their Church of the Assumption.

Emelia found Addie working near her mother, with three additional Pillsbury children nearby. Addie's sisters were diligently on task, but the youngest, eight-year-old Alfred, appeared more interested in cavorting around the stacks of donated supplies. "Alfred," Mahala Pillsbury sternly commanded, "come back here before you make a mess of your sisters' achievements."

Emelia commented, "This looks like an amazing achievement."

"Provisions have been gathered for delivery to six thousand families," Addie said proudly.

Mahala pointed along one wall of the warehouse. "All of the non-perishable food is there, mostly flour, sugar, coffee and some canned fruits and vegetables." She pivoted to the warehouse interior, holding on to Alfred's hand and resisting the boy's attempts to tug free. "We have a lot of warm clothing. It's organized by size and gender into stacks of hats, coats, mittens, pants, socks and shoes."

"Where should I work?" Emelia asked.

"Come with me," Addie said, taking Emelia by the hand and leading toward the warehouse wall with big doors adjacent to the railroad tracks. "Most university students are loading the train," she said. "Each boxcar is identified with the name of a southwestern Minnesota town. Then the cars are filled with food and clothing, which will be distributed from that stop on the railroad route."

Addie and Emelia got busy assembling collections of clothing, making sure that each stockpile contained an adequate assortment of garments for men, women and children. A group of college boys were loading handcarts, which they wheeled out the doors and unloaded into the waiting boxcars. Cold winter air whooshed through the doors each time a cart was rolled in or out, but the boys were working hard enough to keep warm without wearing heavy coats.

Emelia noticed that Addie was exchanging frequent glances with the young men and engaging in friendly conversation. When the girls were alone for a minute, Addie turned to Emelia. "You should talk to the boys." Addie's face was alive with delight.

However, Emelia focused on their humanitarian task rather than this opportunity to flirt with young men. "I guess I've always been more interested in my work than in romance," she said straightforwardly. "Besides, boys don't notice me. They're attracted to girls with hourglass figures. Not somebody like me who's shaped like a barrel."

Addie's expression turned sympathetic. "Do you have any friends who are boys?"

Water Wheels

Emelia remembered her friendly conversation with Halvor Dahl at Jim Hill's farm. "Maybe," she said slowly. "I know a boy at the university, but we don't have much in common."

* * *

Halvor and Governor Pillsbury toured westward out of New Ulm through Sleepy Eye, a small town named after a famous Native American leader. Thirty years earlier, Sleepy Eye's band of Dakota people had lived all along the Cottonwood River valley, where the governor's buggy now traveled. Fifteen years ago, this land was the scene of vicious, deadly fighting between Dakota warriors and white settlers. Hundreds of people were killed on both sides of the US-Dakota War of 1862, which ended with the banishment of Dakota people from the state of Minnesota.

"Do you remember the war?" Halvor asked.

"Of course I do," Pillsbury answered. "Mahala and I were living in St. Anthony with two-year-old Addie. Minnesota was a brand-new state, and we were one year into the Civil War."

"What happened?"

"Well, it's an ugly and complicated story with blame to be found on both sides," he began. "Wild game was becoming scarce, and more settlers were crowding into Minnesota. Believing they had no other choice, the desperate Dakota decided to sell their land and move onto a reservation. However, the US Senate cut the size of their reservation in half. Then, when the Civil War started, food and money promised to the Native people was diverted to support Union Army troops."

"What did they do?"

"Many of the older Dakota urged peaceful patience, but the young warriors were angry and eventually resorted to violence. That brought thousands of US military troops down here to crush the uprising. Unfortunately, justice was never done."

"Justice?"

"Many of the warriors who committed atrocities got away. They fled westward to join other bands beyond the Missouri River.

Meanwhile, all the remaining Dakota people were rounded up in prison camps, where many died. Thirty-eight men were executed by hanging, and eventually, all the Dakota people were relocated outside of our state. The reservation was erased."

Halvor and Pillsbury traveled for miles in thoughtful silence before overtaking a sled being pulled along the snow-covered roadside by a pair of draft horses. A load of chopped firewood was on the sled, being driven by a middle-aged man on the seat beside a young girl. The governor asked Halvor to slow Flag to a walk beside the sled, and he hailed the driver. "Good afternoon. Where are you going?"

"We're taking this load of firewood to Walnut Grove," the man responded. "I would like to sell it all in town."

"I hope you don't mind us driving alongside. I am Governor Pillsbury, and I've come out here to investigate the grasshopper plague. Perhaps you could tell me about it."

"Are you really the governor?" blurted the little girl who sat on the near side of the bench seat. She had a shawl covering her head and ears, but a pair of reddish-brown braids stuck out from underneath. She had withdrawn one hand from a fur muff on her lap and pointed at Pillsbury.

"Settle down, half-pint," the man cautioned while he reached to press her finger down. "Yes, he's the governor. I recognize his face from the newspapers." Then, looking across to the buggy, he apologized, "Please forgive Laura's bad manners. I'm her father, Charles Ingalls."

"Well, Mr. Ingalls, I apologize for failing to introduce my companion here. This is Halvor Dahl." Halvor waved a greeting, and Pillsbury continued, "What can you tell me about those grasshoppers?"

"There were millions of the icky little things," the girl proclaimed, "brown and green with shiny wings. Their eyes bulge out, and they have little hooks on their feet that grab onto your hair and clothes." The words spilled out of her mouth, and she imitated the insects by widening her eyes and shaping her fingers into claws. "Then they spit brown juice on you that makes a terrible stain."

Water Wheels

When Laura took a breath, her father silenced her by gently wrapping his arm around her torso. "Yes," he confirmed, "there were millions of them. So thick in the sky that the cloud of approaching insects looked like a dust storm. They descended onto our gardens and fields and devoured every plant. So many that you could hear their jaws munching the grains of wheat."

"What did you do?" the governor asked.

"My wife and I tried to fill the air with smoke by setting fire to scattered piles of manure-soiled straw, but it didn't work," Ingalls lamented. "When the grasshoppers finally flew away, only a brown landscape remained. There was no shade beneath naked tree branches. There was no grass in the pastures where our livestock had grazed."

"How have you survived?" Pillsbury inquired.

"My brother has a farm in the Zumbro River valley," Ingalls said, "one hundred fifty miles east of here, beyond the grasshopper infestation. I walked over there and did harvesting work for him and several of his neighbors. Earned enough money to get my family through the winter."

"We stayed here," Laura chipped in. "Ma and my two sisters took care of the animals until Pa came home." She nodded her head so the braids bounced on her shoulders. "I can milk our cow."

"A sizable creek flows through our farm," Ingalls said. "Plum Creek. I've made some money by trapping varmints near that stream and selling their fur pelts." Then he crooked his thumb back toward the load of firewood on the sled. "Since Christmas, I've been harvesting trees from along Plum Creek. After I chop and split the logs, Laura helps load 'em onto this sled, and we sell the firewood in town."

Pillsbury nodded to the youngster. "Sounds like you're quite a worker for a little girl."

She straightened herself to sit tall on the seat and declared, "Pa calls me half-pint, but I'll be ten years old next month." The girl pointed at Pillsbury's elegant Hackney trotter and said, "You have a pretty horse."

"His name is Flag," the governor replied. "He is fast, but I'll wager your horses are stronger."

"Sampson and David are our Christmas horses," Laura proudly stated. "Everybody in our family wished that Pa would get a new team of horses. We didn't wish for anything else," She thrust both arms out toward the horses as if introducing celebrities, "and sure enough, Santa Claus delivered them on Christmas Eve."

Charles smiled from behind her shoulder and shared a wink with the governor. Then, in a voice filled with anxious hope, he said, "If we can raise a wheat crop this year, Santa might bring us boards to build a new house for next Christmas."

"Pa is the best carpenter in Walnut Grove," the girl declared.

"Where do you live now?" Pillsbury asked.

"We live in a dugout," Laura said. "It's one big room with sod walls and a dirt floor, but Ma keeps it clean, and she chases all the snakes and spiders out."

Charles seemed a little embarrassed to admit they were too poor to live in a wooden frame house, but he allowed, "It's nice and warm in the winter."

Halvor didn't say anything but turned to gaze across the rolling prairie. He remembered his own family, tucked inside their hillside farmhouse underneath a roof of sod. He visualized his mother and thought to himself with a grin, *Ma keeps it clean, and she chases all the snakes and spiders out.*

It was late afternoon when they neared Walnut Grove, and the temperature was dropping with the setting winter sun. Ingalls halted his team of horses at the edge of town, where the snow-covered roadside gave way to a muddy street. Pillsbury asked Halvor to stop their buggy, and he jumped down to approach the sled on foot. Removing his expensive coat, the governor extended it to Ingalls, whose timeworn garment was thin and tattered.

"I can't take your coat," the man protested.

But Pillsbury laid it on the seat. "This is my thanks for the valuable information you have provided," he insisted. "I'll just buy another coat here in town."

Laura interrupted the exchange. "It was fun to meet a real governor."

Pillsbury was now close enough to see the freckles on her face. "It was my pleasure to meet you," he said. "Maybe someday you will be famous like me."

* * *

Later that spring, Governor Pillsbury declared Thursday, April 26, to be "a day of fasting and prayer" in Minnesota, "to beseech the mercy of God" for protection from another locust invasion. Within a week, the state was hit by an unusually late storm of snow and sleet that froze a large portion of the grasshopper eggs. Fewer insects hatched that year, and they flew away in August, never to return in the numbers that devastated southwestern Minnesota between 1873 and 1877.

* * *

Laura Ingalls Wilder (1867–1957)

Michael Barnes

Born in Wisconsin and raised in four other midwestern states, Laura Ingalls Wilder lived more than sixty of her final years in Missouri. However, her few years in Minnesota are well documented through her children's novel *On the Banks of Plum Creek* and the popular television series *Little House on the Prairie,* based on her book.[45]

Laura was seven years old when her parents, Charles and Caroline Ingalls, moved into a sod dugout home near Walnut Grove, Minnesota. Autobiographical stories about her childhood on a pioneer farm include particularly vivid descriptions of grasshopper infestations during the 1870s.[46]

After the family moved to South Dakota, Laura became a teacher and married Almanzo Wilder when she was eighteen. The couple struggled financially and with Almanzo's health until they established a successful dairy, poultry and fruit farm in Missouri.

It was there in the Ozarks, at age forty-four, that Laura began her writing career with a regular column, "As a Farm Woman Thinks," in the local newspaper.[47]

Not until the 1930s did her "Little House" novels appear in print. The original manuscript, written for adults, was rejected. However, her daughter Rose Wilder, then a professional writer at age forty-five, helped Laura revise the stories into a series of eight children's novels. They were all published between 1932 and 1943 and became enormously popular. In 2014, fifty-seven years after Laura's death, the South Dakota State Historical Society published an annotated version of her autobiography.[48]

Chapter 12
Explosion
1878

Maria Sanford was Emelia's favorite teacher, which was not surprising. The forty-four-year-old professor of composition and oratory was popular with all the college girls and most of the boys. Since being hired as Minnesota's first female professor, Sanford's classes attracted so many enrollees that she had more students than any other teacher at the university. Maria famously roved about her lecture hall, infecting pupils with her excitement for knowledge that made the subject matter exciting and relevant to their personal lives. She placed high expectations on their performance, and they were eager to please her. Outside of classroom hours, sometimes as early as four o'clock in the morning, she privately tutored students to help improve their writing or public speaking skills.

Sanford had purchased a boardinghouse near campus, where she lived with her twenty-year-old niece Emily, and leased rooms to as many as sixteen university students. The boarders could defray part of their monthly rent if they joined in meal preparation and housecleaning. The boardinghouse was also a location for frequent social gatherings of college-age youth, which Maria always chaperoned.

Some controversy swirled around Professor Sanford, generated by other teachers who were jealous of her popularity. They disapproved of the parties at her boardinghouse and complained about the money she was collecting from tutoring and outside speaking engagements. In truth, Maria needed the money. She had repeatedly fallen victim to ill-advised investment schemes that mired her in debt: land speculation in Minnesota, a celery farm in Florida, a rubber plantation in Mexico and failed mining ventures in Colorado and Montana.

She was, in fact, a celebrated public orator, recruited as a spokesperson to endorse numerous causes that she favored: public education, child labor laws, temperance, prison reform, forest conservation and women's rights. The university president and board of trustees never wavered in their support for Maria. They approved of her public speeches, believing they brought good publicity and that she was a wonderful ambassador for the college.

This evening, during the first week of May, was near the end of Emelia's sophomore year at the university. She was attending an event on campus hosted by Professor Sanford, who would be joined by two other female teachers. Harriet Bishop, at age sixty-one, was to provide a historical perspective, and Julia B. Nelson, age thirty-six, was to represent the future. On the university lawn was a large canvas tent with a small, raised platform under one side. Three chairs were arranged on this low platform, soon occupied by the panel of speakers.

Most of the audience gathered haphazardly under the shelter, though some people capitalized on the pleasant spring weather by standing just beyond the edges. Emelia moved to a nearby corner of the tent, which was to one side of the speakers where a girl about her age was seated on a blanket. "Please join me," the girl beckoned for Emelia to share her space on the ground. "My name is Clara Hampson," she said. "I'm a schoolteacher in Minneapolis."

"Thank you for the invitation to share your blanket. I'm Emelia Meier, one of Maria Sanford's students."

"Pennsylvania's loss was Minnesota's gain," Clara stated. Then, leaning close to Emelia, she whispered with a sly grin, "Lucky for us, the president of Swarthmore was a married man."

Water Wheels

Emelia's face tilted with a confused expression.

"I have friends in Philadelphia," Clara said. "Miss Sanford was beloved by her students at Swarthmore, too, but after a decade there, she chose to leave when rumors swirled about her relationship with the college president. He was already married." She paused, then repeated, "Lucky for us."

At that moment, Professor Sanford rose to address the audience. As the woman stepped forward in one of her customary plain black dresses, Emelia found it hard to align Clara's rumor with this dedicated teacher she adored.

"Welcome, everyone," Sanford began. "I am thrilled to share this platform with two of Minnesota's most heroic teachers. I will ask each of them to make opening remarks, and then, as time allows, we will entertain questions from the audience." She turned to the elder Miss Bishop. "Our first speaker will be Harriet Bishop, who came to Minnesota thirty-one years ago before this ground was even a US territory. She established our first public school right across the Mississippi River from Harriet Island, which is named after her. She is a published author of three books, and it will be our honor to hear her remarks."

The tall, angular Bishop stood up and smiled to acknowledge the heartfelt applause. Emelia was struck by how pretty she was in her advanced years. "That first school was an abandoned blacksmith shop," the woman began, "one block above the lower St. Paul levee. We used mud to fill gaps between the logs and covered the inside walls with pine boughs."

Harriet went on to describe her first multiracial and poverty-stricken students. "I provided many of them a bath before we commenced our lessons," she said. "Then I recruited a trilingual interpreter who could translate the lessons from my English into their French and Dakota vocabularies." She smiled. "Our only books were the few texts I had carried from my native New England, along with my Bible. Most of our reading material was provided by James Goodhue, the editor of St. Paul's first newspaper, who gave us unsold copies of his *Minnesota Pioneer.*

"In a few years, Minnesota's population boom required the service of many more teachers. That was when I switched from educating children to training other women to become instructors." Bishop turned, extending a hand toward Sanford. "But like you, Maria, I always recommended the importance of teaching manners and morals as a foundation for academic instruction. I believe our students' knowledge will only be valuable when they use it to promote righteous achievements."

Bishop sat down, and Sanford stood up. "Thank you, Harriet." She pivoted to the next speaker. "We are lucky to have Julia B. Nelson back home for the summer. She has returned to her native Red Wing after spending a tenth consecutive school year in the former Confederacy, where she educates former slaves to become successful participants in American society."

Nelson stood and acknowledged the crowd's polite applause. "I earned my teaching degree from Hamline University during the outbreak of the Civil War," she began. "Six years later, I was a childless widow after my son and husband died five months apart." A somber silence hung within the tent while Julia paused. "So there was nothing to stop me from answering a call from the Freedman's Bureau to provide schooling for Black men, women and children who had never learned to read or write. I taught at a school in Texas for the first four years and have worked in Tennessee since then." She proudly stated, "One of my former students has begun to teach with me and is enrolled to attend Howard University in Washington, DC."

Clara was whispering again. "Some people say that college boy is more to 'Julia B' than just a former student." She had a devilish grin on her face.

Emelia was flustered. She stopped listening to Nelson and turned to confront Clara. "If you have contempt for these women, then why are you here?"

"On the contrary," Clara protested. "I admire their spirit and spunk. They are brave and independent women, paving the way for girls like us to make our mark in the world." Clara's face was alive with excitement. "Their stumbles in life prove that they are human like you and me and that we can overcome obstacles and break through barriers just as they have."

Gradually, Emelia became aware that Julia B. was finishing her remarks. "I enjoy my summers back here in Minnesota," she admitted. "They enable me to join the campaigns for temperance and women's rights, about which I am passionate."

When Nelson sat down, Professor Sanford announced that questions would now be welcome from the audience. Clara's hand was immediately in the air, and when called upon, she boldly asked, "When will Minnesota women gain the right to vote?"

Sanford and Bishop both turned to look at Nelson, who had just proclaimed her enthusiasm for suffrage. The young woman was happy to field the question. "Well, I would initially like to celebrate the fact that our state has recently approved the participation of women in school voting, and I will punctuate that with congratulations for last year's election of Charlotte VanCleve to be a member of the Minneapolis School Board." A spontaneous burst of applause erupted among the female onlookers.

"We have several Minnesota women to thank for this progress, leaders like St. Cloud newspaper editor Jane Swisshelm, Dr. Mary Colburn from Champlin, Red Wing teacher Harriet Hobart and Sarah Stearns, a civic leader in Duluth," Nelson paused to turn and direct attention to Bishop and Sanford, "in addition to these ladies beside me."

When Julia B. sat down, Professor Sanford acknowledged the next question by pointing to a man behind the crowd. "I commend all of you for your opposition to alcohol," began the loud, clear voice, which Emelia immediately recognized as Father John Ireland. He continued, "Do you believe that our state will outlaw the sale of liquor?"

Now it was Emelia's turn to share a secret with Clara. "That's our Catholic bishop," she whispered. Then, with a giggle, she added, "I wonder if he knows that I work for the Hamm's Brewery?"

On the speakers' platform, Harriet Bishop rose to respond. "I saw the life of my former husband destroyed by his addiction to

191

alcohol," she said. "It tore our marriage apart, and I have seen it rip other families apart. Money wasted on liquor is dragging some households into poverty, and intoxicated parents are too often guilty of neglect or violence inside their own homes." She paused. "But in answer to your question, Father Ireland, no, I do not believe that alcohol will be banned in Minnesota."

"But we will keep fighting," came a resolute echo from the priest.

Harriet smiled. "I know you will, Father." Then, turning to Nelson, she said, "And Julia B. will keep fighting too, even after her knock-down, drag-out tussle in Anoka two summers ago."

Nelson's face blushed pink, and several audience members chuckled. They remembered the protest by members of the Woman's Christian Temperance Union of Minnesota, during which Julia B. was roughed up and thrown down in the street by an angry bar owner. Indeed, she remained an active opponent of alcohol.

Boom, boom-boom. Three thunderous explosions erupted in a span of seconds. Emelia felt the ground shake beneath Clara's blanket, and they both jumped to their feet, whirling with everyone else to look northwest toward the origin of the blasts. A dark, tumbling cloud was thrust skyward, with lightning-like flashes flicking up into the black smoke. The university audience stood in stunned silence, which enabled them to hear a few particles of debris land on top of the tent from the violent explosion just over a mile away.

* * *

Halvor was thoughtful during his late afternoon walk to work at the Anchor flour mill. He was halfway through his college career after two years at the university. His life had changed, and his goals had changed. When freshman year started, Halvor had no idea where higher education would take him. He thought perhaps he was simply destined to become a better farmer. However, after two years of college study, his work experience in the mill, and employment with the Pillsburys, the boy had raised his sights on a career in the grain business. He admired Governor Pillsbury but had no desire to pursue a career in government. Halvor knew himself well enough to understand that he was no politician.

He was attaining a rare combination of knowledge as a college-educated farmer. After years of work on the Dahl family farm, he knew firsthand the realities of life in the fields. Now, at the University of Minnesota, he was introduced to the latest advancements in agricultural science and technology. Furthermore, his employment in the Pillsbury flour mill made Halvor aware of the farm economy from a business angle. These three viewpoints gave Halvor a unique blend of understanding, which he hoped to use in a mutually beneficial way. He was aiming for a career in the grain industry that would promote financial success for everyone: farmers in the fields, laborers in the flour mills and himself.

Along his walk to the Anchor Mill, Halvor had passed by the Washburns' two mills, known as the A and B. Built seven stories tall of limestone blocks, the four-year-old A-Mill was the biggest in the city. The five Pillsbury mills were smaller and located another block up Second Street, closer to St. Anthony Falls.

Cadwallader "C.C." Washburn, former governor of Wisconsin, was an absentee owner who lived in Lacrosse, where his older and more expansive lumber company was headquartered. His brother William "W.D." Washburn, thirteen years younger, lived in Minneapolis and managed the Minnesota assets. Most notably, the Washburns built and owned a two-hundred-foot canal that ran along the river's west bank from St. Anthony Falls, providing waterpower to operate everybody's mills. Thus, all the factories, tightly packed along both sides of the Minneapolis canal, paid rent to the Washburns.

At five o'clock, the large day crew of nearly one hundred workers filed out of the Anchor Mill, and Halvor joined the night crew of less than ten who walked in. Most of the men who worked this shift spent their time cleaning the mill or moving barrels of flour to the loading dock. However, since his trip with Governor John Pillsbury to Minnesota's grasshopper-stricken counties, the boy had been promoted. It was now his daily responsibility to tour the mill's production line, inspecting each machine to make sure they were in tip-top working condition.

Halvor was particularly adept at maintaining a new machine called a middlings purifier, which he had initially been introduced to at the Archibald Mill back home in Dundas. The Pillsbury machines were bigger and more modern, but the process was the same. They enabled the mill to process a harder-shelled variety of wheat, known as spring wheat, which grew better in Minnesota's cold climate and produced better bread. The company sold its improved product with the famous label "Pillsbury's Best XXXX Flour."

Continuing his evening shift chores, Halvor was checking a fan and screen combination that filtered flour through a middlings purifier. Suddenly, he felt a quick suction of air from the room and lifted his head. In the next instant, he heard a deafening boom and felt the entire building bounce in place. He found himself flat on the floor with a ringing in his ears, not knowing if one second or a longer period of time had passed.

Halvor scrambled to his feet and quickly flexed each arm and leg to verify that they functioned, then scampered out the door and down the stairwell in search of his fellow crew members. Nearing ground level, he began to hear shouting voices as the ringing in his ears gradually subsided. Halvor emerged from the stairwell in time to see a pair of his coworkers exiting the building. He followed them out onto Second Street and immediately turned to face the fireball that had replaced the Washburn A-Mill.

The heat was unbearable. Everyone instinctively backed farther up the street, and Halvor shielded his face with both muscular forearms, peeking between his wrists at the brilliant, blinding blaze. People were yelling to be heard over the noise of the fire, a howling roar punctuated by loud crackling pops. The smell of smoking timbers was unmistakable, and he could taste the acrid air, filled with tiny, falling cinders.

This had been a quiet, late spring evening with only a gentle breeze, but the fire was creating its own wind. Oxygen was sucked into the inferno and whooshed upward by the scorching, swirling flames. The A-Mill had seemingly vanished in the explosion. Two adjacent buildings, the Diamond and Humboldt flour mills, were partially demolished, and the wooden beams that remained standing were all ablaze.

Soon, bells and horns could be heard from approaching horse-drawn fire engines. However, the intense heat stopped them from advancing nearer than a block from the source of the flames. One steam wagon pulled up right in front of the Anchor Mill, where its handsome matched pair of dapple-gray Percherons were panicked by the chaotic spectacle. The driver was yelling, "Whoa!" and pulling tight on the reins, but his horses were jerking madly in every direction.

Halvor spontaneously ran to the Percherons, approaching from the side to avoid being trampled under dangerous, heavy hooves. He grabbed a harness trace in one hand and reached for the near animal's bridle with the other, but just then, a glowing orange ember swirled down onto the horse's back. It screamed in pain and reared upward, lifting Halvor completely off the ground. When his feet landed back on the street, he quickly swatted the ember from the dapple-gray hair and re-gripped the leather harness lines. Moving to control the heads of both Percherons, he commanded in the firmest, steadiest voice he could muster, "Whoa-a-a. E-e-easy."

Now he could see their panic-stricken eyes. "Whoa-a-a. E-e-easy." Cautiously, their attention moved from the arena of pandemonium to focus down on the short, stocky human in front of them. "Whoa-a-a. E-e-easy." He was calm, and their tense, quivering muscles began to relax. Halvor noticed the driver jump down from the seat and begin to unhitch his team from the wagon tongue. Working his way forward, the driver finally unhooked the yoke, and the Percherons were loose.

"Thanks," he said. "You were amazing."

"I've been handling horses all my life," Halvor admitted. Then, giving the reins to the driver, he said, "They're a beautiful pair."

195

"Thanks to you, I still have 'em," he remarked and began leading his team up Second Street, safely away from the fire.

Other firemen quickly maneuvered the steam engine into place and started the mechanical pump. They connected hoses and began to spray water on the outer edge of the fire's perimeter. Obviously, they were hoping to contain the blaze and stop it from reducing all of Minneapolis to ashes. Halvor and other men from the Anchor Mill voluntarily joined a fire crew that began to douse the building where they had been working only minutes before. They labored all night long. In addition to the three exploded mills, the spreading fire consumed two more buildings, but every other structure was saved.

Tragically, eighteen people died. The initial blast killed the entire night crew of Washburn's A-Mill, and four additional men perished in the chain of explosions that destroyed the Diamond and Humboldt mills.

* * *

C.C. Washburn arrived in Minneapolis by train the morning after the explosion. He walked over the still-smoldering debris from his collapsed A-Mill before talking to newspaper reporters. "First of all, my brother and I are grieving for the people who lost their lives in this tragedy. We have already made contributions to initiate a fund that will provide money so the surviving family members can begin to recover from the loss of their loved ones." Indeed, Washburn himself was the most generous contributor to this fund.

"Looking forward," he continued, "I promise the local citizens that this flour mill will be rebuilt as quickly as possible, bigger and better than before. Meanwhile, our workers will not be unemployed. Some of them may participate in the reconstruction of the A-Mill, while the remainder will be temporarily relocated to expanded operations in our other Minneapolis mills."

In addition to Washburn's comments, the newspapers printed an eyewitness account of the explosion. "A stream of fire poured out of the A-Mill's basement windows," testified the local resident.

"Then, each floor above the basement became brilliantly illuminated, fire bursting from the windows as each story ignited, one above the other. Walls cracked open, and the roof blew off, blasting high into the air. Then, a cloud of black smoke billowed up, with flashes like lightning sparking back and forth. When the roof came back down, it collapsed all seven stories of the mill into a heap of limestone rubble."

A pair of university professors supported this account. They conducted controlled experiments with flour dust, observing similar explosions if the dust was ignited. Perhaps, they suggested, a burning lantern had fallen, or dry spinning millstones had produced a spark.

The Washburns followed up on this theory and recruited a Philadelphia company to demonstrate their system of filtering flour dust out of the air. The company sent William De la Barre, an Austrian engineer who installed dust collectors into the Washburns' other Minneapolis mills. C.C. was so impressed with the devices and De la Barre that he hired the man to supervise construction of the new A-Mill. As promised, it was bigger, more productive, and safer when it reopened two years later.

Five years after that, a monument was erected in Minneapolis's Lakewood Cemetery to memorialize the eighteen fatalities from the explosion. The stone obelisk is thirty-seven feet tall, with etchings of wheat, a millstone, and a broken gear beside the names of all eighteen people who lost their lives on May 2, 1878.

* * *

Michael Barnes

Minnesota Teachers who Worked for Women's Rights

Harriet Bishop (1817–1883)

In 1847, Harriet Bishop, a thirty-year-old New England schoolteacher, joined a cohort of young women who trained to establish schools on the American frontier. Harriet volunteered for St. Paul, where she taught a multiracial group of children inside an abandoned blacksmith shop built of logs. Her only books were a few texts she carried from her native Vermont and a Bible, prompting the Dakota parents of her students to call her "Good Book Woman."[49]

Bishop rallied St. Paul donations to provide clothing and shelter for poor families and to build a new schoolhouse, which also served as a church, courtroom and polling place. Eventually, she began training other teachers to spread around the region and wrote three books, all of which focused on Minnesota.[50]

In later years, Bishop campaigned against alcohol and for women's rights. She was an organizer of the Minnesota Woman's Christian Temperance Union in 1877 and helped found the Minnesota

Woman Suffrage Association in 1881. Harriet Island, across the Mississippi River from where she established Minnesota's first school, is named in her honor.[51]

Maria Sanford (1836–1920)

Already a teacher of ten years at Swarthmore College and a successful seminar speaker, Sanford became the University of Minnesota's first female professor in 1880. A beloved instructor of composition and oratory for twenty-nine years, the university dedicated Sanford Hall in her name.[52]

Her career was not without controversy. Several ill-advised financial investments put Sanford in perpetual debt. Consequently, she sought to augment her university salary with side jobs, most notably as a public orator. A tireless traveler on the speaking circuit, Sanford was a spokesperson for many causes, including education, child labor, health care, prison reform, forest conservation, temperance, minority rights, and women's suffrage. Her speech "An Apostrophe to the Flag" became a standard for patriotism during World War I.[53]

Julia Bullard Nelson (1842–1914)

A Hamline University graduate, Julia Bullard Nelson began teaching near her family's Red Wing home in 1861. She married a returning Union soldier after the Civil War and gave birth to a son, but both the infant and her husband died of illness within a year. The childless widow answered a call from the Freedman's Bureau and ventured into the former Confederacy, where she taught Black men, women and children who were uneducated during slavery. She spent seventeen years in that endeavor, first in Texas and later in Tennessee. Nelson hired Jeremiah Patterson, one of her former Tennessee students, to manage the Red Wing area farm she inherited. Together, they opened a store in town and named it the Equal Rights Meat Market.[54]

"Julia B." returned to Minnesota during each summer when schools were not in session. She immersed herself in this state's efforts to ban alcohol and win voting rights for Minnesota women. In 1874, she was knocked to the ground while protesting in front of an Anoka saloon. She later edited the *White Ribbon,* Minnesota's temperance newspaper. Nelson was a leader of the Minnesota Woman Suffrage Association from its founding in 1881 and served as president for six years. Known as an excellent public speaker, she became a nationally active suffragist in her later years.[55]

Clara Hampson Ueland (1860–1927)

Born in Ohio, her father died of illness when Clara Hampson Ueland was four. She and her brother were brought to Minnesota by their widowed mother, who had two sisters living in Faribault and Minneapolis. Clara was an excellent student and began teaching her own class of eleven- and twelve-year-olds when she was only seventeen.[56]

Eight years later, she married Norwegian immigrant Andreas Ueland, who became a prominent Minneapolis attorney and judge. In 1890, the prosperous young couple built a country estate on three acres of unpopulated land beside the lake called Bde Maka Ska. Seven children gradually filled their spacious two-story home. Clara homeschooled her three girls and four boys until the age of eight but led a successful campaign to provide free kindergarten for all Minneapolis youth.[57]

All their children went to college, and her daughters' campus activism partially inspired Ueland to help gain voting rights for women, in addition to other progressive causes. She founded the Equal Suffrage Association of Minneapolis, which recruited women and men into the movement. Then, as president of the Minnesota Woman Suffrage Association, she led its final five years to victorious passage of the Twentieth Amendment. A significant turning point came in 1919, when Clara Ueland was elected first president of the newly formed Minnesota League of Women Voters.[58]

Chapter 13
Graduation
1880

"Halvor Dahl."

Halvor heard his name announced. He stood and walked forward to shake hands with the University of Minnesota president, who handed him a college diploma. This was graduation day.

Soon, the announcer reached the middle of the alphabet. "Emelia Meier," he said.

Emelia marched across the stage to receive her diploma, and like Halvor, she peered into the audience to share an emotional look of recognition with her parents. Both graduates recognized the support and sacrifice they had received from their mothers and fathers. The parents recognized this accomplishment for their children, and they beamed with pride.

Later, the Dahls and Meiers found themselves seated around the same table at the graduation luncheon. When introductions were complete, Heinrich nodded to his daughter and said, "After thirty years in America, she is our family's first college graduate."

"Halvor is *our* first," Goran echoed, "since we came from Norway. He was only five years old at the time." Halvor and Emelia both blushed and exchanged modest glances.

"Neither of us would be here if it weren't for you," the girl said, looking at all four adults around the table.

Hildegaard spoke up. "Our investment in your education has already paid for itself." Looking at Emelia, she continued, "The hardware store profits have boomed with improvements you have recommended since coming to college. First, you talked us into selling coal fire furnaces, and then you convinced us to supply indoor plumbing equipment. Both ideas have been enormously successful."

Ingrid's face sparkled with a delightful giggle. "I'm laughing because Halvor has done the same thing. We used to throw away the offal from our wheat—that's the hull and bran that are ground off the seeds," she explained, motioning toward her son. "But since he's come to the university, we have learned to feed those parts of the wheat to our livestock. Offal is a nourishing food supplement that we don't even have to pay for."

That evening, after their families had gone home, the graduates met again at a party in Maria Sanford's boardinghouse. Halvor eagerly approached Emelia, to whom he was attracted like a magnet. This girl had fascinated him since their first meeting at Oliver Kelley's Strawberry Picnic twelve years earlier. "That's impressive," he said, "those ideas you came up with to improve your family's store. Are you going to take it over someday?"

"No," she answered, "my older sister Johanna is in line to inherit the family business. She helps to manage the hardware store with my mother now, and her new husband Tim is father's assistant at the lumber yard." Emelia shrugged her shoulders as if that arrangement were unimportant and added, "Mother and Father are only in their mid-forties. They will be in charge for another twenty years."

"So, what are you going to do?"

"I could move from part-time to full-time at the Hamm's Brewery," she said, "but I have an interview to start working for James J. Hill. He said that he would have an opportunity for me after graduation."

"Wow," Halvor gulped. Then, while awkwardly shuffling his shoes, he hesitated before asking, "Do you have any plans to start your own family?"

Water Wheels

Emelia's first impulse was to snarl, "That's none of your business." Instead, she maintained her cool demeanor and slowly said, "No, I don't even have a boyfriend." Then, when she detected the hint of a smile at the corner of Halvor's mouth, she added, "I don't need a boyfriend." The only change in Emelia's straight-faced expression was the independent arch of one dark eyebrow.

She remembered her conversation with Halvor at North Oaks, the Hill family's summer estate. He was a nice boy, and while she had no romantic interest in him, she could be polite without encouraging his courtship. She inquired about his plans. "What are you going to do after graduation?"

He began, "I have an interview scheduled with Mr. Pillsbury—"

"The governor?"

Realizing her confusion, Halvor stopped and started over. "I know the governor because I traveled with him during the grasshopper plague."

"You traveled with the governor?" Emelia was surprised to learn that this ordinary farm boy was personally acquainted with the state's chief executive.

"Yes, but my interview is with his nephew Charles, president of the Pillsbury flour mills."

Emelia knew that Charles was one of the illustrious Pillsburys. In addition to managing the five family flour mills in Minneapolis, Charles was an elected member of the Minnesota state senate. She kept listening while Halvor explained his part-time college job and his winter-time buggy tour of southwestern Minnesota.

In the same way this pair had once shared dangerous encounters with the outlaw Jesse James, they now compared their connections with the grasshopper plague. "I know the governor's daughter Addie," Emelia said. "She's a student at the university, and we volunteered together collecting food, clothing and money for grasshopper victims."

It dawned on Emelia that Halvor's flour mill job may have brought him near to the A-Mill explosion. "Where were you when the Washburn Mill blew up?"

He flashed a grin. "I guess I can smile about it now," he said, "but that blast knocked me flat on my back. I was at work in the Anchor Mill one block away."

"Oh, my gosh," she gasped. "Were you hurt?"

"No," he confessed, "just dazed."

"I saw it," she gushed. "We were attending a symposium here on campus, and when we heard the explosion, everybody whirled around to look at the fire and smoke."

Halvor explained how he calmed the fire engine horses in the street and stayed through the night to help the volunteer firefighters.

Emelia smiled at her recollection of a childhood memory, and she proceeded to tell Halvor about the wild buggy ride to the scene of her father's burning lumber yard.

Before long, a pair of student musicians appeared and began to play some popular songs, such as "I'll Take You Home Again, Kathleen" and "Come and Meet Me, Rosa Darling." They were ballads, not really dance music, and neither Halvor nor Emelia were skillful dancers. Nonetheless, he asked, and she consented.

By the end of the evening, she realized that he might be more than an ordinary farm boy. Was she guilty of looking backward at where he came from? Maybe, Emelia thought, she should look forward to where he was going.

* * *

"Let's talk about your future."

Three members of the Pillsbury family surrounded Halvor. Thirty-seven-year-old Charles conducted the interview from behind his large office desk inside Pillsbury Flour Company headquarters. Sixty-four-year-old George Pillsbury, Charles's father, was seated to Halvor's right. Recently retired from the family's New Hampshire place of origin, the still-vibrant family patriarch was ready for a new adventure in Minneapolis.

To Halvor's left was twenty-eight-year-old Fred Pillsbury, Charles's younger brother. Fred was a tall, handsome, fun-loving youth whose favorite hobby was racing his own thoroughbred trotting horses. Halvor and Fred were already friends, partly because of their mutual affection for horses but also because they were co-promoters of wheat "offal" as a byproduct for Pillsbury flour mills. Fred stabled his horses and Holstein dairy cattle on a 120-acre farm near Lake Minnetonka, where the livestock flourished with a diet supplement of wheat bran.

Charles began the interview. "We are going to build a new flour mill on the St. Anthony side of the river. We're naming it the Pillsbury A-Mill, and it will be the biggest flour mill in the world, with the most advanced technology." He nodded toward George and continued, "My father will be in charge of the construction process, which we expect will last two years."

The elder man spoke up. "We're going to tour the best flour mills in the United States and Europe. Our new mill will be equipped with electricity and elevators. The wheat will be completely ground by smooth steel rollers instead of grindstones, and dangerous dust will be removed from the air by modern exhaust fans."

Charles turned to his younger brother. "During these next two years, Fred will prepare to become on-site manager of the A-Mill, and you… " Charles paused and looked directly at Halvor. "You will be in training to assume the position of head miller."

Silence fell over the room. Halvor quickly glanced at the other three faces, each waiting for his response. "Yes," he blurted out. "I'll gladly accept if you think I'm up to the task."

Fred was on his feet, clapping Halvor on the back. "We don't want to lose you," he declared. "You're the best man for the job."

Charles gave him a look of steady confidence. "If we didn't think you were up to this, we would not be offering you the position."

George stood up and extended his right hand to Halvor. "Welcome aboard."

* * *

"Congratulations on your graduation from the university." James J. Hill leaned back in the high-backed desk chair behind the large desk in his downtown St. Paul office.

"Thank you," said Emelia, maintaining a businesslike expression and posture in the chair opposite Hill's desk. Her hair was pulled into a tight bun on the back of her head, and she wore her most professional dress.

A relaxed smile spread across the balding and bearded man's confident face. "This interview is not an interrogation," Hill said. "In fact, I have already decided to offer you a job. I have spoken about your qualifications with some of your college professors and with Theo and Louise Hamm."

Emelia relaxed a little. "What did those people have to say about my qualifications?"

"They confirmed what I've seen for myself while knowing your family over twenty years," he said. "That you're extremely smart and dedicated to your work. Perhaps too dedicated to work."

Emelia was puzzled by that latter comment, and she waited for Hill to continue.

"Your friends and family are worried that you totally pour yourself into work at the expense of your social life." He paused. "They wonder if you're happy."

Emelia thought for a moment before saying, "People say the same thing about you, Mr. Hill."

"Aha-ha-ha," he chortled. "So, you've been checking up on me as well."

"Like you," she said, "I would like to know about a person before I agree to work with them."

"So, what else do people say about me?"

"That you're a workaholic with a perfectionist's attention to detail." Emelia felt self-conscious, knowing about Hill's blind right eye, but she did not look away from their shared scrutiny of each other. "I have been warned that you're a controlling, domineering employer with a fiery temper."

The burly man leaned forward to rest his powerful forearms on the desk surface. "I like you better already," he said. "Most of my employees are afraid to be honest with me, even after they get hired." Hill folded his fingers together. "You and I will make a good team. If anything, we're too much alike—honest, ambitious and temperamental."

After a few moments of mutual silence, Emelia inquired, "Okay, Boss, what's my job?"

Hill withdrew a scrolled map from a desk drawer and flattened it upon his desktop. It was a map of Minnesota, which he spun around so she could see it right side up. Emelia stood and leaned forward, using both hands to prevent the map edges from rolling back together.

Stabbing his index finger onto the map location of the capitol city, Hill explained, "I have led a group of investors to buy the St. Paul and Pacific Railroad." He began dragging his finger to the northwest. "We have renamed it the St. Paul, Minneapolis and Manitoba, and extended our tracks to join the Canadian Pacific Railway." He placed the palm of his hand across the international border and looked up into Emelia's face. "My investments in this region have grown so large as to require a separate accountant to keep track of the money. I would like you to be that accountant."

"For the railroad?" she asked.

"Yes, the railroad," Hill said, and then consecutively poked a string of dots located throughout the Red River Valley, "but there are towns growing beside this train route where I am spending and collecting increasing amounts of capital." He stood. "Your first order of business will be a journey by rail to explore this region. Along the way, I'll introduce you to a couple of my fellow investors."

* * *

Halvor was seasick aboard the steamship *Germanic* and the ocean liner was only halfway through its first day of an eight-day voyage across the Atlantic. The SS *Germanic* was a premier vessel among passenger ships of the day; nearly five hundred feet long, she had three decks built to carry seventeen hundred passengers. A giant propeller could thrust the ship across calm waters at eighteen miles per hour, but she was also outfitted with four sailing masts in case the steam engines malfunctioned. However, despite the size and stability of the boat in moderate sea waves, the boy's stomach was twisting and turning.

Fred Pillsbury entered the small room that he and Halvor were sharing. "There you are," he said. Halvor remained seated on his bunk, hunched over a chamber pot held between his knees. Fred gripped him by the arm and gently lifted him. "We need to get you out on the deck where you'll feel better." The two young men made their way to a railing near the center of the ship's starboard outside wall. "Look out at the horizon," Fred instructed, "while I get you a drink of water."

It was a beautiful view. Cumulous clouds towered high into the pale blue sky like floating white mountains. The clouds temporarily masked the sun, but its slanting rays glittered off the blue-green ocean surf. Nevertheless, this panorama was lost on Halvor. As Fred had directed, he kept an eye on the southern horizon while gripping the railing with both fists and clenching his upset stomach. Halvor suddenly realized that the entire surrounding skyline was resting on water. The North American continent had disappeared behind them, beyond his view of the earth's western rim.

When Fred reappeared, Halvor accepted the glass of water. "Thanks," he said weakly, "I hope I can keep it down."

"Dehydration will contribute to motion sickness," Fred explained, "so let's make sure you have fluids." However, he hastily added, "No liquor though. That would make it worse."

Halvor managed a feeble smile. "Alcohol is the last thing I need."

"Well, you do need fresh air," Fred said, "so take in some deep breaths and try to keep your vision focused on the horizon."

"What difference does it make what I look at?"

"Not everyone gets seasick," Fred said, "but some people can be disoriented by the combination of movements experienced on a boat." He held his hand out level. "Between ocean swells, a ship will roll," he rocked the hand side-to-side. "Yaw," Fred swiveled his hand to pivot like a compass needle, "and sway." The flat hand slipped sideways. "Then, over wave crests and into troughs a ship will pitch," he dipped and then raised his fingertips, "heave," he raised and lowered the entire hand, "or surge back and forth." He thrust his hand forward and then pulled it back. "That's a combination of six movements that your body doesn't expect. So, it will usually help if your eyes can remain locked on one thing that is not moving."

"Like the skyline," Halvor deduced.

"Like the skyline," Fred confirmed.

After a while, Halvor started to feel a little better, but he remained on the deck, where he could breathe fresh air and see the horizon. Additionally, Fred recommended that he remain near the middle of the ship, where the yaw and pitch would be minimized. Eventually, by watching the boat's approach to each ocean swell, Halvor began to anticipate and predict how the *Germanic* might move in response. This awareness was particularly helpful.

The boy rejected the idea of supper that first night at sea, but by the evening of the second day, he felt ready to join the Pillsburys at their first-class dining room table. This voyage to Europe was a business trip. Charles and Fred had scheduled a series of marketing meetings, where they hoped to negotiate an increase in international sales for Pillsbury flour. George and Halvor, on the other hand, were going on a tour of the newest and most advanced flour mills in the world.

Notwithstanding the official purpose of this voyage, the Pillsburys were cruising in style. Halvor owned one formal suit of clothes, which he had purchased since going onto the full-time company payroll, and formal attire was expected at dinner. The first-class dining room was a luxurious space with courteous waiters, white linen tablecloths, and silverware that was truly silver. The food was delicious, and Halvor was finally healthy and hungry enough to enjoy it.

As scheduled, the SS *Germanic* landed in the Netherlands seaport of Amsterdam after eight days at sea. During the coming week, Charles and Fred would meet flour buyers in that city, as well as Brussels, Paris and London. They delivered complimentary barrels of their prize-winning Pillsbury's Best XXXX flour at each appointment.

From Amsterdam, George and Halvor traveled by train into the recently established Austro-Hungarian Empire, the sprawling central European dual monarchy that was the continent's largest wheat producer. The cities of Vienna and Budapest, both located in the fertile Danube River Valley, were home to a pair of modern flour mills that George and Halvor had arranged to visit.

It was more than just coincidence that Vienna-born William de la Barre was exploring these same mills on behalf of C.C. and W.D. Washburn. Both Minneapolis competitors were anxious to investigate the safer and higher quality "new process" used along the Danube.

The first difference that impressed George Pillsbury was the outside of the European flour mills. Their ornate, artistic exterior made the buildings pleasing to the eye, while typical American mills were simply utilitarian. Construction of the Pillsbury A-Mill would be George's responsibility, so this attention to architectural beauty got his attention. Halvor noticed the contrast but was far more anxious to see the internal variations.

Upon entering the Vienna and Budapest mills, the boy immediately noticed a lack of dust in the atmosphere. In fact, there were places where he felt a movement of fresh air passing through the building. When asked about the ventilation system, his tour guides proudly showed their multiple batteries of exhaust fans located on each floor.

Halvor paid particular attention to the steel rollers that ground the wheat in both mills. He was already convinced that the new technology was more consistently precise than stone grinding wheels. This investigation made him suspect that the process was also quieter and cleaner.

One surprising observation Halvor made was the packaging of finished flour into bags instead of barrels. Another unexpected circumstance he witnessed was the presence of women and girls in the workforce. When he asked about both practices, Halvor was told they were related. "The cotton sacks are better in two ways," his guide explained, "less expensive and not as heavy as barrels." He continued, "We already had some women working in our mill, and we discovered that they could more easily handle the lighter bags."

After their tours of Austro-Hungarian flour mills, George and Halvor returned to Amsterdam by train. Back aboard a steamship, they skirted the North Sea to London where they reunited with Charles and Fred. Then they traveled through the English Channel, across the vast Atlantic, and home to the United States. The westward voyage gave both pairs ample time to compare notes from their European missions.

For Halvor and Fred, the three-week tour had been an exciting adventure and educational experience. Upon returning to Minneapolis, both young men resumed their tutorial internships—Fred with his older brother Charles and Halvor with the existing Pillsbury Company head millers. However, Halvor had come home from Europe with a few pieces of knowledge that made him the tutor for a change.

* * *

The Meier family descended from their Dayton's Bluff neighborhood into Lowertown St. Paul. The early morning fog got thicker and thicker as they approached the Union Depot train station. From above, Emelia had seen the serpentine vapor cloud that hovered close to the Mississippi River surface with wispy fingers stretching among the city buildings. Now, just a few blocks from the lower levee on the Mississippi River, she could feel the cooler, moist air on her face.

Her father halted their horse outside the depot, and Emelia jumped to the ground before lifting her carpetbag suitcase out of the carriage. When she bid goodbye, fifteen-year-old Kat wore an envious expression suggesting a wish to accompany her sister on an adventure such as this. "Good luck," she called as the carriage pulled away.

Emelia stood and watched them fade down Third Street into the misty fog. Her bag was indeed made from a rectangle of carpet, folded once and sewn up the sides, with a pair of handles to grip and hold the top together. It contained clothing to last a few days and her grooming supplies. Held tightly under her other arm was a thin leather briefcase that contained her accounting ledgers and pages to record the information she would gather on this trip to the Red River Valley.

When her family disappeared, Emelia turned to enter the brand-new Union Depot. Construction of this common depot, shared by the nine railroad companies that traveled through St. Paul, had been James J. Hill's idea. He hired well-known local architect LeRoy Buffington to design the building and paid most of the construction costs for the structure. Hill was to be Emelia's tour guide on this excursion to the Canadian border and back.

Once inside, she approached the ticket counter but was intercepted by a dark-skinned man in uniform. "You must be Miss Meier."

When she answered, "Yes, I am," he held out his hand to take her carpetbag.

"I'm T.J. Brown, Mr. Hill's porter," the man stated. "He told me to escort you into his private railcar. Please follow me."

The porter pivoted to exit through a south door and walked out onto the railside platform, beside which stood a train emblazoned with the printed title "St. Paul, Minneapolis and Manitoba Railway." Farthest to her right, Emelia saw the train's locomotive, which was motionless but quietly humming with a thin plume of steam swirling upward through the fog. T. J. Brown led her to the tail of the train, farthest to her left.

Upon reaching Hill's extraordinarily long private railcar, they climbed three steep steps into the interior. There, a narrow hallway led along the left wall, all the way from front to back. "You can take either of these two forward sleeping compartments," said the porter. "Mr. Hill always occupies the rear bedroom."

"I'll just take the room next to his," Emelia answered.

T.J. opened the second sliding door and set her carpetbag on the floor inside. "You're welcome to explore the car," he told her. "The other passengers probably won't arrive for another hour, closer to scheduled departure."

Water Wheels

"I know I'm early," Emelia admitted. "My family dropped me off on their way to work." The porter walked away, and she entered her sleeping compartment. The bed was elevated like a top bunk above the side windows. Beneath the bed, facing each other were matching bench seats, padded and covered with fabric. On either side of the doorway were narrow closets, one with shelves and the other with a rod to hang clothes.

After stowing her belongings, Emelia ventured down the hallway toward the back of the car. Hill's bedroom door was closed, and she left it that way. Next was a tiny bathroom with a toilet and sink. Looking up, she spied a tank that held the running water supply. Farther back, she found the porter busy inside a small kitchen.

"Hello, Miss," he acknowledged her. "I'm just checking our food supply and making sure my utensils are properly stored." Each piece of kitchen equipment was tightly contained, and every cabinet door was closed with a latch. T.J. Brown chuckled. "This kitchen has a tendency to lurch around a little."

Continuing to the rear of the train, Emelia found a luxurious space with matching easy chairs in the back, a couch on one side and a dining table opposite. The space was surrounded by windows that afforded a near-circular view, and the floor was covered with plush carpeting. She walked all the way to the back of the car, turned around and settled into one of the overstuffed armchairs, only to discover that it would also swivel completely around.

She was looking out the back windows when a familiar but unexpected voice spun her around. "I was told that Jim Hill's newest employee would be aboard this train." There stood John Ireland, her Catholic bishop. "Good morning, Emelia," he said with a friendly grin.

"Father!" She was surprised by his presence. "What brings you here?"

"I'm traveling to the colonies."

Emelia's blank expression made the priest aware that she needed more of an explanation. He walked to the back of the railcar and settled into the matching easy chair. "Jim Hill and I have both participated in the settlement of Irish immigrants into several colonies in western Minnesota."

She listened.

"Already there are more than one thousand families, most of whom were suffering in unemployed poverty after immigrating from Ireland to eastern US cities. With Jim's help and support of the Catholic Church, we have relocated these people onto unoccupied farmlands."

"What's in it for Mr. Hill?" Emelia knew her boss well enough to suspect that he must have a profit motive in addition to his generosity.

"Well, he could explain that better than I," the bishop began, "but these colonies are all located along railroad lines. On this trip, I plan to visit Red River Valley settlements at DeGraff, Morris and Graceville, all of which are served by the St. Paul, Minneapolis and Manitoba Railway."

Emelia picked up the train of thought. "These one thousand families need supplies and equipment to build their towns and operate their farms, all of which will be delivered by trains."

"And the trains run both directions," Ireland added. "If these farm communities are successful, there will be railroad cargos of crops and livestock products delivered back to Minneapolis and St. Paul."

There was silence in the railcar while Emelia considered the many pluses and minuses of Red River agricultural trade that she would record in James J. Hill's accounting books. After that pause, she looked at the priest and said, "Mr. Hill should be here shortly. We are scheduled to leave soon."

Ireland laughed. "Oh, he won't be late. In the first place, he owns the train, so they won't leave without him. In the second place, he adheres to a very disciplined schedule."

"Yes, I know that."

"Jim Hill and I are quite a bit alike," the bishop commented. "We are both forty-two years old, barrel-chested, stubborn, ambitious… and we are both early risers. I was in church, listening to confessions before six o'clock this morning, and I'm sure he was working in his office by that time."

Emelia wondered, "Does Mr. Hill offer confessions?"

Ireland tilted his head. "Perhaps you don't know. Jim Hill is a protestant."

"But I have seen him in the Catholic Church with his family."

"Yes, he attends mass with Mary and the children," the priest granted, "and he is a very generous donor to our church. However, he has never officially joined our religion."

Emelia turned to look out the window and thought to herself, *If Mrs. Hill could be married outside of the Catholic Church, then I could...*

"Hello!" James J. Hill's booming voice interrupted her private thoughts, and Father Ireland stood to shake hands with her boss.

Emelia heard a short triple-toot of the locomotive's steam whistle, followed by revving of the engine. One by one, she heard the clink of couplings as each car inched ahead. Hill instinctively anticipated the train's movement and reached out to grasp one of the handrails. However, Ireland was caught off balance, and he plopped awkwardly backward into his cushioned chair when the car jolted gently forward.

The priest managed an embarrassed smile at the exposure of his railroad inexperience, "I was lucky for a soft landing," he snickered.

Hill and Ireland discussed their mutual interests in the Irish colonies scattered across western Minnesota, for the remainder of the morning. The business tycoon sat sideways beside his private dining table, sipping a cup of coffee that was kept hot and filled by frequent visits from T.J. Brown. Emelia and the bishop faced forward from their matching easy chairs. Ireland leaned forward in conversation most of the time while the girl reclined. She was silent but attentive to every word.

Hill described the expansive land grants along railroad routes, which amounted to hundreds of thousands of acres. Ireland explained his efforts to provide each settlement with a priest and a church, to which Hill responded by stating that this very train was carrying three cars of lumber and building supplies. A well-known opponent of alcoholism, the bishop declared his intent to ban liquor from the colonies. Hill chortled, "Good luck with that." Shaking his head, the businessman remarked, "I believe the Irish are much too fond of their beer and whiskey."

Ireland was anxious to report that many of the colony farms were growing bountiful wheat fields in the Red River Valley. "That's good," Hill hesitated, "but you know my preference for diversified agriculture."

"Yes," the priest assured him, "I am urging the farmers not to put all of their eggs into one basket."

"Thank you," Hill said. "Remind them that crop rotation will keep their soil fertile and provide defense against insects."

"Many of the farmers have expressed gratitude for the livestock you have donated to help them breed herds of cattle, hogs and sheep."

"That's good," Hill affirmed. "Meat, milk, eggs, hides and wool are year-round products, not just at harvest time."

Hours passed quickly, and soon, their noses told the riders that T.J. was preparing lunch. They shared a small but hearty meal, and not long after, the train pulled into the town of DeGraff, where Ireland disembarked. He would also visit Morris and Graceville, traveling by horse-drawn buggy, before catching the St. Paul, Minneapolis and Manitoba on its southbound return trip.

After the bishop's departure, Hill excused himself into his sleeping compartment, where he had an office desk beneath his bed. From the hallway, Emelia could see over the man's shoulder when he sat down and pulled a sheaf of papers onto the desktop. She proceeded into the next compartment and retrieved her notebook before sitting down to record as much information as she could remember from the morning's conversation.

Soon, the tracks curved straight northward to run alongside the flow of the Red River. The girl may have dozed off on her padded bench seat, but before she realized the afternoon's passage, the porter called her to supper. Her boss was already seated at the dining table when Emelia carefully settled onto an adjacent chair. "I may have fallen asleep," she admitted. "Your private car rolls so smoothly."

"I caught a catnap myself," Hill grinned. "The smooth ride is partly due to this car's especially long length, almost seventy-five feet from end to end. But I also have it equipped with extra heavy-duty springs that provide softer support than typical suspension for a railcar."

During and after supper, Hill prepared Emelia for the next business associate she would meet on the train. "Norman Kittson is a partner of mine who used to be a competitor. He is in his mid-sixties, which makes him a quarter-century older than me, but the man is still a sharp wheeler-dealer. He started as a fur trader competing against Henry Sibley until the American Fur Company got smart enough to make him a partner. Norm established a trading post at the village of Pembina, and he has earned the trust of people up and down the Red River Valley on both sides of the Canadian border."

"Canada?"

"Yes. He and I became partners in the Red River Transportation Company ten years ago, and we own five steamboats that carry cargo between Fargo and Winnipeg."

"Steamboats?"

"Yes, we have a shipping monopoly on the river, which has helped both of us become millionaires." Hill paused and looked out the window. "However, the steamboats will become obsolete now that our train tracks connect with the Canadian Pacific Railroad."

"So, Kittson is a partner in the St. Paul, Minneapolis and Manitoba Railway?"

"Yes, a very important partner."

"In that case," said Emelia, "I look forward to meeting him."

"That will come in the morning," Hill said. "Our train will stop at the international border sometime after dark tonight, and Norm will meet us there for breakfast." The man stood up and stretched, then called toward the kitchen. "Are the dishes done, T.J.? It's time for a smoke."

The porter came around the corner and tossed an apron back onto the kitchen counter. He strode to the rear of the car, between the easy chairs and out the back door, which Hill held open onto a small outdoor platform covered by the car's extended roof. The business tycoon produced a pair of big cigars, handed one to T.J. and struck a match to light both tobacco rolls. The two men stood relaxed beside the platform railing, watched cigar smoke trail away behind the rolling train, and shared satisfied smiles.

Feeling like an intruder, Emelia left the dining area and retired to her compartment, where she sat alone and looked out the windows, watching the distant Dakota plains pass by. Gradually, the cloudless western summer sky changed in color from blue to golden, then orange, pink, purple and finally black. She changed into her nightgown, let loose her hair, and climbed up onto the bed.

Lying on her back in the darkness, Emelia could hear the distant purr of the locomotive engine and consistently repeating clinks when each railcar rolled over a joint between steel rails. She could feel the vibration of revolving wheels and the train's gentle sway from side to side. It was a soothing combination of sounds and sensations that would surely put her to sleep in a few miles. However, the girl lay awake because she could not suppress her excitement to be a part of this adventure. Minnesota was growing by fifty thousand people a year, stampeding here from Europe and eastern states to find opportunities in agriculture, lumber and transportation. It was an economic and cultural revolution, and how exciting, she thought, to play a role in the amazing transition.

* * *

Sometime during the night, the train had eased to a stop beside the small villages of St. Vincent, Minnesota, and Pembina, North Dakota, divided from each other by the Red River. It was an hour after sunrise when Norman Kittson bounded up the back steps of James J. Hill's private railcar and entered from the rear platform. There was a spring in the step of the man's wiry frame. To Emelia, he looked much younger than his sixty-some years and seemed elegantly dressed for this time of day.

"Good morning, Jim," Kittson cheerfully greeted his host and extended a small package wrapped in paper. "I brought you some good Canadian bacon." Hill accepted the package and pivoted to carry it to the kitchen while the visitor turned to Emelia. "What a pleasure to meet you, my dear." Kittson bowed slightly and gently squeezed the fingers of her extended hand.

"This is the girl I've told you about," Hill said, returning. "She's a financial whiz."

The group sat down at three sides of the dining table, and T.J. was quickly serving coffee while they began to talk about railroad business.

Hill said, "Norm, you have done marvelous work gaining cooperation with the Canadian Pacific."

"We have an international alliance with them now," Kittson said. "Our St. Paul, Minneapolis and Manitoba trains are allowed to travel all the way to Winnipeg, and the Canadian Pacific Railway can use our tracks down to Grand Forks."

"That's about seventy-five miles, both directions from the border."

"In addition," Kittson continued, "we agree to pull their cargo to final destinations, and they will do likewise for us."

"This deal should benefit both railroads."

"Yes, they recognize the mutual advantages. Plus, it has been a big help that both of us were born in Canada."

"You from Quebec and me from Ontario," Hill nodded, then reached out to grip Kittson by the shoulder. "But you are the one who earned their trust with your history of cultural and economic loyalty." Hill turned to Emelia and explained, "Norm married into the Metis culture of mixed white and Native ancestry decades ago. Since then, he has forged a reputation for honest trading with every race and nationality."

"What's next for our railroad?" Kittson asked.

"We will keep laying tracks to the northwest, as straight and level as we can," Hill answered. "Maybe someday, to the Pacific Ocean."

* * *

Michael Barnes

The Pillsburys

John S. Pillsbury (1827–1901)

John S. Pillsbury departed from the family's native New Hampshire domain in 1855 to settle in Minnesota and open a hardware store. He married Mahala Fisk one year later when he was twenty-nine and she twenty-four. The couple built a home in St. Anthony at the corner of Fifth Street and Tenth Avenue, where they raised four children and lived the remainder of their lives.[59]

John entered politics at age thirty-six and served twelve years in the state senate before being elected governor in 1875. Minnesotans chose him to lead the state through three terms that spanned the devastating four-year grasshopper plague. As governor, Pillsbury visited the most afflicted counties twice and, with Mahala, organized a statewide charity campaign to aid victims of the infestation.[60]

Nicknamed "Father of the University," John joined the board of regents in 1863 and served on that body for thirty-seven years.

222

Water Wheels

All four Pillsbury children attended the University of Minnesota. He raised money to fund the university by managing timberlands under the federal Morrill Act, donated personal funds to pay college debts after financial panics and the Civil War and paid to build the Pillsbury Science Hall on campus. Generous supporters of many other civic projects, the couple established the Pillsbury State Forest, opened several public libraries, and gave to numerous disaster relief efforts. Mahala was a founder of Northwestern Hospital for Women and Children, the predecessor of today's Abbott Northwestern Hospital.[61]

Charles A. Pillsbury (1842–1899)

An 1863 graduate of Dartmouth College, Charles A. Pillsbury arrived in Minneapolis when he was twenty-seven with his wife, Mary Ann. The larger Pillsbury family had recently purchased a flour mill near St. Anthony Falls, and Charles came to manage the facility.

Proving enormously profitable, the Pillsbury Company expanded, purchasing four additional flour mills over the next six years.[62]

Charles served eight years in the state senate while his uncle John was governor, but he devoted most of his time to business rather than politics. The Pillsbury mills were renowned for adopting new technology, which enhanced the reputation of their "Pillsbury's Best XXXX" flour that was sold around the world. Charles is credited with beginning one of the nation's first employee profit-sharing programs, and he opened the Pillsbury A-Mill in 1882, the largest and most modern flour mill of its time. Charles is credited with streamlining the Pillsbury Company into a vertical monopoly, with ownership into each vital part of the grain business: farmland, grain elevators, flour mills, railroads and banks.[63]

Charles and Mary Ann had four children in Minneapolis, two who died in childhood and twin sons, both of whom became executives in the Pillsbury Company[64].

Fred C. Pillsbury (1852–1892)

Water Wheels

Fred C. Pillsbury and his brother Charles were sons of George A. Pillsbury, born in New Hampshire ten years apart. Eighteen-year-old Fred came to Minneapolis in 1870 and went to work as a clerk in his uncle John's hardware store. However, he moved to employment with the booming flour mills within five years.[65]

Fred maintained a close relationship with the University of Minnesota's agriculture department and brought scientific advancements to the Pillsbury Company. He maintained a 120-acre livestock farm near Lake Minnetonka, where experimental seeds and feeds were tested. Fred was an enthusiastic trotting horse racer and member of the State Agricultural Society, which was key to promoting the Minnesota State Fair during its early decades.[66]

Fred and his wife Alice had a family of five children. Unfortunately, he died of diphtheria at age thirty-nine when the children were between the ages of three and thirteen.[67]

George A. Pillsbury (1816–1898)

225

George A. Pillsbury lived most of his life in New Hampshire, where he was a successful businessman and civic leader. But after his parents died, George and his wife Margaret moved to Minneapolis to be near their sons Charles and Fred.[68]

Shortly after his arrival, at age sixty-two, George assumed the construction manager job for the Pillsbury A-Mill, which would become the world's largest and most modern flour mill. Simultaneously, the elder statesman became active in local politics, winning election to the school board and Minneapolis city council. George pushed successfully to provide city parks, improve the sewer system and eliminate government corruption, which won him the position of mayor in 1884. After leaving city hall, he took on one more construction project—the building of the Minneapolis Grain Exchange, now listed in the US National Register of Historic Places.[69]

Chapter 14
Steamboat Race
1882

Emelia Meier looked up from her desk at James J. Hill Company headquarters when the office secretary knocked on the frame of her open door. It was after five o'clock on this early October afternoon, and she was almost ready to go home.

"A young man is here to see you," said the secretary.

Emelia glanced at her empty appointment calendar. "I was not expecting anyone."

With a raised eyebrow, the secretary added, "He says his name is Halvor Dahl."

Emelia stood behind her desk when Halvor entered. He was wearing a dark, conservative suit, more expensive and finely tailored than she had seen on him before.

"Hello, Emelia," he smiled nervously, not knowing whether to stand or sit in the leather chair that faced her desk.

"It's nice to see you, Halvor." She settled into her chair and gestured for him to be seated. "What brings you over to St. Paul?"

"I wondered if you would like to see the comet with me."

Since they had not seen each other in more than a year, Emelia asked, "What made you think to ask me?"

"You're the smartest girl I know," Halvor said without hesitation. "I thought you would be interested in the historic event."

She was indeed curious about the heavenly phenomenon that scientists were calling the "Great Comet of 1882," so she asked, "How would we see it?"

"Skies are expected to be clear this week," Halvor answered. "The best time to see it is before sunrise, between four-thirty and five-thirty in the morning." He slid forward to the edge of his seat. "We should try to watch from a high elevation, with a view toward the southeast."

"I know just such a spot," Emelia offered. "The crest of Summit Hill. It's about two hundred fifty feet above the river and only a few blocks up the bluff from here."

"How about Friday?" he suggested. "I'll pick you up at quarter past four, right in front of this building."

Sure enough, a few days later, Halvor was waiting on the street with a carriage borrowed from Fred Pillsbury. He gave Emelia a hand up onto the seat and offered a blanket to cover her knees against the cool, crisp predawn air.

They trotted quickly away from the downtown streetlamps and up Wilkin Street to the summit, where an ornate Victorian house was under construction. Emelia pointed at the half-built mansion. "That house is being built by Norm Kittson, my boss's partner." Then, directing Halvor to circle across the avenue, she said, "Mr. Hill has purchased three adjoining lots on the south side of Bluff Street. He's planning to build an even bigger house right here."

"This should be an excellent spot to see the comet," Halvor remarked.

During the next half hour, several other people gathered on the promontory, where they watched the comet blazing low along the horizon. One of the observers, a professor from Hamline University, shared some of the scientific information he knew. "The head of a comet is a huge chunk of ice and dust. This one is extraordinarily big, maybe two hundred miles in diameter."

"What about the tail?" Halvor asked, pointing at the glowing stream that flared behind the head.

"Comets orbit the sun in very elongated ovals," the professor said, "and have no tails at all when they're millions of miles into freezing outer space. But when they circle close to the sun, like this one, some of their ice melts away to leave a visible vapor trail."

Emelia wondered aloud, "How fast is it going?"

"Astronomers believe this comet is traveling eighty-four thousand miles per hour, and that tail is sixteen thousand miles long."

The sun had not risen by five-thirty, but from beneath the horizon, it cast enough light into the eastern sky that the comet began to fade from view.

"I'm hungry," said Halvor. "How about some breakfast?"

Emelia agreed, suggesting the Windsor Hotel might be the only place open at this hour. "It's expensive," she said. "I'll split the bill with you."

The food was good, and they shared an easy conversation, exchanging stories about the launch of their young careers, working for two of Minnesota's most famous business tycoons.

As usual, James J. Hill was already at his work desk when Halvor delivered Emelia back to the office. She stood in the doorway and watched her friend drive away. "That was nice," she thought to herself. "He's nice."

* * *

It was an early December afternoon when Jim Hill and Norm Kittson burst into the downtown St. Paul office. They stamped their feet and unbuttoned winter coats, trying to warm themselves while buffeting tiny snowflakes from their garments.

Hill stuck his head into Emelia's doorway. "Come join us." She quickly collected a notebook and stepped across the corridor into his much more spacious office.

Kittson stood and gently grasped her fingertips. "My pleasure to see you again, Miss Meier."

"I saw your new house a couple of months ago," she said. "It looks beautiful."

"I'll be glad to spend the winter in St. Paul," he commented. "I've grown too old for the North Dakota blizzards." He gave a gentlemanly nod. "Your boss and I have just returned from Minneapolis, where we spent the morning assessing the progress of his new projects at St. Anthony Falls."

Hill stated, "Our underground canal to provide waterpower into St. Anthony is working perfectly, and construction of the Stone Arch Bridge looks good."

"Looks good indeed," Kittson exclaimed. "It's a beautiful structure of form and function, high and wide enough to support two trains at once, traveling opposite directions across the Mississippi River."

"Thanks for your endorsement," Hill said, "but Emelia's duties are not directly connected to either one of those projects." He turned to her. "Rather, Norm is here to report about potential trouble for the St. Paul, Minneapolis and Manitoba Railway." He leaned back and waited for his elder partner to proceed.

"Well, there *was* trouble thirteen years ago," Kittson began. "The Red River Valley erupted in a violent rebellion when the Canadian government tried to take greater control of the valley where Native and Metis people of mixed ancestry had lived for generations. An educated Metis named Louis Riel led the establishment of a provisional government that demanded property rights, religious liberty and political representation in Canada's parliament."

Emelia looked up with her pen in hand. "Sounds reasonable."

"Yes, but Riel's people imprisoned some Canadian protestants and killed one of the white leaders. Eventually, Manitoba became a Canadian province, and many Native rights were preserved. However, Riel was pursued as a criminal."

"That was thirteen years ago?"

"True," Kittson admitted, "but he's still a polarizing individual. English Canadians believe he should be hanged as a traitor, while French Canadians and Catholic Metis consider him the Father of Manitoba. They have elected him a legislator to Canada's parliament three times, even though he's hiding in exile in the United States."

"So how is this connected to our St. Paul, Minneapolis and Manitoba Railway?"

Water Wheels

"I recently visited Riel at his home in Montana," Kittson said. "It is clear that he considers himself God's chosen leader of the Metis people, many of whom live in the Saskatchewan Valley, where Canadian National Railway tracks are being laid. If he returns to Canada and another violent rebellion explodes, our shipments to and from the Pacific Ocean could be disrupted."

Hill rocked forward and bellowed, "All the more reason for us to begin laying our own westward tracks on the US side of the border."

"Your own transcontinental railroad?" Kittson reacted to Hill's ambitious proposal. "Sounds like you intend to be an empire builder."

* * *

While James J. Hill was planning his massive railroad project to the Pacific Ocean, another group of Minnesota merchants was plotting a railroad connection to the Atlantic. W.D. Washburn was spearheading the "Soo Line," officially titled the Minneapolis, St. Paul and Sault Ste. Marie Railroad, with fourteen other primary investors. They were a team of Minneapolis bankers, grocers, lumbermen and flour millers, including John and Charles Pillsbury.

By laying tracks across northern Wisconsin, the Soo Line sliced between Lake Superior and Lake Huron to connect with the Canadian Pacific Railway. This route shortened the distance to northern Europe by three hundred miles and, more importantly, allowed the Minneapolis entrepreneurs to set their own shipping rates rather than pay more expensive cargo fees charged by rival railroads. It was a fantastic success. Original Soo Line stockholders saw the value of their investment quadruple in the next sixteen years.

This railroad competition between W.D. Washburn and James J. Hill was only one piece of a rivalry that developed between the two men, who could hardly have been more different. Washburn got started in Minneapolis with a boost from his wealthy brother after graduating from Bowdoin College. Hill's schooling ended at age fourteen when his father died, and he started as a dockworker on the St. Paul riverfront. Washburn was a political orator who spent twelve years in the US Congress while trusted employees managed his business affairs. Hill tried to influence politicians from behind the scenes, but he never trusted others to control the daily details of his numerous enterprises. A tall, handsome man, W.D. wore stylish clothing and enjoyed an extravagant social life. The stocky, muscular Hill always dressed in a plain dark suit and disdained social revelry in favor of lengthy workdays or quiet family weekends.

The winter of 1882–83 found Washburn at the busiest point in his life. He and his wife Lizzy were building an eighty-room mansion on ten acres in Minneapolis, which they named Fair Oaks. It would be home for their six children and a showplace for political and business parties. Older brother C.C. Washburn had died the previous spring, leaving fifty-one-year-old W.D. in charge of their joint flour mill operations. In addition to his railroads, W.D. independently owned timberlands and sawmills, the *Minneapolis Journal* newspaper, and a brand-new hydroelectric company,.

Lake Minnetonka became a focal point for the rivalry between W.D. Washburn and James J. Hill. They both owned railroads that skirted the lake: Washburn's Minneapolis and St. Louis Railway along the south shore and Hill's Minneapolis, St. Paul and Sault Ste. Marie Railroad to the north. Tourists could exit either train to dine or lodge at their choice of deluxe resort: Washburn's Lake Park Hotel or Hill's Hotel Lafayette. In the summer of 1881, Washburn launched a luxury steamboat, the *City of St. Louis,* to tour guests around the lake. Not to be outdone, Hill floated an even larger vessel, the *Belle of Minnetonka,* the very next year. So, it came as no surprise when a match race between the two steamboats was scheduled for the last Saturday in May of 1883.

* * *

A remarkable coincidence occurred several days before the steamboat race when America's most famous riverboat pilot appeared in Minnesota. While researching for his next novel, *Life on the Mississippi,* Mark Twain landed on the St. Paul riverfront.

232

Water Wheels

He grew up in Hannibal, Missouri, as Samuel Clemens and steered steamboats up and down the Mississippi River for several years before the Civil War temporarily halted river commerce. Now, using the pen name Mark Twain, he was the famous author of numerous best-selling stories, including *Tom Sawyer*. The purpose of this two-week voyage upriver from New Orleans was to rekindle his memories of life on the Mississippi and inspire creative composition.

Twain was welcomed to St. Paul by, among others, James J. Hill and Harlan Hall, editor of the *Daily Globe* newspaper. After providing Hall with answers to a string of interview questions, the author dropped a humorous quote on the local journalist. "If you don't read the newspaper, you're uninformed. If you do read the newspaper, you're misinformed." It was difficult to see the sly smile that curled beneath Mark Twain's drooping mustache.

Hill shared information about the forthcoming steamboat race and invited the famous writer to be his guest aboard the *Belle of Minnetonka*. Until race day, the tycoon suggested that Twain reside in a rent-free room at his Hotel Lafayette.

"Thank you, I accept." Then, well aware of Hill's multimillionaire status, the humorist said, "I can turn a phrase, Mr. Hill, but when it comes to turning a profit," he paused before poking fun at his own poor track record with financial investments, "I am seldom able to see an opportunity until it ceases to be one."

* * *

One glimpse of shaggy blonde hair told Halvor that his friend Emil Lindstrom had arrived from the north woods. The slender young Swede stepped down from the train and searched helplessly for a familiar face amid a throng of people on the depot platform. Halvor was not tall enough to be seen wiggling through the crowd, but he suddenly appeared within handshake distance. "Welcome to Minneapolis."

"Pony!" Emil shouted. He dropped his travel bag and reached out both hands to grasp Halvor by the biceps. Their eyes quickly scanned each other up and down, looking for physical changes that may have occurred during their six years apart. Emil had grown a blonde goatee that formed a neat oval around his mouth and chin. Otherwise, each young man found the other basically unchanged, though a little thicker in the midsection. The Swede was as cheerful and talkative as ever.

The idea for this visit originated with an exchange of letters between the two friends. Emil expressed his desire to see the big city, and Halvor suggested this final weekend in May. Halvor was taking Friday off from his job to tour Emil around Minneapolis. On Saturday, they would attend the big steamboat race on Lake Minnetonka.

"Let's get out of this crowd," Halvor suggested, and he began guiding Emil from the train depot toward his boardinghouse in St. Anthony. They paused on the Tenth Avenue Bridge to look up the magnificent Mississippi River toward St. Anthony Falls. Halvor pointed at the palisade of twenty flour mills, including Washburn's rebuilt A-Mill on the west bank and Pillsbury's new A-Mill on the east bank. "The flour milling industry exploded in Minnesota during the last decade," Halvor said, "to make this the number-one flour-producing location in America."

"Why?" Emil wondered.

"It was a simultaneous combination of factors." Halvor pointed at the waterfall. "First, there's the immense waterpower provided by this river." He swept his hand to gesture beyond the western horizon. "And upper midwestern farmland has proven ideal for growing grain." Halvor paused. "Since the Civil War, Minnesota's population has more than doubled with wheat farmers and potential factory workers. Then, technology advanced with farm machinery, new milling equipment and railroad transportation." He nodded at a cargo train just now rolling across the brand-new Stone Arch Bridge.

"Could you show me where you work?" Emil asked.

"Sure," Halvor answered. "Let's drop your bag at the boardinghouse and get something to eat. Then I'll give you a tour of the biggest flour mill in the world."

Water Wheels

After supper, the evening sun cast a glow on the Pillsbury A-Mill's exterior. "It's a beautiful building," Emil said.

"Yes," Halvor agreed, "old George Pillsbury insisted on hiring local architect LeRoy Buffington, who designed these gray limestone walls with recessed arching windows."

Once inside the seven-story building, Emil noticed several workers offered friendly greetings to Halvor, calling him by name. The Swede was also fascinated by glowing interior light bulbs rather than burning lanterns. "We generate our own electricity with hydropower," Halvor said. Then, he guided Emil into an elevator that lowered them into the basement.

It was noisy here, with the sound of rushing water that entered the building through an underground canal to turn whirling turbines. "Natural flow from the Mississippi is all we need in spring and summer," Halvor shouted over the noise before pointing to machinery in a darkened corner, "but when the river level drops in fall and winter, we have steam engines to power the entire mill."

Halvor showed Emil where the raw wheat seeds entered the building and where they passed through a series of steel rollers to separate their layers. They walked into an adjoining area. "This is a new section of the mill we call the 'bran house.' Here, parts of the wheat we used to throw away, the hull and bran, are processed into livestock feed."

"Less waste and more profit?"

"Yes," Halvor confirmed, "and the feed is proving especially nutritious for animals that are eating it."

Eventually, they reached the end of the process, where finished flour was collected into cotton bags just inside the railroad dock. Emil was surprised to see a team of girls handling twenty-five-pound sacks, labeled Pillsbury's Best XXXX.

"We brought these ideas home from Europe," Halvor said. "Cotton bags are cheaper than wooden barrels and pack more tightly into a train car. We buy the sacks in different sizes from twenty-five to one hundred pounds, and the female workers can easily handle the smaller ones."

235

Walking back to the boardinghouse, it suddenly occurred to Halvor that he had not noticed any old scars from Emil's battle with the white wolf. He turned to look and saw that the mangled ear was hidden beneath his friend's shaggy hair. The vicious gash that Cookee had stitched from Emil's left nostril, down and around his chin, was now concealed by the outline of his well-trimmed blonde goatee.

In that moment of silence, Emil detected Halvor's stare and guessed what he was thinking.

"You can barely see the teeth marks." The young Swede grinned and stroked his wispy whiskers.

Halvor self-consciously glanced aside. "You look good either way."

"That's what my fiancée says."

"Your fiancée?"

"Marta and I will be married next month," Emil declared. "I'm a top hand cook now, and all my years of logging camp wages have enabled us to buy a farm along the western shore of Little Lake. Hammer has helped me build a home for us near a small bay in the lake's northwest corner.

"Next month?"

"I hope you can come," Emil beamed. "Swedish weddings offer amazing smorgasbords."

* * *

On Saturday morning, Halvor and Emil joined a crowd of people who boarded a special run of W.D. Washburn's "Tootin' Louie" train from Minneapolis to the village of Excelsior. The little town was home to four hundred residents on the southern edge of Lake Minnetonka.

The boys made their way to the Lake Park Hotel, Washburn's luxury lakeside resort. With the beginning of summer, many tourists would arrive to fill the hotel's two hundred guest rooms. An abundance of these would be wealthy southerners escaping their sultry temperatures to enjoy the weather and water in Minnesota.

Water Wheels

Halvor led Emil to the grand hotel dining room, where he intended to treat his weekend guest to a gourmet lunch. Upon arrival, he found Fred Pillsbury and his wife Alice seated with another young couple. Halvor approached their table. "Hi, Fred. My friend Emil and I have come out to watch the big steamboat race."

Fred stood up. "Nice to meet you, Emil." He opened his hand to the others. "This is my wife Alice and our friends, Andreas Ueland and Clara Hampson. Why don't you join us for lunch?"

"Oh, we shouldn't intrude," Halvor said.

But Pillsbury objected, "Nonsense, we're all on Team Minneapolis. As fellow flour millers and partners in Washburn's Soo Line Railroad, we have to stick together." Fred motioned for a waiter to bring two more chairs, and he sat back down before introducing Halvor. "This is Halvor Dahl, the head miller at our new Pillsbury A-Mill. He and I work closely with the University of Minnesota agriculture department, where he is a recently honored graduate."

"And he saved my life." Emil's abrupt statement dropped a moment of silence over the table. But the talkative Swede was soon entertaining the group with tales of wolves and lumberjacks and "Pony's" horsemanship skills.

Halvor simply listened to the conversation, but he learned that Andreas Ueland was, like himself, a Norwegian immigrant. After only twelve years in America, Ueland was a licensed attorney providing legal advice to the Pillsburys. Clara, his fiancée, was a beautiful blonde-haired schoolteacher in Minneapolis who clearly had a mind of her own.

When lunch was complete, Fred said, "We were invited on Washburn's boat. You should join us."

"Whoa," Halvor protested. "We came to *watch* the steamboats, not *ride* on one."

However, Fred insisted, and Emil accepted for both. "This will be fantastic," he declared, marching out onto the pier where the *City of St. Louis* was moored. Flags flew atop the one-hundred-sixty-foot vessel propelled by matching paddle wheels, one on each side.

The group climbed a stairway to stand forward on the second deck, where Pillsbury described the racecourse. "It's a four-mile race in the shape of a horseshoe," he said. "Out of Gideon's Bay, the pilot will bear northeast past Big Island, out into the main body of the lower lake. Then we'll curve around to the left and charge back southwest into Lafayette Bay, just below James J. Hill's hotel."

* * *

Emelia was among a group of passengers who rode the Minneapolis, St. Paul and Salt Ste. Marie train out to Mr. Hill's Lafayette Hotel on the morning of the big steamboat race. She was slightly the oldest in her trio of girlfriends; Louisa Hamm and Mamie Hill were one and two years younger than she. They walked to the hotel on the crest of a peninsula ridge, from which tourists could view north or south down onto Crystal Bay or Lafayette Bay. Hill's resort was newer and larger than Washburn's Lake Park Hotel. Three hundred rooms were lodged beneath a multi-gabled roof, and a covered veranda ran the entire seven-hundred-foot length of the building.

The girls had just encountered the famous author Mark Twain in his trademark white suit when they neared a magnificent hedge of blooming lilac bushes. Growing beside a curving path, the purple blossoms were gorgeous, and their fragrance more pleasant than expensive perfume. Just then, a stray dog emerged from the bushes and lifted one hind leg to relieve himself upon a lilac blossom. Mamie giggled as she and Louisa turned red in front of the esteemed writer. Whereupon, Twain remarked, "Man is the only animal that blushes... or needs to."

After lunch, the guests of James J. Hill walked down to the shore where his boat, the *Belle of Minnetonka*, was tied to a large dock. The *Belle* was huge, almost double the *City's* length, and equipped to carry one thousand additional passengers. Hill's supporters who climbed aboard were mostly business and social associates, primarily with St. Paul connections. Everybody found a spot to relax and enjoy the lake scenery during their leisurely trip to the village of Excelsior, where the race would begin.

Water Wheels

Along the way, Emelia and her friends were approached by a slender-shouldered young man about their age. "I'm Richard Sears," he announced, "owner of the R. W. Sears Watch Company."

The girls introduced themselves, and Sears took a step forward upon hearing the famous names of Hamm and Hill. "Where is your store?" Emelia asked.

"I don't have a store," he responded. "Rather, I advertise all over the state and use train delivery to fill mail orders."

When the start of the race at one o'clock was imminent, two people made their way to the tip of Sunrise Point, which marked the starting line. One hoisted a large US flag, and the other held a pistol in hand. The sun-drenched flag was flapping smartly in a northwesterly breeze, which would blow sideways against the steamboats for most of the race.

Emelia turned back to Sears. "I have heard Mr. Hill talk about doing business by mail order."

"That's how I got his invitation onto this boat," boasted the young Minnesotan. "He wants to talk with me about the relationship between mail order business and railroad delivery."

The *Belle's* pilot circled his big vessel around Gideon's Bay and slowly pulled parallel to the *City's* starboard side. From her vantage point on the middle deck, Emelia could see passengers on the rival boat, and there was Halvor Dahl. He was in a happy group of young men and women.

Then, Emelia recognized one of the women, Clara Hampson, with whom she had shared a blanket at Maria Sanford's symposium the night that Washburn's mill exploded. They had met again two years ago at the founding convention of the Minnesota Women's Suffrage Association in Hastings. Clara was beautiful, and Emelia caught herself wondering if she and Halvor were a couple. *Why should I care?* she scolded herself.

"Someday, I will be selling a lot more than watches," Sears declared. His voice jogged Emelia out of her inner thoughts, and he continued, "The Sears Company will publish a catalog with hundreds of mail-order products."

At that moment, Emelia saw across the *City's* bow, the starting pistol was fired into the air, and the US flag waved in a figure-eight. Suddenly, the steam engines of both boats roared to life, smoke billowed out of their twin exhaust pipes and the rival vessels surged forward.

Washburn's smaller craft was lighter in the water and pushed ahead initially. Past Gale Island and Point Charming, Hill's more powerful boat gradually gained until it nosed in front at the two-mile halfway point. However, rounding Big Island into the wide-open lower lake, the *Belle's* massive size was exposed to the strongest wind and waves. The more maneuverable *City* made a tighter turn through shallower water and once again got sideways to the breeze.

Emelia was wearing her hair down today, and it unfurled behind her shoulders as Hill's larger craft slowly fought to turn against the wind. Bigger waves crashed against the forward hull, scattering a sparkling spray of mist through the sunlight. It was exhilarating to feel the water droplets glisten against her face, but now Emelia saw that the *Belle* faced an even larger deficit than at the start. The steam engines rumbled louder than ever, but soon, only one mile remained to close the gap. It was not enough. The bow of Washburn's sleeker boat was narrowly in front when the finish line flag was waved from Huntington's Point.

The St. Paul contingent was noticeably quiet, and the Minneapolis passengers were conspicuously loud as their boats cruised into Lafayette Bay. When the *City* approached the dock, dozens of rambunctious Washburn supporters climbed over the boat railing and jumped into the lake to celebrate. Emelia looked down to see a fully clothed Halvor Dahl, standing in waist-deep water and waving for her to join him.

She heard Richard Sears's voice of disapproval behind her. "That is bad behavior."

Then, from along the railing, white-suited Mark Twain offered a retort. "Be good... and you will be lonesome."

Emelia looked sideways at the author, that word "lonesome" sticking in her mind. Suddenly, she had one leg over the railing and was sailing through the air. She splashed into the lake and was instantly in Halvor's arms, where they shared the wettest embrace in Minnesota.

* * *

Cadwallader Colden "C.C." Washburn (1818–1882)

C.C. traveled west from his native Maine when he was twenty-one, settling in Wisconsin Territory, where he became an attorney specializing in real estate. Washburn was soon purchasing forest land and harvesting trees to sell for lumber, then reselling the cleared land to pioneer settlers.[70]

A Republican politician opposed to slavery, C.C. was appointed a general during the Civil War. He served twelve years in the US House of Representatives and was eventually elected Governor of Wisconsin in 1871.[71]

Washburn made Lacrosse, Wisconsin, his home and headquarters for his lumber empire that stretched into the major river valleys of western Wisconsin. Ironically, flour milling became his most profitable business despite his late entry into the industry and his absence from St. Anthony Falls. He did take charge after the 1878 A-Mill explosion and supervised the reconstruction of a bigger, more efficient and safer factory.[72]

William Drew "W.D." Washburn (1831–1912)

Thirteen years younger than his brother C.C., W.D. followed him to the upper Midwest after graduating from Bowdoin College. He became the manager of the family's Minneapolis Mill Company at age twenty-seven, which included a water canal from St. Anthony Falls that powered more than a dozen Minneapolis mills.[73]

During the nineteenth century's final two decades, W.D. was the leading political, business and social celebrity in Minneapolis. He was a US Senator, partner in the Washburn-Crosby flour mills, a lumber baron in his own right, president of the Soo Line Railroad, owner of North Dakota coal mines, a hydro-electric company, and a Minneapolis newspaper. With wife Lizzy, they raised a family of seven children and built Fair Oaks, a ten-acre showplace estate where Minnesota's powerful elite came to party.[74]

C.C. was a more conservative business executive than W.D. and the older brother saved his family from bankruptcy during the Panic of 1873. After Cadwallader's death, however, William Drew's risky ventures and lavish lifestyle ended in the loss of the entire W.D. Washburn fortune.[75]

Questions for Readers

Minnesota's Department of Education recommends that students learn "Minnesota Studies" during the middle grades. Learning standards and benchmarks are established for state history, civics, economics, geography, and sociology. Here are five sample questions designed to use *Water Wheels* as a resource for learning about Minnesota in each of these categories.

1. HISTORY: Several historic events occur during the story *Water Wheels*, including natural phenomena (Blizzard of 1873, Grasshopper Plague, Great Comet of 1882) and man-made calamities (Panic of 1873, James Gang Bank Raid, Washburn A-Mill Explosion).

   Can you pretend to be a television reporter on the six o'clock news, and record a two-minute video in which you describe one of these events?

2. CIVICS: Every chapter in *Water Wheels* is followed by brief biographies of authentic Minnesota individuals. These people were entrepreneurs, politicians, authors, and religious or social leaders.

   In your opinion, which of them had the greatest positive impact on lives of Minnesotans? Why?

3. ECONOMICS: One hundred and fifty years ago, Minnesota was America's #1 producer of flour.

   Can you draw a cartoon strip, or story board, or picture map to show the process of making flour, from farm field to grocery store?

4. GEOGRAPHY: Families of the two main characters in *Water Wheels* were immigrants from Germany and Norway, and according to U.S. census bureau statistics from the year 1880, nearly half the people in Minnesota were first or second generation European immigrants.

   Can you make a chart, listing ways that immigrants' lives became better or worse when they moved from their native country to Minnesota? Try to list three examples in each category.

5. SOCIOLOGY: Emelia Meier grew up during a time when America was a male-dominated society.

   Can you describe three ways that women of today have greater equality than they did one hundred and fifty years ago? Try to explain how that happened.

Acknowledgments

I am indebted to my family for the creation of this book—precious partnership of my wife Kelly, generous support from my parents Bill and Marge, steadfast affection from sons Greg and Andy, and the inspiring curiosity of grand-daughters Madison, Claire, Sylvia, and Lucy.

Sincere gratitude to my friend and fellow teacher Barb Parrish for guiding the grammar and educational direction of this text.

My appreciation for the Minnesota Historical Society of which I am a member. Their online and printed publications are a treasure trove of stories, and preserved historical sites that offer unique opportunities to touch our past.

Thank you to Calumet Editions, especially Ian Graham Leask and Gary Lindberg, for their publishing expertise and faith in the *North Star Kids*.

About the Author

Water Wheels is the second book in Michael Barnes' "North Star Kids" series, following *Twisting Trails*, published by Calumet Editions in 2020. The series provides young adults with historical fiction adventures, which are based on factual Minnesota people, places and events.

As a retired social studies educator who taught history, geography, sociology, civics, and economics, Barnes is uniquely qualified to write these books. A resident of Minnesota for more than fifty years, Barnes has enjoyed unique wonders in every corner of the state. An avid outdoorsman, he has fished Minnesota lakes and rivers and hunted its fields and forests. He is a married (Kelly) father of two (Greg and Andy), and four granddaughters (Madison, Claire, Sylvia and Lucy).

Endnotes

1 Minnesota Historical Society, Oliver Kelley Farm, https://www.mnhs. org/kelleyfarm.

2 Thomas A. Woods, *Knights of the Plow: Oliver H. Kelley and the Origins of the Grange in Republican Ideology* (Iowa State University Press, 1991).

3 Ibid.

4 Oliver Kelley Farm.

5 Minnesota Historical Society, State Grange of Minnesota, MNOpedia, https://bit.ly/3KfmolP.

6 Martin Ridge, *Ignatius Donnelly: The Portrait of a Politician* (Minnesota Historical Society Press: St. Paul, 1991).

7 Zac Farber, "Ignatius Donnelly: Paranoid Progressive in the Gilded Age," May 30, 2018, https://bit.ly/3pWHDSQ.

8 Ridge, *Ignatius Donnelly*.

9 Rhoda Gilman, "Donnelly, Ignatius (1831–1901)," MNOpedia, https:// bit.ly/3Y9tLRA.

10 James M. Moynihan, *The Life of Archbishop John Ireland* (Harper & Brothers Publishers: New York, 1953).

11 Kate Roberts, "Ireland, John (1838–1918)," MNOpedia, https://bit. ly/3DApyNk.

12 Marvin R. O'Connell, *John Ireland and the American Catholic Church* (Minnesota Historical Society Press: St. Paul, 1988).

13 Moynihan, *The Life of Archbishop John Ireland*.

14 Bob Sandeen, "Bob Looks Back: The Great Storm of 1873," Nicollet County Historical Society, https://bit.ly/3Yb3Adk.

15 Paul Clifford Larson, *Icy Pleasures: Minnesota Celebrates Winter* (Afton Historical Society Press: Afton, Minnesota, 1998).

16 Dana R. Bailey, *History of Minnehaha County, South Dakota* (Higginson Book Company, 1993).

17 "Mary Dreis Giesen (Mrs. Peter J. Giesen)," St. Paul Historical, 2021, https://bit.ly/3qIDYIG.

18 Virginia L. Martin, "Giesen's: Costumers to St. Paul, 1872–1970," *Ramsey County History*, Winter 1994.

19 Ibid.

20 St. Paul Historical, 2021, https://saintpaulhistorical.com/items/show/18.

21 Eileen M. McMahon and Theodore J. Karamanski, *North Woods River: The St. Croix River in Upper Midwest History* (University of Wisconsin Press: Madison, 2009).

22 Agnes M. Larson, *The White Pine Industry in Minnesota: A History* (University of Minnesota Press: St. Paul, 1949).

23 Ibid.

24 Washington County Historical Society, https://www.wchsmn.org.

25 K. B. Stewart and Homer Watt, "Legends of Paul Bunyan, Lumberjack," *Wisconsin Academy of Sciences, Arts, and Letters* 18, no. 11 (1916).

26 William B. Laughead, "The Marvelous Exploits of Paul Bunyan," Red River Lumber Co: Minneapolis, Minnesota (1922), https://bit.ly/463Vs1d.

27 Michael Edmonds, *Out of the Northwoods: The Many Lives of Paul Bunyan* (Wisconsin Historical Society: Madison, 2009).

28 Theodore Hamm Brewing Company, https://bit.ly/3PdExT5.

29 Ron Dansley, "Theodore Hamm: the German Immigrant Who Built a Brewing Dynasty in St. Paul," June 15, 2023, (blog), https://bit.ly/47JbgYH.

30 Ibid.

31 Ibid.

32 Doug Hoverson, *Land of Amber Waters: The History of Brewing in Minnesota* (University of Minnesota Press: Minneapolis, 2007).

33 Dansley, "Theodore Hamm."

34 Rich Grant, "Discover Old West Outlaw History in Northfield, Minnesota," https://bit.ly/3ssGHX4.

35 Ted Yeatman, *Frank and Jesse James: the Story Behind the Legend* (Cumberland House Publishing; Nashville, 2003).

36 Ibid.

Water Wheels

37 John Koblas, *Faithful unto Death: the James-Younger Raid on the First National Bank* (Northfield Historical Society Press: Northfield, Minnesota, 2001).

38 Grant, "Discover Old West Outlaw History in Northfield, Minnesota."

39 Koblas, *Faithful Unto Death.*

40 Larry Haeg, *Harriman vs Hill: Wall Street's Great Railroad War* (University of Minnesota Press: Minneapolis, 2013).

41 Albro Martin, *James J. Hill and the Opening of the Northwest* (Oxford University Press: New York, 1976).

42 Ibid.

43 Joan Brainard and Richard Leonard, *Three Bold Ventures: The History of North Oaks* (Beaver's Pond Press: Edina, Minnesota, 2007).

44 Claire Strom, *Profiting from the Plains: The Great Northern Railway and Corporate Development of the American West* (University of Washington Press: Seattle, 2003).

45 Kathryn R. Goetz, "Laura Ingalls Wilder, 1867–1957," MNOpedia, 2014, https://bit.ly/3sjzxo3.

46 Laura Ingalls Wilder, *On the Banks of Plum Creek* (Harper Collins Publishers: New York, 1937).

47 Pamela Smith Hill, ed., *Pioneer Girl: The Annotated Autobiography of Laura Ingalls Wilder* (South Dakota Historical Society Press: Pierre, 2014).

48 Ibid.

49 Norma Sommerdorf, "No Grass Beneath Her Feet: Harriet Bishop and Her Life in Minnesota," *Ramsey County History* 32, no. 2 (Summer 1997).

50 Winifred D. Wandersee Bolin, "Harriet E. Bishop: Moralist and Reformer," in *Women of Minnesota: Selected Biographical Essays* (Minnesota Historical Society Press: St. Paul, 1998), 7–19.

51 Sommerdorf, "No Grass Beneath Her Feet: Harriet Bishop and Her Life in Minnesota."

52 Kathryn R. Goetz, "Maria Sanford: 1836–1920," MNOpedia, https://bit.ly/45t3aSn.

53 Geraldine Bryan Schofield and Susan Margot Smith, "Maria Louise Sanford: Minnesota Heroine," in *Women of Minnesota: Selected Biographical Essays* (Minnesota Historical Society Press. St. Paul, 1998), 77–93.

54 Frederick L. Johnson, "Julia B. Nelson: The Rock on Which the Effort for Woman Suffrage Has Been Founded in This State," *Minnesota History* 67, no. 3 (Fall 2020).

55 Ibid.

Michael Barnes

56 Elizabeth Loetscher, "Clara Ueland: 1860–1927," MNOpedia, https://bit.ly/3OyWCdO.

57 Barbara Stuhler, Gentle Warriors: *Clara Ueland and the Minnesota Struggle for Woman Suffrage* (Minnesota Historical Society Press: St. Paul, 1995).

58 Ibid.

59 "John Sargent Pillsbury: 1827–1901," MNOpedia, https://bit.ly/3L0Ovph.

60 Lori Sturdevant with George S. Pillsbury, *The Pillsburys of Minnesota* (Nodin Press, LLC: Minneapolis, 2011).

61 Ibid.

62 Molly Huber, "Charles Alfred Pillsbury: 1842–1899," https://bit.ly/44eTBFs.

63 William J. Powell, *Pillsbury's Best: A Company History from 1869* (The Pillsbury Company: Minneapolis, 1985).

64 Huber, "Charles Alfred Pillsbury: 1842–1899."

65 Sturdevant, *The Pillsburys of Minnesota.*

66 Ibid.

67 Ibid.

68 Ibid.

69 Isaac Atwater, ed., *History of Minneapolis*, https://bit.ly/47PfDkY.

70 Karel D. Bicha, *C. C. Washburn and the Upper Mississippi Valley* (Garland Publishing, Inc.: New York and London, 1995).

71 Ibid.

72 Iric Nathanson, "Looking Back at the 1878 Washburn A Mill Explosion," https://bit.ly/3OFEwqC.

73 Kerck Kelsey, *Prairie Lightning: The Rise and Fall of William Drew Washburn* (Pogo Press: Lakeville, Minnesota, 2010).

74 Ibid.

75 Ibid.

www.ingramcontent.com/pod-product-compliance
Lightning Source LLC
Chambersburg PA
CBHW031948080426
42735CB00007B/316